MW01233455

Warren Brewin has lived in New Zealand most of his life and has travelled extensively with various business roles as CEO, MD or general manager and also socially with friends and family. On his travels he has met many people from diverse religious beliefs, which along with his thirst for knowledge and extensive research helped spawn his ideas on how today's social media is impacting the virtues of ancient belief systems which are explored in the Truth of Religion section in this book.

Warren's considerable business experience in restructuring and turning around the fortunes of failing companies into profitable efficient organisations has provided him with the knowledge to extol the Truth of Business in this book. An absolute commitment to integrity in business is the foundation stone of his enduring success.

Warren was a competitive badminton player, having won Auckland titles and played in England competitively in his early twenties. He also has won many tennis club championships in his earlier life. Warren's lifelong passion for sports is revealed through the deep insights in this book in the Truth of Sport. He still runs regularly and loves nothing more than a bush run, followed by a swim in the beach where he lives and a cold beer.

Warren is the loving father of two wonderful teenage children, Jack and Renee, and has gone through the pain and difficulty of the breakup of a seventeen-year-old marriage. These experiences led Warren to explore the fundamental basis of different relationships and this provided inspiration for the section on the Truth of Relationships. His passion for politics and global economics is revealed with clear views on Brexit, the rise of nationalism or possible homogenisation of Europe.

We live in a world full of greed, lies, war, corruption and deception but Warren believes the truth is the most important criterium that governs all life's challenges and opportunities, and by embracing it fully, we can all exist harmoniously while striving for our individual freedoms.

Warren enjoys his current CEO role and loves to spend time with his two awesome children and his amazing new partner, Ronger, and her daughter Sunny. In his spare time, he likes to drive his BMW Turbo E30 too fast, play his guitars and have the odd game of tennis. Warren has an IQ of 135 (BMI certified top 2%) and has exceptional analytical thinking, visual perception and pattern recognition.

Dad, who taught me life's important ways, especially the value of being honest, and who is the inspiration behind this book and my lifelong hero.

For my son Jack and daughter Renee, my greatest treasure, I love you endlessly.

For my family – Mum, Russell, Paul and Kris – how lucky we are to have had Dad in our lives and be the family we are.

For my love, Ronger, who inspires me with every breath and has shown me new worlds.

Warren Brewin

THE TRUTH IS WHAT
YOU BELIEVE

AUSTIN MACAULEY PUBLISHERS™

LONDON • CAMBRIDGE • NEW YORK • SHARJAH

Copyright © Warren Brewin (2021)

The right of Warren Brewin to be identified as author of this work has been asserted by the author in accordance with section 77 and 78 of the Copyright, Designs and Patents Act 1988.

All rights reserved. No part of this publication may be reproduced, stored in a retrieval system, or transmitted in any form or by any means, electronic, mechanical, photocopying, recording, or otherwise, without the prior permission of the publishers.

Any person who commits any unauthorised act in relation to this publication may be liable to criminal prosecution and civil claims for damages.

This is predominantly a work of non-fiction however any names, characters, places and incidents as developed in the Relationship section are used fictitiously, and any resemblance to actual persons, living or dead, events, or locales is entirely coincidental.

The author of this book does not dispense medical advice or prescribe the use of any technique as a form of treatment for physical, emotional, or medical problems without the advice of a physician, either directly or indirectly. The intent of the author is only to offer information of a general nature to help you in your quest for emotional and spiritual well-being. In the event you use any of the information in this book for yourself, which is your constitutional right, the author and the publisher assume no responsibility for your actions.

Any people depicted in stock imagery provided by Getty Images are models, and such images are being used for illustrative purposes only. Certain stock imagery © Getty Images.

A CIP catalogue record for this title is available from the British Library.

ISBN 9781788784719 (Paperback)
ISBN 9781528986342 (Hardback)
ISBN 9781528986366 (ePub e-book)
ISBN 9781528986359 (Audiobook)

www.austinmacauley.com

First Published (2021)
Austin Macauley Publishers Ltd
25 Canada Square
Canary Wharf
London
E14 5LQ

The Truth of Religion

In approximately 550 BC, Buddha wasn't in the slightest aware of Google when he said, ***"I am the sum total of everything I thought,"*** and this has always been a really godly statement to me. I am what I believe and think, how could I be anything else?

God has changed over the years and the undisputed king of all gods today is Google – the all-seeing, all-answering modern-day miracle of internet wisdom. Google is even a mightier god than Jimi Hendrix, and I know you are finding that hard to believe right now, but even though Google can't play the guitar, I still think Google comes up with the best answers.

That's why I currently rate Google ahead of even the longest serving and most amazing God of all time – the creator of the universe – because Google is just much quicker and more direct in answering the mysteries of life. You don't have to pray and wait for an answer any longer and you also get multiple answers. You even get to choose the one you like and want to believe in. Given that the truth changes over time, God 2000 years ago was an entirely different proposition to the way we view His holiness today.

Of course it must be reasoned that Google is part of the universe and was therefore really created by the all-time great God, so Google is really only the greatest truth of our time. No doubt the Creator will invent something to outwit Google and I have the feeling that this might be the resurrection and awareness of the importance of nature; well, that's what I would like to see anyway.

Whether you believe in Google or the almighty God, or both, or some other God is your choice entirely.

Larry Page and Sergey Brin, the founders of Google, are obviously closely connected to the almighty and are instruments of his modern powers. You've really got to hand it to God for keeping himself so contemporary and letting humans develop all these amazing things and earn all the cash, so they can have a great life and make others' lives easier.

All the while God remains humble in his invisibility and does not get any economic acknowledgement for his incredible prowess at being the ultimate master of all things. His believers pray and love him and that is enough for Him. This selflessness is an example to all of us and something that most of us don't get as the material world we live in has many of us measuring each other by what we have, and not what we do making us who we are.

There are so many gods and religions and probably the one you believe in will come true, so if you believe you will go to heaven, then that's what will be.

Most of us live in our own realms and cannot easily comprehend how others can exist, but if you really believe something, then it is amazing what can happen on our planet.

In Deshnoke, India, there is a temple dedicated to rats. Some Hindu tribes believe rats are reincarnated spirits of storytellers, so they take special care of them. I guess Hindu doesn't really appeal to those that know about heaven. However, these people are happy and easily coexist with rats and also highly venomous King Cobras that share their houses with them. Amazingly, no one gets bitten as the snakes are not feared by the locals; they are immortalised as are the rats.

Thousands of rats live in the temple where they are fed milk and other tasty treats, which some pilgrims eat afterward because it's considered a blessing to eat food that has been nibbled by the rats. It's true, but to a modern-day Western world person, the idea of cohabiting your home with rats and deadly cobras would be something they would not contemplate as they would not believe it could end in any other way than disaster. Yet this state does exist and it is a happy one.

Buddha was right, what you believe ultimately shapes and determines your life story.

Varanasi, or the city of the dead, is one of the holiest cities in India, but to people of a different faith, this place may seem very disturbing. It is considered an honour to be cremated in Varanasi as Indians believe to do so will allow the soul to escape the cycle of reincarnation.

A couple of hundred people are cremated each day on funeral pyres that never go out and the ashes are poured into the Ganges River. Old and dying people travel to Varanasi and wait to die.

The world's largest gathering also happens in the Ganges at the Kumbh Mela otherwise known as the Pitcher Festival. It's held every three years over 55 days with about 110 million people attending marking an incident in Hindu mythology where deities battled demons and won the right for nectar that granted them immortality.

The masses gather to wash away their sins and get a chance at redemption for the guilt they may be carrying in their lives. There is 3400 million litres of sewage dumped into the Ganges every day yet the belief is that the river cleanses itself and, amazingly, there are no claims of illness spread through this extraordinary phenomenon. 110 million people create a powerful belief system, or religion as what is religion if not a belief system. Not as great as the following Google has generated in a remarkably short time but not far behind!

It is the miracle of the universe that we can all be so different, yet our core essence is determined on what we believe in and, in that regard, all humans are indelibly linked. We believe in different things but we all believe in something.

There are about 21 major religions in the world today according to Yahoo as searched on Google. Yahoo is a secondary god and lives in Google's shadow as a deity of information as do all modern internet gods.

The top six of these 21 religions in order, and excluding Google, are: Christianity – 2.1 billion, Islam – 1.3 billion, Agnostic/Atheist – 1.1 billion, Hinduism – 900 million, Chinese traditional – 394 million and Buddhism 360 million.

I was surprised that Tom Cruise's Scientology was not up there but these things constantly baffle me as this is usually the only religion referred to in Woman's magazines, so my view may have been distorted somewhat!

The point is that there is an abundance of people who believe in different gods. Atheists don't have a god; they mostly believe in the universe and look for science to answer the meaning of existence.

Clearly to the believer of each religion their own religion is the right one, and we all need to respect that. As a young child going to a Presbyterian Church, I never thought that there could ever be another god. As I grew up through my teens, I considered those who believed in something different to me to be bonkers. How could anybody believe in Buddha and who was he anyway?

Now I know that it was me who was misguided, misinformed and missing out. It is really interesting to see how these various religions compare and this depicted in the next chart taking a quick comparative view of the top six religions plus Scientology.

Religion/Sect/ Belief System	Origins and History	Followers Worldwide (estimates)	God(s) and Universe	Human Situation and Life's Purpose	Afterlife
Atheism	Appears throughout history (including ancient Greek philosophy), but especially after the Enlightenment in the 19th Century.	1.1 billion	There is no God or divine being. Beliefs about the universe usually based on scientific discovery and evidence.	This life is all-important as they don't believe in afterlife. Humans are solely responsible for the world we create.	Does not exist.

Chinese Religion	Indigenous folk religion of China.	394 million	Dualistic yin and yang; mythological beings and folk deities.	Purpose is a content peaceful life and afterlife, achieved through rituals and honouring of ancestors.	Judgement, then reincarnation or temporary hell until one gains a Buddhist-type paradise.
Christianity (Catholic, Protestant, Orthodox)	Began with Jesus Christ in c.30 AD, Israel.	2 billion	One God who is an eternal being who created, controls and preserves all things.	All have sinned and are thereby separated from God. Salvation is attained by living an honest life without sin.	Eternal heaven or hell.

Hinduism	Indigenous religion of India brought to the country by Aryans in about 1500 BC.	900 million	One Supreme Spirit called Brahman who has many forms and pervades the whole universe.	Humans are in bondage to ignorance and illusion, but can escape. Purpose is to gain release from rebirth, or at least a better rebirth.	Reincarnation until you can gain enlightenment.
Islam	Muhammad (PBUH), 622 AD, Saudi Arabia	1.3 billion (Sunni: 940 million)	One God (Allah in Arabic) the all-powerful, all-knowing creator and judge.	Humans must submit (Islam) to the will of God to gain Paradise after death.	Paradise or Hell.

| Buddhism | Founded by Siddhartha Gautama (the Buddha) in c. 520 BC, NE India. | 360 million | Varies: Theravada atheistic; Mahayana more polytheistic. Buddha taught nothing is permanent. | Purpose is to avoid suffering and gain enlightenment and release from cycle of rebirth, or at least attain a better rebirth by gaining merit. | Reincarnation (understood differently than in Hinduism, with no surviving soul) until gain enlightenment. |

Scientology	L. Ron Hubbard, 1954, California	70,000 or up to several million, difficult to determine	God(s) not specified; reality explained in the Eight Dynamics, the pinnacle of human survival.	Human consists of body, mind and an immortal spirit; capable of great things. Gain spiritual freedom by removing past painful events from your mind.	Reincarnation.

In Scientology, an engram is a mental image picture of an experience recording pain. Scientology is a relatively new religion nowhere near as modern as Google which Larry and Sergey started off in a garage in 1998.

Google now has 1.17 billion believers (users) which is staggering growth when you consider that Buddhism started in 520 BC and has 360 million followers. Google is consulted a staggering 3.5 billion times a day for divine wisdom, that's 40,000 a second on average as found on Google 30 April 2017.

https://www.google.co.nz/search?q=how+many+google+users+worldwide&oq=how+many+google+users&aqs=chrome.1.69i57j0l5.5303j0j1&sourceid=chrome&ie=UTF-8

If you ask the question who is God, there are clearly many different answers all of which are correct according to the specific religion so it follows that…

THERE IS NO SINGLE GOD AND ALL GODS ARE TRUE.

For world peace to endure and become an everlasting state, this is something that everybody needs to understand and believe. We all need to respect our different heritages and evolve in harmony, with the knowledge that we don't have to force our beliefs on to others.

A religious war is one that is caused by or justified by religion and can be one religious group wishing to spread its faith by violence. Many so-called religious wars have also ulterior rationale which may include economic or political motivations such as access to trade routes, the confiscation of strategically important or wealthy land or even dynasty changes.

Some would argue that the paragon of virtue the USA is guilty of this deception and only goes to war to help the disadvantaged or maintain world equilibrium where there is economic benefit. Saddam Hussein in the end was proven to have been an absolute master at hiding the development of nuclear arms, wasn't he! Surely, the USA had no interest in oil.

However, it is true also that Saddam used chemical warfare against Iranian and Kurdish civilians during and after the Iran/Iraq war of the 1980s and pursued a nuclear programme, so perhaps the world's policeman was entirely justified in its action, it just depends on what you believe which is entirely derived from the information you have been given.

Therefore,

THE TRUTH IS AN ASSIMILATION OF INFORMATION RESULTING IN A CONCLUSION BASED ON THE INFORMATION AVAILABLE, ACCORDING TO THE INTELLECTUAL CAPACITY, POLITICAL AND EMOTIVE PERSUASION OF THE INDIVIDUAL.

The issue we all confront in the new world is that war, religion and politics all get used and confused to suit geopolitical, racial or economic power drives fuelled by greed, necessity or fanaticism. This, however, has not always been the case as the excerpts below from Wikipedia and learn peace extol. The incredible thing is the magnitude of deaths throughout history attributed to war detailed in the chart below.

MAJOR WARS

Lowest estimate	Highest estimate	Event	Location	From	To	Religions involved	Percentage of the world population
3,000,000	11,500,000	Thirty Years' War	Holy Roman Empire	1618	1648	Protestants and Catholics	0.5%–2.1%
2,000,000	4,000,000	French Wars of Religion	France	1562	1598	Protestants and Catholics	0.4%–0.8%
1,000,000	2,000,000	Second Sudanese Civil War	Sudan	1983	2005	Islam and Christian	0.02%
1,000,000	3,000,000	Crusades	Holy Land, Europe	1095	1291	Islam and Christian	0.3%–2.3%
130,000	250,000	Lebanese Civil War	Lebanon	1975	1990	Sunni, Shiite and Christian	

Wars have often been fought with religion given as the reason or cause with peace as the intended outcome. However, these beliefs are often entwined with the personal views of individuals and groups within each religion which complicates the rationale and outcome.

Religions tend to start wars for one of three reasons:

Ironically, one is the belief that violence and killing is wrong. Another view is that a war should be fought because it is in the interests of the greater good and therefore the war should be fought according to the just rules. The third is the belief in a holy war where disciples think it is their duty to make war on those who do not believe in their chosen religion or threaten it. This is the primary drive of what many see as fanatical Muslims behind the Islamic State movement that changed the world when planes smashed into the Twin Towers in New York, September 11, 2001.

Most religions have their core belief system rooted in non-violence and Buddhism, Hinduism and Sikhism all have their roots in India. The great Indian leader Mahatma Gandhi summed up the countries core essence when he wrote in 1947 as part of India's strive for Independence:

"I object to violence because when it appears to do good, the good is only temporary; the evil it does is permanent."

Religions like Hinduism and Jainism believe that people should endeavour to become detached from their day to day worldly existence and that war is justified to help the weak and disadvantaged, but throughout history, Hindu has not been an aggressive religion by comparison. In fact, the thinking of Gandhi and how he managed to reclaim Indian sovereignty from the British was established way back in the 10th Century when Muslims invaded India.

Around 986, AD Sultan Mahmud and Amir Sabuktigin wreaked havoc after several battles reaching Punjabi Hindus. The Hindu King sent a message to the Sultan saying that war should be avoided to which the Sultan replied that his aim was to *"obtain a complete victory suited to his zeal for the honour of Islam and Musulmans."*

The response from King Jaipal was enlightened indeed as he completely disarmed the Sultans glory seeking pursuit with the ultimate sacrifice, stating,

"You have seen the impetuosity of the Hindus and their indifference to death. If you insist on war in the hope of obtaining plunder, tribute, elephants and slaves, then you leave us no alternative but to destroy our property, take the eyes out of our elephants, cast our families in fire, and commit mass suicide, so that all that will be left to you to conquer and seize is stones and dirt, dead bodies, and scattered bones."

The history of what happened next is vague but it seems the Sultan promised peace for a large ransom which King Jaipal refused to pay angering the Sultan to a level of violence that included burning villages and towns, destroying temples and killing on an uncountable scale.

The Hindus in the end tried to fight a just war but the Muslims were obsessed to make holy war on those who didn't believe in their religion or threaten it.

In later years, Gandhi fine-tuned this passive resistance that ultimately infuriated and conquered British rule. Gandhi believed you should engage in struggle but in a non-violent way.

Buddhists believe it is better to be killed than to kill as evidenced in the Vietnam War (1961–1975) when monks burnt themselves to death in protest against the war between the American and Communist armies. Of all religions, Buddhists have the best record for non-violence and always seek to be ethical and like Taoism and Confucianism seek to assimilate human life within the bounds and wonder of nature. Confucius and LaoTse were the founders of these religions and lived in the same era as Buddha.

Christianity, Judaism and Islam have all at some stages in their history adopted the rationale of the holy war to satisfy and justify ideals that certainly don't have their sole pursuit based on the core religious belief. The larger Christian religions like Roman Catholics, Church of England and Methodists all support the idea that war is sometimes unavoidable, however undesirable it is.

Islam means to surrender to the will of God (Allah) and the base ideology was developed by the Prophet Mohammed (570–632). The Islamic teaching encourages disciples to exert themselves in the way of God with their duty being to lead wholesome lives and grow the belief system through education and prayer which is referred to as Jihad. Jihad also implores the defence of Islam through holy war.

Increasingly in our modern world, there are those that don't necessarily align to any set religion and don't choose to believe in God, but still aspire to the humanitarian ideals that religions bring, like treating others as you wish them to treat you. They all have varying views on the need for war and the very reason war still exists is that in all religious and non-religious states there is no enduring solution for peace that has conquered human aspiration.

Clearly, the different religions all interpret and justify different situations with what they perceive the best solution for their objectives at the time of confrontation. When you boil it all down, the difference between them is minimal, none really want to enter into conflict but will to rectify a situation where they perceive they have been treated badly. Probably Gandhi is right that violence is only a temporary solution, and the Iraq conflict with the US, covered later in this section, is a classic example of retaliatory action spiralling out of control resulting in the advent of ISIS.

War is ultimately the result of conflicting views or ambitions and therefore can only be eradicated by finding common ground where parties agree to a compromise and accept each other's position. If Gandhi's view is accepted, then both parties should move straight past the cost of war and the unfathomable waste of life and focus immediately on the common ground.

Unfortunately, emotion and fervour often clouds rational thought and we destroy each other for a belief that will never be accepted by the opposing force, so really – acceptance and understanding is the only sustainable end game.

When you consider the meaning of religion, it is really interesting and a search on Google revealed the following three meanings I found to be most relevant:

1. The belief and worship of a superhuman controlling power, especially a personal God or gods.
2. A particular system of faith and worship.
3. A pursuit or interest followed with great devotion.

I find all of these meanings to be very relevant, but also not what a lot of people would also associate with religion, which would include some association and affinity with the pursuit of peace. However, nowhere in the meanings above does this exist showing a distinct shift in perception from the more detailed and historical views developed in the 500 to 600 BC period.

In fact, the first meaning where one worships a superhuman controlling power is perfectly set up to the contrary, where the divine being's belief can be used as an excuse for war and history is littered with differences in beliefs that have led to massive atrocities.

The second system can be attributed to any system where faith and worship satisfy the believers. This might be the Hitler Youth or the Ku Klux Klan (KKK). It might also be the Baha'i Faith who believes the crucial need facing humanity is to find a unifying vision of the future of society and of the nature and purpose of life.

From the 1920s, the Nazi Party targeted the youth and educated them in Aryan Supremacy and this ultimately became a fervour that justified some of the most heinous crimes in humanity, against the Jews, through the period of the Second World War. The KKK attacked and intimidated blacks particularly in the Southern States of North America to intimidate them. This may have included killing them and burning down their houses.

Both the Nazi Party and the KKK had white supremacy as a core belief system that was used to justify their actions. As always, good prevailed and these misguided uprisings failed, but they are simply referred to so that the meaning of what religion really can be when the meaning of point 2 above is understood.

Point 3 has Google written all over it, doesn't it? It doesn't matter where you go in the modern Western World today, Google is omnipresent. If you want to know something, there is simply no better medium. When I look back, we used the Encyclopaedia Britannica which cost my parents a small fortune, but at the time was among the best information sources available.

Google has become so much more as it now provides you with instant access to knowledge which you can then use in so many ways. As I write this, 1/12/14, the European Union has started an action to consider the breakup of Google in Europe because it has 90% market share in a free market environment where the best rise to the top.

This is typical of the most financially and socially troubled continent on the planet where they try to control competition and in many countries like France, Greece and Italy are slow to accept the new world order being forged by great new innovators like Google. Rather than embrace this wondrous new deity to their advantage, they choose to break it down and use some inferior search engine system that will further stunt their ailing region and escalate the speed of their demise.

They surely have no concept of the God they are dealing with, and seek to politicise the failings of the web and create phobias around privacy that seem to have no real legitimacy. This endeavour is not supported by the European Commission.

"This call isn't supported by the findings of the European Commission or the outcome of a similar investigation by the Federal Trade Commission in the U.S.,"

Mr Aubert wrote in the email, which was reviewed by The Wall Street Journal.

He said that any solution of the EU's antitrust investigation *"should be in proportion to the degree of concern identified by a thorough and rigorous legal and economic analysis."*

The truth is:

YOU CAN'T HIDE FROM COMPETITION.

I also think that the European Union needs to understand the loyalty and following that Google has with its believers before they undertake such an action as to try and deny the masses a basic right to the truth by the best service available. This must surely be a foolhardy retrograde step.

What Google is alleged to be doing as I understand is to favour its own products by way of using the hierarchy search engine optimisation system to its own advantage. What successful organisation doesn't try and self-promote? Really, what a load of malarkey!

The point is that even if Google is doing this, which in my view is done by companies worldwide, whether they be retailers stacking margins on favoured brands or wholesalers setting prices and features to make the maximum return, makes Google no worse than other businesses. Google offers a choice so the punter can search through and find the best deal or information that best suits them. If they don't, more fool them.

They also have the choice of other search engines and it is up to the competition to develop a product that is more preferred than Google.

It's no different to buying something at shop A and finding out that shop B sells it cheaper, except Google gives you all the options and in this way is really a very fair modern-day deity. Try switching search engines away from Google for a week, I have and it was one of the most horrible experiences ever.

This is going to be another hard lesson for Europe and the tragedy is that successful economies like Germany are now being dragged down with the gargantuan debt in some of these Mediterranean countries. They have not faced up the productivity threat that has come from China, Korea, Japan and other Asian powerhouses where the joy of work is a treasure to behold, not a God-given right. The French riot in the streets if they have the threat of their 37.5-hour week taken away from them. It is so ridiculous that an employee in Apple faced heavy warnings for working 20 minutes over time and the company possible fines.

Yet they complain about the Asian Tiger and low-cost merchandise. God help them. Sacré bleu! Now we see them attempt to try and break up a new-age god because they are too blind to see the brilliance on offer.

With this type of mediaeval thinking Europe, as we know it, is doomed. God (Google) is no longer divine simplicity with no parts; it is a multi-headed business that is speeding up progress at a rate that only the brave can withstand. It is doing this by arming everyone with access to divine information at a level never seen before. If the European Union thinks they can break up Google's search engine and gain from it, they are misguided as to what is good for them.

Religion, as it was, is being pushed aside by a new society that believes money, entertainment and information is more important than taking their children to a church on Sunday, and handing over a donation in the interest of lifelong support they are too busy to feel.

Larry Page, Google's CEO and co-founder, once described the *"perfect search engine"* as something that *"understands exactly what you mean and gives you back exactly what you want."* I am often amazed by Google's intuitiveness and for leaders of Europe to not recognise this is sad indeed. Often the top-ranking response tells me exactly what I need to know but the brilliance of the system is that you scroll down for more information and have choices. The reason that Google has 90% share is that they are the best at this by miles and have now ascended to divine status.

The EU will tamper with this force at their peril.

But Europe may well attempt this as history shows they have an unbelievable desire to control religious desires, and the quest to quell Google's ability to serve you is very great as the 90% market share is testimony to.

That's where Google is so brilliant, they are the god that serves you and demands nothing. Very different to Jesus' old man!

If we wander back through European history, we see that the Thirty Years' War (1618-48) began when Holy Roman Emperor Ferdinand II of Bohemia attempted to curtail the religious activities of his subjects, sparking rebellion among Protestants. You can see in the preceding chart on historic wars that this war caused up to 11.5 million deaths, and I'm not suggesting that trying to curtail Google will lead to such a violent reaction that we saw four centuries ago, but I am saying that the consequences will adversely affect Europe's already fragile stance on the world stage, and that the downstream impact will only create reduced competitiveness and a divorcing from the realities of progress.

And we are revisiting history again now with the birth of ISIS, the Islamic State of Iraq and Syria where Sunni extremists and Jihadi terrorists operate in conflict with 60 countries around the world. The United Nations has held ISIS guilty of human rights abuses and war crimes and Amnesty International has reported ethnic cleansing by the group on an historic scale.

So what is the difference between Islam and Muslim? Part of the problem with all that happens in this part of the world is that it is squarely labelled against these religions, so what do they stand for, what is there core essence?

Remarkably, they are very similar as shown where Islam refers to the religion or community of believers in the faith as a whole and Muslim refers to the person who submits to the will of God, or a believer of Islam.

I cleared that up because I think a big part of the issues Western people have with Muslims is a lack of understanding. If the base of these religions is to submit, accept and surrender the will of God, that is paradoxical to the act of an aggressive terrorist beheading innocent Western journalists, to gain ransom money to buy more arms to fuel their war efforts against the West.

Or is it the Islamic State warning the Americans and others to get out of Iraq and leave their people alone. It just depends which story you believe, doesn't it? But the latter is exactly what is said by the man with the knife on this website. http://www.military.com/video/operations-and-strategy/terrorism/a-second-message-to-america/3763859346001/

When you consider that America has since the 1980s, in the war between Iraq and Iran, and the subsequent Persian Gulf War, sought to maintain a level of control over the Persian Gulf, it is easy to hypothesise that the real interest is oil. The Gulf States are an important oil-producing region but the share of world production has dropped from 37% in 1973 to 28% in 2006, but at the time held 55% of the world's reserves, so they now have a diminished global importance.

Given that America in October 2013 produced more oil than it imported for the first time in almost 20 years, due to technological breakthroughs like hydraulic fracturing, one can easily see how the reliance on the Gulf States reduced substantially. The US production has increased by a staggering 50% since 2008 lending credibility to the rationale that oil is no longer the main reason that the US is in this region, and its role of world policeman may have some real justification.

But what is the real truth in all this never-ending commotion in this area that was the world's oldest civilisation?

Mesopotamia was the first known civilisation that man can chronicle and is thought to have existed from about 3300 – 750 BC, which is a bleeding long time ago. This civilisation existed in what we know as modern day Iraq, known then as Babylonia, and Sumer and the Assyria highlands. Hammurabi, the exalted prince, and divine ruler of the region at the time is credited with bringing many of the laws that controlled the civilisation.

Much of Hammurabi's code was based around the presumption of innocence, with both the accuser and accused having rights to submit their version of the truth, and an 'eye for an eye' and a 'tooth for a tooth'.

To my mind, these are basic life rules that apply today and I contend that Newton's third law – for every action, there is an equal and opposite reaction applies to more than just the physical sense it is intended. This rule applies to emotional drivers, and religious protectionism, and nationality, and in fact, this is simply summed up in the eye for an eye theory.

That is what it is, an equal and opposite reaction to create justice in the eyes of the force retaliating to a perceived injustice from the opposing force. That is why I believe the ISIL murderer has done what he has done. He grew up in the world where this theory was a base law that pervaded the region and the only way they know of reacting to the horror that they see the US bring with weapons of mass destruction is to cause equal and opposite terror by the best means available to them.

Neither action do I condone but history also shows that sometimes force is required to create peace and no more graphic example was the horrific destruction of Nagasaki and Hiroshima to get Japan out of the World War II. The Japanese fight with a ferocity and conviction to their cause few nations can rival, so brute force was the fastest and best method, however tragic it was.

If God is the belief system that determines the truth, then this equally applies to the many scientists who struggle with the theory that physics created the universe in the absence of God. Scientists and Musicians also share a similar bond in that they both search in their own way for the meaning of life.

This surely must be the continual quest for the truth which ultimately creates the harmony and love we all strive for in our day-to-day existence.

To find the true answer to anything, ASK WHY FIVE TIMES. This is an excellent solving problem method as not until you get down to the core of the matter can you truly determine the solution.

Not only must you discover the truth, the parties involved in the dispute must then both accept it so that the pursuit of a peaceful and positive existence can be achieved.

Sakichi Toyoda originally developed the five times technique in the Toyota Motor Company and it goes without saying how that brand has an intrinsic value that makes it a global giant in the auto industry. People don't buy Toyotas because they are stylish, or because they have status or because they are the fastest. No, they buy them because they know they will be reliable and fit for purpose and are a low-maintenance vehicle.

That dedication to excellence of quality in no small way will be attributed to ask why five times method that gets to the nitty-gritty of the issue so that a solution can be determined. The dedication to excellence at Toyota is like a religion and it's interesting to note that the brand's entire media assault in New Zealand is based around the word believe.

Toyota New Zealand believes that inspiration and respect come from shared values and beliefs. No doubt this is part and parcel of how the brand engages so closely with its loyal customers.

The first Queen Elizabeth of England and Ireland (7th September, 1553 to 24th March, 1603) was a Protestant and also embodied a similar belief system to that of Toyota. She had to rule a much-divided country which was similarly divided between the Protestants and the Catholics who many of her advisors believed would lead a crusade against heretical England.

Elizabeth was known as the Virgin Queen and, in the movie named after her, she says in response to a drive to attack the Catholics that she will not punish them for their beliefs but will punish them for their deeds. She outlines her belief below in an excerpt from Wikipedia which is well worth a look if you have further interest.

http://en.wikipedia.org/wiki/Elizabeth_I_of_England

Elizabeth I in her coronation robes patterned with
Tudor roses and trimmed with ermine.

*"My lords, the law of nature moves me to sorrow for my
sister; the burden that is fallen upon me makes me amazed,
and yet, considering I am God's creature, ordained to obey
His appointment, I will thereto yield, desiring from the
bottom of my heart that I may have assistance of His grace
to be the minister of His heavenly will in this office now
committed to me. And as I am but one body naturally
considered, though by His permission a body politic to
govern, so shall I desire you all ... to be assistant to me, that
I with my ruling and you with your service may make a good
account to Almighty God and leave some comfort to our
posterity on earth. I mean to direct all my actions by good
advice and counsel."*

Throughout the ages, the divinity of gods has been
paramount in religious discussion and, in later centuries,
science has provided theories that compete with religion for
the reason of our existence.

This was all brought to the fore again at the end of the Second World War when the second atom bomb was dropped on Nagasaki to finally force the stubborn, resilient Japanese into surrender and bring the war to an end on the evening of August 14, 1945.

Robert Oppenheimer was a brilliant theoretical physicist that is credited as the father of the atom bomb and he reflected weeks after the war ended that we all now need to question whether science was good for man. *"We have made a thing, a most terrible weapon, that has altered abruptly and profoundly the nature of the world. A thing that by all standards of the world we grew up in is an evil thing. And so by doing, we have raised the question of whether science is good for man."*

Oppenheimer later in life admitted that he was haunted by an ancient Hindu scripture as a result of what they developed – *"Now I am become death, the destroyer of worlds."*

He often suffered with depression, and while he saw physics clearly, the mystery of the universe surrounded him like fog.

Oppenheimer was ejected from his position of political influence in 1954 and, interestingly, epitomised by many as the failure of scientists to realise that others would not use their research for the purpose they believed most appropriate. Einstein said *"Time is opportunity unfolding,"* and the implied progress of this interpretation, which I totally agree with as the best explanation I have heard, means that even the most well-intended design may end up being used to cause devastation of enormous consequence.

I doubt Ernst Rutherford conceived the atom bomb when he split the atom. He was a strong supporter of education and scientific research, but was aware of the misuses to which science could be put. During World War I, he said he hoped that an efficient way of extracting the energy of the atom would not be discovered until men were at peace again. Before the outbreak of World War II, he argued for a ban on using airplanes in war.

However, that turned out to be a wishful thought and dropping the atom bomb changed the world forever.

The whole of Europe, North America and Russia all lived in the spectre that this unspeakable evil could be repeated, and we still don't know whether that bomb was the start of something or the end of something. The thought of horrific destruction has held a fragile peace that then flourished into an era of peace and prosperity for many years.

One third of a million innocent civilians were victims of this massive shift in the world's understanding of what it was that maintained peace. Gandhi's theories were out the door, now peace was delicately balanced by the threat of devastating power.

While I don't like the world having a policeman, I think that the US by and large does a reasonable job of pushing democratic principles, however, as we have seen in countries like Iraq, it is not what everyone wants and this is why ISIL are fighting back. They don't want the West controlling their way of life and they don't want political systems influencing their religious beliefs.

Therefore it is true that:

WHEN YOU FORCE A BELIEF ONTO A COMMUNITY OR COUNTRY, THERE WILL BE AN EQUAL AND OPPOSITE REACTION TO THAT FORCE, ALBEIT NOT NECESSARILY OF THE SAME NATURE.

As mentioned earlier, an example of this is where ISIS fights the superior arms of the US with terror tactics to create a similar level of fear but through the best means they have.

Even a peace-loving Buddhist choosing no action is an equal and opposite reaction to an aggressor attacking their rights, as the belief is that love will negate hatred and create equilibrium and peace.

This is why I continue to contend that it is respect of others' religion and belief systems that will ultimately lead to harmony and this can only be derived from both parties maintaining a true representation of their position. This also needs to have a commitment to open sincere communication as a foundation stone and is a basis of building trust and resulting harmony, which is ultimately really what religions seek.

One of the most amazing books I have ever read is Shantaram by Gregory David Roberts which is a really interesting blend of fact and fiction to create a must-read novel.

In the book which is based on the real-life story of a prison inmate, who escapes a high-security Australian jail to live in the slums of Mumbai, India with drug lords, has an amazing revelation one night. He is sitting with these drug lords, smoking a pipe of hashish as I recall it and they are sitting together in a circle.

Every night they do this, they establish a subject that each person must speak on after they have inhaled from the pipe. The subject this particular night is to define God.

After several hours of deliberation, the concluding thought is along the lines of God being the ever-increasing speed and complexity of life. That is certainly a true phenomenon and I respect the thought but think God has a much wider sphere of influence than just the complexity of life. Searching for the truth is indeed probably the most complex equation known to man and Albert Einstein had a brilliant perspective which I have copied below.

"Be a loner. That gives you time to wonder, to search for the truth. Have holy curiosity. Make your life worth living."
– Albert Einstein

Here we see the greatest brain of all mankind seeing the holy relationship with the truth and recognising that searching for the truth makes your life worthwhile.

The innocence of the truth, however, should not only be the domain of the young. It is up to us all to recognise the value of honesty and the freedom and peace that reside within it.

THE INNOCENCE OF THE TRUTH SHOULD NOT SOLELY BE THE DOMAIN OF THE YOUNG.

I don't believe anyone knows what or who God really is but I am a believer, and like the theory of this book have changed my thinking numerous times as to what God is.

My current view, which has inspired much this book, is that my GOD IS A BELIEF SYSTEM THAT SEARCHES FOR THE TRUTH.

God is what we refer to when we try to understand the mysteries of time, the universe and how we came to exist.

This is the only common ground that I can find in all religions. We all need something to believe in, it is the thing that makes us get up in the morning; it is the energy source that drives ambition, inspiration and, ultimately, success. So whether your god is the divine being that Christianity observes or one of the many gods that the Hindu believe in, or Jimi Hendrix, the heavenly guitarist, who created sounds I have not heard of before or since, we all use that belief to fuel who we are. It is the gas in the tank that gets us through our daily existence.

Some religions have one supreme being while others have many deities of variety of ranks.

Deities in some religion may take a human form, whereas to other religions, such an idea would be considered sacrilegious and even impossible that their God could be perceived in a concrete form. Often deities are believed to be immortal and assumed to possess consciousness, knowledge, desires and personalities beyond the abilities of humans.

In the times before science could explain the catastrophes that can be caused by earthquakes and great floods, before electricity was understood, gods were often attributed to have been the source of these miraculous events and the ultimate controllers of human life. Some gods were deemed to be the determiners of law and morality, the judges of human worth, and the designers of the universe. Often mistakenly, they were attributed to have super-natural powers that were a natural result of the law of physics.

How God relates to nature is a mystery but there is a relationship there and we consider this later.

If you don't believe in something, whatever it is, even if it is a non-belief like atheism, then, ultimately, you have no real identity, no purpose, and will sink into a spiral of nothingness. To those people who find themselves on the slide to nowhere, religion and the church can provide that meaning and support, that faith that gives the energy and purpose to carry on.

On the back of this need, another new religion in the vein of Google has sprung forth.

Enter Facebook, the social media phenomenon that must have the pope and other religious leaders shaking in their robes and searching for a new way of connecting with their followers. If it isn't, it should be, as one of the core reasons for religion as we have already outlined is that people find a sense of community and wellbeing and comfort from their church and religion.

In 10 short years, Facebook has established 1.23 billion believers and is now in $1/3^{rd}$ place behind Christianity (2 billion) and Islam at 1.3 billion believers. This level of commitment took centuries for these other established religions to grow and develop, so where is this all heading?

GOD CAN DESTROY LONELINESS.

But here is the rub, so can Facebook, and it's quick and convenient and you can keep in touch and share all sorts of things with friends and family. Personally, I have no interest in it, but utilise it from a business perspective, and watch with interest how the youth are fascinated by images of themselves and seem to be able to communicate more effectively through electronic formats like email, texting or social media.

The pressure this open access to everything puts on young children is immense and I've witnessed some real rubbish go on with my 13-year-old daughter on Facebook, that no child that age should have to deal with. Just kids placing comments that are ill considered and selfish with no thought of the position they put someone in. However, she is dealing with it admirably and growing up with a fine set of values none the less.

No doubt youth suicide is impacted as a result of the spread of social media and that is where religions need to get smart and bring communities together and breathe life into the wholesomeness of believing in something good and connecting with nature. As I grow in years, my appreciation of the wonder of nature calms me when turmoil at work or my personal life comes around.

Cyber bullying and impact cults play their part in this change in children's lives today.

Research conducted by the School of Public Health at the University of Sydney, Australia, concluded that one of the most mentioned sources of suicide stories were social websites. There was also a reported rise in feelings of hopelessness and suicidal tendencies among the participants surveyed.

Religion has a huge future if the leaders can navigate the way forward and restore credibility to their faith that has also been lost through the unsuitable behaviour of some of their ministers. They must, however, recognise the need of the youth today and move swiftly before Facebook, Google and other social media enterprises undo the base foundation essence that has been so long a part of our moral integrity.

It's also hard to see these social media sites taking a highly moral stance and adopting standards that bring today's youth up with the sense of righteousness that we all hope our children will grow up with. Because if they don't, what will become of society?

Dating apps like Tinder now set up more than 4 million matches a day! This app pulls together profile information from Facebook and is quick and easy to set up and seems to be the latest way to arrange casual sex further fuelling this gradual decline of the youth today with instant gratification being a main driver in all things they do. The challenge for religions today, if they are to survive and prosper into the future, is to not only understand the social changes with today's youth but also find a way to engage with them by adopting modern media formats and throwing off the shackles of past ideologies as to the correct and only way churches interact with their disciples.

There is no more glaring evidence of this failure than as reported this week, January 2015, in Europe by the fact that empty churches are now going on sale and one has been turned into a skate park. The Church of St Joseph in Arnhem, the Netherlands, was once a place for a thousand worshipers to express their beliefs and now it has been humbled into a skating arena where kids show off their skills while being watched over by a mosaic likeness of Jesus and stone saints. If religions worldwide can't get this incongruity, then their future may well be on a slippery slope that is beyond redemption.

It is interesting that this has been widely understood and adopted by Islam as they cleverly deploy social media to accelerate the impact of their retaliatory acts of violence, creating mass media coverage and an amplifying affect that is simply incredible.

"In a study by Gabriel Weimann from the University of Haifa, Weimann found that nearly 90% of organised terrorism on the internet takes place via social media. According to Weimann, terror groups use social media platforms like Twitter, Facebook, YouTube and internet forums to spread their messages, recruit members and gather intelligence."

It is clear that social media can be a potent medium for spreading terror, so why can't it be used to spread the positive influence that religion can bring to society that it has over the ages?

The latest terror attacks that have just occurred in Paris, France, have further attacked the common rights of Western freedom by Jihad extremists. A million people are expected to march the streets of Paris on January 11, 2015 in defiance against the terrorist extremism that killed 17 innocent people and three terrorists and show their love for liberty.

Is the equal and opposite reaction simply that the Islam extremists are trying to take away the freedom of those who they feel are taking away their freedom by infiltration of their lands and manipulative political agendas?

So not only must religions find ways to drive peace, but also governments of influence must also adopt similar visions and find ways to create solutions, not exacerbate existing tensions that are as old as the ages. Whether human nature will ever allow peace to prevail is probably the underlying conundrum that will perpetually cause conflict, as different races, different religions and different countries strive for supremacy so that they feel good.

Interestingly, there are now thirteen countries around the world that will now punish those that openly espouse Atheism, or reject the official state religion, which in all these countries is Islam, by death. Beyond Islamic countries, there is also widespread discrimination against free thinkers. The Freethought Report 2013 was issued by the International Humanist and Ethical Union (IHEU), and this report shows that *"the overwhelming majority of countries fail to respect the rights of atheists and freethinkers although they have signed UN agreements to treat all citizens equally,"* as said by the IHEU President Sonja Eggerickx.

If you recall my point made earlier in this section that it is true that you can't hide from competition, then it follows that those who follow this line will fail. The evidence is right before their eyes, but I wonder if the leaders can see it, and if they do, then they don't understand the remedy. You cannot quell human spirit, as it springs eternal, and just when you think you have it under control, it will spout forth.

Freedom to choose what you believe in, who you love, where you work, what you do and how you act all must have some boundaries that keep us all civilised. The Communist regime in China under the leadership of Xi Jinping is learning this in Hong Kong as riots continue as the Hong Kong people refuse to give up the freedoms they have had under British administration.

The parties attempts to eliminate religious beliefs, in mainland China, for absolute commitment to communist ideology, will also ultimately fail.

The blatant murder of journalists that speak out the truth as they see it is also a flagrant abuse of human rights but equally so is invading a country under the guise of eliminating the development of weapons of mass destruction, when it is proven they didn't exist. Religion is a very central core to all these conflicts even though human rights or other political/economical agendas are part of the picture.

It's true therefore that,

RESPECTING EACH OTHER'S RELIGIOUS BELIEFS PLAYS A PIVOTAL ROLE IN FOSTERING RELIGIONS ABILITY TO HELP CREATE A BALANCED SOCIETY WHERE FREEDOM IS A RIGHT OF THE PEOPLE.

I have discussed my theory on the truth with others including my son who I have huge respect for. He believes that the truth can only be a single definitive state, and to some extent, I agree with him, and my theory on God being a force that searched out the truth encompasses this view, given it can apply to all religious beliefs and scientific quests in an area that can easily be defined as abstract with no real way of determining the answer.

If God is the belief system that determines the truth, then this equally applies to the many scientists who purport the theory that a big bang created the universe in the absence of God, whether they like it or not!

The only constant I can see in all religion and science that binds their essence together is the unswerving desire to discover the truth.

The continual quest for the truth, which ultimately creates the harmony and love we all strive for in our day-to-day existence is like water to the flower.

What will be absolutely fascinating over the next few decades will be the role that the church and religions play in defining the truth that sustains the moral code humans need to exist by.

Will Facebook, Google, YouTube and the like, create such fanatical followers that religions become a redundant force in human development?

Let us pray!

The Truth of Sport

Will sport descend to the parlour state where success is dictated by the athlete with the best chemist or will the genuine rivalry and human endeavour of honest sportsmen prevail in the pursuit of excellence?

The outcome is not in the hands of sportsman but rather in the hands of the administrators who need to stop hiding behind the ridiculous fear that exposing cheats will destroy the game! It won't! It will return sport to the glory that is associated with the greatest sporting events like the Olympics, World Soccer Cup, Wimbledon and the Tour de France to name a few. To see athletes push themselves to their limit and beyond in a genuine pursuit is always fascinating to an audience and deeply rewarding to the victor.

It is essential to define the meaning of sport to fully appreciate the many and varied interpretations of what is and what are not acceptable, in the quest of glory and individual or team excellence.

My preferred meaning is the one below obtained online by the Free dictionary by Farlex because it contains the physical element, covers off rules or customs and considers that it may be competitive but is not always so as some choose to play for fun.

That is a rationale that I have only come to understand as I have aged and the body simply won't do what youth made possible.

An activity involving physical exertion and skill that is governed by a set of rules or customs and often undertaken competitively.

Now tell me, have you ever heard of a guy called Lance, amazing cyclist, in fact, he won an unbelievable seven Tour de France races and had a heart-lung oxygen capacity that was paranormal. He's a fantastic guy who overcame testicular cancer and went on to be a world-beater that also gave heavily to charity via the Livestrong Foundation he created in 1997.

Yet this incredible thing happened, it did turn out to be unbelievable. The truth that he had so vehemently hidden for many years came out, as it always does and his cheating was exposed. The following excerpt is taken from the BBC.com confirming his most sudden fall from grace.

"Lance Armstrong has been stripped of his seven Tour de France titles and given a lifetime ban by the United States Anti-Doping Agency (USADA).

USADA said Armstrong's decision not to fight the charges against him triggered the lifetime ban and led to his results dating back to 1 August 1998 being erased.

He won the Tour de France in 1999, 2000, 2001, 2002, 2003, 2004 and 2005."

YOU CANNOT HIDE THE TRUTH

Lances lies were of epic proportion and so his fall from grace has been brutal from the status once greater than man demi-god. Not only did he bully his teammates into cheating with him by using performance-enhancing drugs, he used expensive lawyers to muzzle media reporters.

This is easily the greatest hero to zero sporting humiliation in history and it's hard to feel any sympathy for Lance.

It would be most interesting to be a shrink and have Lance sitting on the couch to try and understand how he now sees himself and what he believes his future will hold. He is probably the only person in the world who still thinks he is innocent. It will take a significant realisation and a massive amount of humility for Lance to win back favour from the public, as his lies and deceit have left him in a very dark place.

Lance was so absorbed in himself, anybody who got in his way would be persecuted and vilified especially if they were to call him a drug cheat, but as is so often the way with bullies, they come up against someone that won't back down.

In 2002, Mike Anderson was hired as his bike mechanic and personal assistant. Within two years, Mike's life turned into hell as his employment was terminated and he endured the full force of Armstrong's legal armoury, spotlighted in world media, as he had found evidence in Armstrong's Spanish town house.

Mike was forced to leave Austin Texas and ended up moving 12,000 kilometres away to Upper Hutt in New Zealand where he runs a small bike shop. Mike had the conviction of integrity that drove him to defy the legal might of Armstrong as the excerpt below from Sports Illustrated reveals.

SI: You're one of a number of people who were telling the truth and who Armstrong tried either to intimidate or ruin. There has been speculation as to whether he'll address that with Oprah.

Anderson: And doing it! Not trying, but doing it. He certainly ruined me, and [Greg] LeMond, and Frankie [Andreu], and Emma [O'Reilly]. Professionally. Financially. He did a really good job of polarising the cycling fans in the U.S. against Greg. He ruined Greg's bike company. He told me he was going to do it when I worked for him! It's a cautionary tale, I think, of what happens when people get too much power.

SI: A lot of media figures are now piling on Lance, but when you were in the newspapers after Lance sued you, that certainly wasn't the case.

Emma O'Reilly was a former US Postal Service cycling team masseuse and she was labelled a prostitute and an alcoholic by Armstrong.

Betsy Andreu, wife of former pro-cyclist Frankie Andreu, discovered a vial of Frankie's EPO in her fridge in 1999 and persuaded her husband to abandon performance-enhancing drugs which ultimately led him to being ostracised by the US Postal team. It was Betsy and Frankie that testified that, in 1996, Lance told cancer doctors in their presence that he'd doped with steroids, cortisone, growth hormone and EPO.

For that, Lance tried to destroy them both.

Betsy comments, *"I wasn't going to lie for him and Frankie wasn't going to dope for him and we've been living with the repercussions for years. If you were on the wrong side of Lance, you were on the wrong side of the UCI (Union Cycliste Internationale), who cared more about their cash cow; you were on the wrong side of sponsors, of the many in the fawning media who helped perpetrate the lie. You were on the wrong side of the fans."*

What I find so utterly amazing about this story is that so many people are prepared to turn a blind eye, or not attempt to believe the truth if it suits them financially not to. It is further evidence of how morally bankrupt much of society is today as pursuit of the mighty dollar expunges any thought of wrongdoing.

The lie took on its own dimension and grew over time as Lance had to tell more and more lies to cover up the illusion he had created. How many lies were told and friendships sacrificed in his blind belief that he was going to get away with it? He even sued his former university friend Mike Anderson and claimed that he was trying to blackmail him for $US 500,000.

The lie continued to spiral out of control until the US Anti-Doping Agency released the damning report vindicating Mike Anderson and others like Betsy and Frankie Andreu.

'IT'S NICE TO KNOW THE TRUTH MATTERS.'
– Betsy Andreu.

You said it, Betsy, it does, and only through courage and that belief does it remain so. People like you are what continue to make the truth the binding agent of humanity as without it we descend into depravity, lawlessness and complete social disorder.

The Bible says the truth will set you free. Lance Armstrong better hope his attorneys and public relations advisers are atheists.

"If the disgraced cyclist does publicly confess to the doping that cost him his seven Tour de France titles, he could put himself in risk of criminal prosecution," said New York trial attorney Stuart Slotnick and this is in fact what happens.

There are a few moments in life that you witness something absolutely incredible and so striking was the moment that it lives vividly in your memory forever.

One such moment for me was the 1988 Seoul Olympics 100 metre Men's Final. Ben Johnson exploded from the blocks and put plenty of clear air between himself and another pre-race favourite, Carl Lewis.

It was the classic good-guy-bad-guy race and Johnson was the bad guy. The explosive power was phenomenal and awe-inspiring.

Johnson not only won but broke the world record in dramatic fashion. 9.79 seconds.

He collected gold medal and only hours later was stripped of his medal for the taking of banned substances. Some after the race commented that they were not so much surprised that he was taking drugs, rather that he had been caught.

Check the race out on YouTube and you will see what I mean. The glamour event lived up to all the hype and the world stopped as Ben blew away the Good Guy in undeniable fashion.

The real amazing truth is that the supposed Saint Guy Carl was just like Ben and Lance, he cheated too! It was also proven that he took banned substances and received a letter from the US Olympic Committee that he had failed tests that could ban him from the games, yes, in 1988.

Dr Wade Exum, former USOC Director of Drug Control, has stated the facts and uncovered evidence that Carl Lewis failed his drug test in the lead up to the games and shown a letter from Barron B Pittenger that shows Carl Lewis's test was positive for specimen B for pseudoephedrine, ephedrine and phenylpropanolamine and that this abuse was cause for a ban from the 1988 Olympic Games in Seoul Korea. Wade Exum says that this was covered up by a term called inadvertent use. Carl says it was a something for a cold.

The USOC said this inadvertent use was based on the athlete not meaning to take it or not meaning to get an advantage from using it.

Whatever, Ben took the rap alone.

Twenty-five years later, after being found guilty of doping on September 27, 1988, Ben had this to say, *"I was nailed on a cross, and 25 years later I'm still being punished. Rapists and murderers get sent to prison, but even they get out eventually. I know what I did was wrong. Rules are rules. But the rules should be the same for all."*

This is where administrators have failed sport so badly – the rules were interpreted and used differently.

Alan Hubbard, working then for London agency United Newspapers, has said in this article, *"The baddies are winning; the chemists are always one step ahead, working on measures to mask tests. It was interesting the IOC awarded the 2020 Olympics to Tokyo. Spain and Turkey have been quite well-known for having drugged athletes. Japan is not just a safe pair of hands but a clean pair of hands."*

I disagree with his prediction and believe as always that the truth will prevail as it is fundamental to our ongoing sustenance and success of humankind that it does. The fact that the IOC has gone in favour of Japan is indeed a meritorious decision and it is for that reason, and because history shows time and time again that the truth prevails, I believe substance abuse will be driven out of sport. It must be as anything less is a failure in human endeavour and integrity.

Amazingly Linford Christie, who came third in the great race, or dirtiest race in history as it is often referred to, and was later elevated to silver was also drug cheat. He tested positive for the stimulant pseudoephedrine at the 1988 Seoul

Olympics, but he escaped sanction after the International Olympic Committee's disciplinary committee voted by a margin of 11 to 10. Incredibly, it was reported that two judges on the panel were asleep when the vote was taken, so one wonders how their votes were recorded.

Furthermore in the same article, there is further reason to believe that the truth will win as the following excerpt clearly shows the dilemma these cheats have in reconciling their blatant and obvious abuse with their own self-image.

In 1999, Christie was found guilty of using the performance-enhancing drug, nandrolone, following a doping test after an indoor meet in Germany. He was found to have more than 100 times normal levels of the metabolites of nandrolone in his urine. Various explanations were offered to explain the results, including eating avocado, or using nutritional supplements.

True, avocado!

The IAAF rejected that explanation and gave Christie a two-year ban from athletics, despite UK Athletics feeling that there was reasonable doubt whether the drug had been taken deliberately, a decision which ignored the usual drug testing principle of 'strict liability'.

Christie denied any wrongdoing and denied his spectacular physique was the result of steroid abuse. He stated, *"It does not follow that all athletes who are big take drugs... Only by testing all athletes will the sport be kept clean of drugs."*

However, after the ban the British Olympic Association advised that Christie would not be eligible for any future Olympic Games.

Carl Lewis, second place getter in the great race and later awarded the gold which he must surely treasure, believes that the system allowed it and so it was okay. But what Wade

Exum (former USOC director) is saying in the YouTube link below is that the whole level playing field was a myth. Ironically, he says at the end of the interview that if they could not do anything to take doping out of sports, when this was his job, then doping was meant to be in sports.

At least Ben told the truth that he cheated and didn't lie. He was open when questioned that he had taken banned substances but stated that they were different to the ones the Olympic Committee accused him of taking which lends weight to the scenario that Ben was not treated fairly and ended up being a victim of unfair treatment.

If Carl Lewis is a drug cheat and shouldn't have been at the games, then he should be stripped of the gold or he should hand it back to the Olympic Committee to see if they can determine a genuine competitor who won the race or void the event.

There can be no double standards in competitive sport where the stakes are so high. If sport is *"an activity involving physical exertion and skill that is governed by a set of rules or customs and often undertaken competitively,"* which I believe it to be, then Ben is either the gold medal winner of drug cheats or they all need to hand the medal down to the first clean competitor which is really the only fair and just outcome.

Ben's integrity is intact in so far as he admitted it as soon as he was caught and that I can respect. An entirely different approach to Lance and Carl it would seem given the commentary that he failed three times.

http://www.youtube.com/watch?v=dGiEKeJnmpg&feature=related

Interestingly, this YouTube link showing Carl Lewis infringed has been withdrawn as I have just checked it – 25/1/15. The reason and apology stated in it is due to several copyright infringements.

"Proof That Carl Lewi..." The YouTube account associated with this video has been terminated due to multiple third-party notifications of copyright infringement.

Is it that or is somebody trying to hide the truth? If so, who and why?

There is an incredible link between Carl and Lance in the way they treat the reality of being caught and guilty. They both have an overriding need to substantiate their credibility to their adoring public to such an extent that the truth is insignificant.

In January, 2015, Lance was interviewed and said if he had his career over, he would *'probably do it again'.*

When I started writing this book several years back, I was wondering whether Lance would ever admit the truth. It is not surprising that even after he was forced to fess up that he still feels it necessary to justify his ego by saying that it was the right thing to do because others were doing it at that time.

No, Lance, just because others are cheats and liars, it doesn't make it right to break the rules in the quest of false glory, because that is what is what it was, false glory, as you never really won.

That is why you were stripped of your titles.

Carl, in 2003, finally admitted he was the beneficiary of taking banned substances with the statement, *"Who cares I failed drug test?"*

"There were hundreds of people getting off," he said. *"Everyone was treated the same."*

It's a real shame that the YouTube internet site has been taken down as the evidence was there for everyone to see. What is really incredible about this statement is Carl obviously cared himself at one stage as he tried to protect his image and happily took the medal from Johnson.

As I investigated further, I found an article in *The Age* dated April 19, 2003, that confirmed the embarrassment the US Olympic Committee where Exum claimed that more than 100 athletes of failed drug tests that were covered up and went on to win 19 Olympic medals from 1988 to 2000.

These included Lewis and the tennis player Mary Joe Fernandez and Lewis's training partner Joe deLoach who went to win the gold in the Olympic 200 m in 2000. Interestingly, Joe was caught taking the same three banned substances as Lewis that contained substances found in medicines used to treat a common cold. The lads were obviously under the weather!

The more I dig into sporting abuse of the elite, the more I find that many of those at the very top are taking every advantage they can.

So what is the most important thing? A gold medal won by cheating or admitting you cheated and endeavouring to resurrect your integrity? Imagine how hard that must be to face, when the world media has extolled you as the greatest sportsman in your field, and now you are at an age that you will never be able to again be the hero in history that you're cheating created.

Ben on the other hand told the truth about his lie and in the end that is the truth in my book. The truth evolves and as humans we need to be able to exonerate ourselves by admitting our failings. People coming clean should be forgiven but the ill-gotten victories expunged. If they have owned up to the situation and accepted their mistake, the lie has been sentenced to the past and no longer current. It is replaced by the new truth which ultimately becomes the mark of the man.

However, the victories created with dishonest abuse of substances cannot be changed. It happened and must be dealt with in history accordingly, so like Lance all cheats should have their titles stripped. No exceptions.

Ben has a similar view and his statements below referring to Lewis affirm this.

"We know several times before the Olympic Games he tested positive."

"And for him preaching the word that he's clean and working with kids, I challenge him to come on this campaign, tell the truth, tell the world that he has used performance-enhancing drugs."

"He would be ashamed but he would be a man to come forward and we can work together. If he can't come face to face, we know what he is. He is not a man."

Unfortunately, for people like Carl, the internet is easily accessible and all sorts of fallacies get laid bare on this free medium of information. There are also large amounts of fake news pumped through social media sites, so one has to be as discerning as possible when determining sources of information and endeavour to use credible sources.

IF YOU LIE, AND THEN REVEAL THE TRUTH ABOUT THE LIE, YOU WILL REDEEM YOURSELF AND SENTENCE THE LIE TO THE PAST AS IT WILL BE SUPERSEDED BY THE NEW TRUTH. IT DOES NOT HOWEVER EXONERATE ANY DAMAGES THAT MAY HAVE BEEN CAUSED BY THAT LIE.

The biggest perpetrators of deception, in my opinion, are the imposters that accepted gold and silver knowing full well that on the same basis of the race day Ben blew them off the Park.

If you want to read more, then I urge you to dial Ben Johnson into YouTube and the links will be there to see all manner of comments, not many in favour of Carl that I could see, so Betsy Andreu is right – the truth does matter and always will.

While Ben may not threaten Einstein's intellectual capacity, which none of us do, it is quite clear that Albert wasn't ever going to threaten Ben out of the blocks. Yet both of them come from completely different worlds and have a disarming simplicity about them. They both have an incredible single-minded belief in what they are pursuing which is a common trait in all successful people.

They believe and they commit. They are fearless in the pursuit of their future and know that as long as they do their best they have not failed.

Ben believes that if he was racing today against Usain Bolt, he would run a 9.3 or 9.4 because he is the fastest runner of all time and he also contends that it was money that was the reason that caused him to be disqualified. He says that if he had not changed from the American brand Adidas to the Italian brand Diadora, then he would be the champion in the history books.

Maybe he's right.

He further contends that the drugs that he was convicted of he never took, but freely admits that he was taking steroids but different to those that resulted in him being stripped of the proudest moment of his life.

Whatever the real truth is with Ben's story at least he has confronted the truth and been honest with himself and taken his medicine while others bask in their shadowy limelight.

Greed is an unbelievably powerful motivator for some people, whether it is for power or money or both as they often go hand in hand. Greedy people will sacrifice friendship and peace, which has an indeterminable value, and even sacrifice the sustainability of our planet.

So let us consider what motivates Ben, Lance and Carl.

A competitive streak that all top sportsmen have and the thrill of competing at the very top of the world is an attribute found in all successful people and they hate losing. The glory of success will also be a factor, the burning hunger to be in the history books. Yes, the ego is truly satisfied when everyone acknowledges you as the greatest human alive, and any sacrifice is okay because the desire is so great that any eventual consequence does not enter into the reality of being a superhuman that other mere mortals idolise.

The fame and fortune also brings financial freedom, security and, if the individual is half decent looking, the attention of the opposite sex. This in turn can bring additional income from brand endorsements often paling the earnings from the main pursuit. So it's easy to see why how something that might start as a little boost to assist energy levels turns into a sustained programme, when success starts nourishing your ego, and that feeling of invincibility takes hold.

So how great is the fall when truth finally knocks on the door and you can't tell it to go away.

The identity crisis they confront when their self-image is shattered is extreme.

The following quote by Lao Tzu provides a really interesting option for all three but at the time of writing acceptance has really only come to Ben yet he continues to believe he was the greatest sprinter ever and he may well have been. Lance has been forced to admit he did it but is contrite and says he would do it all again, otherwise, he undermines his achievements and his ego won't allow that.

He at least accepts what he did and yet there seems to be no such acceptance from Mr Lewis, only an admission qualified by the fact everyone was doing it, so it was okay.

If cheating is to be punished, the rules must be standardised globally and across all sport. Why was Ben stripped of the title and Carl not?

"When I let go of who I am, I become who I might be."
– LAO TZU

I really like this quote which became a life-changer for me. I was hunting around for a car battery in the little town of Silverdale, Auckland one morning. I saw a battery sign and rolled into the auto-electrical workshop. The owner was unbelievable and had a replacement battery fitted in no time with exactly the same crank power I needed, probably not as much as a steroid induced cyclist could crank but it got the SUV sorted again.

When I paid and had a scan of the invoice, this quote from Lao Tzu was staring me in the face and I thought about it for days. It is so true that you build an image of yourself and how other people perceive you mainly based on your life experience to date.

Remember Buddha in the Truth of Religion – *"I am the sum total of everything I thought."*

Based on this belief you can change your thoughts and change your identity.

YOU ARE WHO YOU BELIEVE YOU ARE, AND
ULTIMATELY, YOUR HAPPINESS IS DEFINED BY
THAT BELIEF, HOWEVER MISGUIDED IT MAY BE.

Lance and Carl are probably perfectly happy within
themselves as they have convinced themselves they did
nothing wrong.

The best example in the sporting world I have seen of
someone cleverly confronting their abuse of drugs is Andre
Agassi who diffused the minefield in a brilliantly executed
book where he extolled the drugs he took as actually
inhibiting his playing ability yet the results during and after
this period were his best. Rivals like Boris Becker and Pete
Sampras summed up their thoughts on Andre in the excerpts
below and not surprisingly they differ from Andre's self-
perception.

Again it's all about the ego driving the identity and what
Agassi has done so brilliantly is that he has admitted it like
Ben, so he has gained some public forgiveness. Cheats who
admit their faults are not nearly as despicable as the villains
that try to get away with it.

Boris has this to say: ***"Andre didn't just take drugs, he
also tested positive for drugs and then got away with it, and
that's not good at all for tennis, especially for the governing
bodies. People are going to be thinking, 'How could this
happen? How could he get away with this?'"***

Boris hit the nail on the head in many ways, notably, how
Agassi evolved but, more importantly, how the tennis
administration failed its duties just as was to be revealed in
cycling when Lance's world started to unravel. This is
covered in more detail later.

Pete Sampras was Agassi's main rival during this era
where the big serve volley player took a dominant career over
his ground-stroking competitor. How different the records
might have been we will never know.

Sampras acknowledged he and Agassi are drastically different people despite their tremendous success on a tennis court and everything they did for the rise of their sport in the U.S. Agassi said he sometimes hated tennis and going out to practice for hours at a time. He said he sometimes deliberately lost matches, too.

"We were going in two different directions," Sampras said. *"I think he was sort of lost and not sure what he wanted, and I knew exactly where I wanted to go. In order to be the best player in the world, tennis has to be your life."*

Andre admitted his lie and developed a new truth that has been widely accepted and he continues to be seen as a star and has done enormous deeds in children's education with the foundation he developed.

The point I want to reiterate here is that if you are a liar and want redemption, the best thing to do is own up before you get exposed. That's why Andre has got through this so well, the truth came out on his terms whereas Lance was exposed by his peers but continued to live in denial and believed that he could get away with it.

Interestingly, the public react very differently to his sporting rivals that were competing with him unaided. They are less likely to give him the credit that the public continued to do.

Amazingly, in Agassi's book, which is a must read, he talks openly about how he was caught taking drugs at Wimbledon and how it was all hushed up at the time so that the sports integrity was maintained.

Excuse me! What are the administrators thinking and why do they think the sports integrity will be maintained when they allow cheating to occur? To my simple mind, allowing cheating is in no way maintaining the sports integrity. It's like a head master allowing children to take drugs so he preserves the school's reputation that no one has ever been expelled. I have seen this at a local school, amazing really.

This behaviour is a result of weak leadership, so weak that they are not prepared to deal with the truth of the matter. There is no excuse and the leadership should be replaced with credible people that will value the sport or school before anything else, as they are engaged to do. If the administrators cannot uphold the rules fairly for all, then chaos and mal-intent will reign. There can only be one set of rules and they must always be managed as they are required to be under the appropriate bodies governing constitution.

Cycling is confronting their demons and tennis needs to do the same.

You only need to look at the websites that exist questioning whether Rafael Nadal is a substance abuser to wonder if where there is smoke, there is fire.

From my perspective, there appears to be significant questions being asked and we already know the tennis administration will not always disclose the truth, as in the Agassi case, they failed to disclose his failed drug test.

The call from five of the top world's 10 tennis players including Federer, Djokovic, and Murray for more drug testing to be done in the sport may be targeted at Nadal and Murray at one stage was quite vocal about this.

If it is established that he has been an abuser, will the Tennis Federation give the titles to the finalist that was beaten? If he is guilty as so many people believe, just how brilliant really is Roger Federer who managed to regain his number one status and win a 19th Grand Slam title, presumably with the God-given talent he has.

Federer extended his lead over Nadal to beat him in the Australian Open final in 2017 in what is one of the greatest comebacks of all time, following his own knee injury and surgery. Trailing 3-1 in the final set Federer unleashed a barrage of brilliance that Nadal simply has no answer to, and took the deciding set 6-3 in what was another epic match between the two rivals.

Federer now believes he can beat Nadal and that is most evident in his consecutive wins at the Australian Open, India Wells and Miami and, most recently, Wimbledon taking his tally to 19 Grand Slams. Along with this belief has come a strategy to take the backhand earlier and with top spin as opposed to a defensive slice which historically played into Nadal's strength, endless physical energy, almost inhuman desire and a wicked topspin forehand.

PROGRESS COMMENCES WHEN YOU BELIEVE BEYOND KNOWN FACT OR ABILITY.

Federer went on to win another Australian open to take his total to 20, and is closely followed by Nadal who is now on 19.

This dilemma must have been the same real problem facing the Cycling administrators when Lance was stripped of his titles as the sport seems so riddled with drug cheats that they could well face the same situation all over again to determine who was next in line that wasn't cheating.

One can only admire all those people that persisted with uncovering the massive lie even at the cost of exposing the sports credibility. In fact, the opposite has happened, the process of seriously eliminating drug abuse in sport adds to its credibility and tennis needs to take a cold hard look at the processes before it finds itself in the same situation as cycling, having a prolific champion that may not be legit.

One thing I will say is that Roger doesn't appear to the physical attributes or personal ethic that would condone substance abuse. He also has the most incredible stroke making ability I have ever seen in tennis over the last 40 years and I am an avid tennis fan. Having played to a level of winning several Club Champion singles titles, I have some basis for my opinion as I have followed closely the top players in the world for decades.

If Lance could have 500 drug tests and never be proven guilty and Rafael has the same chemist, as has been speculated, then he may have nothing to fear from the testing process.

Interestingly, in late April and early May 2013, we now have the Spanish judge ruling to destroy all the evidence of blood doping samples found at the premises of Dr Fuentes other than cycling. This smack of hypocrisy is clearly an attempt to cover up potential damage to other sporting heroes and Andy Murray used twitter on May 1 to slam this decision as one of the biggest sports cover-ups in history. He rightly questioned why the court would order blood bags to be destroyed and called the decision *'the biggest cover up in sports history'* and *'a joke'*.

Fuentes has admitted working with other sportsmen including boxers, soccer players, tennis players and athletes, and evidence from 35 different cheats may be lost. WADA, the World Anti-Doping Agency, is appealing the decision.

It is interesting that Nadal was back playing just prior to the decision to destroy the samples; something that I believe is at the heart of Roselyne Bachelot's public comments covered later in this section. All suspects in this case should be lined up before WADA that should have the power to lie detect with the best possible equipment so that the truth can be found and their character either verified or vilified whichever is appropriate. As you will read later in this section, using science and the law is not the only way to determine an athlete's failure to follow the rules or otherwise.

There should be an international law that overrides any country's judiciaries ability to determine legal outcomes that disadvantages athletes from other countries. The fact that Spain was able to adjudicate to impact the lives of so many athletes is simply not right.

Perhaps a lie detection programme, independently managed is the way to go. There is some evidence that lie detectors are not bulletproof which is why I suggest testing several parties, all at once, on the same questions and then see what prevails. The broader the test, the more likely the truth will emerge, and given this deception creates such massive amounts of money, the Global Legal System needs to take a much stronger and more unified stance to stamp out this corruption.

Rumours do little to reveal the truth; in fact, they usually make things worse as the story can be embellished by everyone who tells it.

That is why Andy Murray is right, why should honest people have to compete with cheats if they are proven to be so? It's the proving that is the difficult part especially when the courts choose to destroy evidence.

Nadal came out after all the speculation about his cheating and said that he thinks it is wrong of the judge to destroy the evidence that was held for the Fuentes' case as Fuentes had mentioned that tennis was one of the sports he was involved with creating speculation around Nadal.

Nadal stated that the drug cheats that Fuentes admitted he has worked with from a number of sports should be named, *"so that at least they can feel the contempt of fellow sportsmen and feel ashamed."*

I totally agree with his sentiment. This will eliminate all the speculation and establish the facts.

Yet despite this Judge Julia Patricia Santamaria never once during the whole case asked for the names of these athletes. Both WADA and the anti-doping Spanish authority have said they will appeal the decision of the judge to destroy the evidence, which given the circumstances and the potential damage to Spanish sport seems unlikely to succeed. I don't know how the Spanish Judicial System works but one reason the judiciary moved to destroy the evidence could be to protect the country's image and that of its leading athletes.

Nadal further protested, *"Unless that decision is reversed, it means the world may never know the names of those people who used Fuentes's services in order to gain an unfair advantage in their sport.*

"I find it unfair that the names of the cheats are not given, whether they're Spanish or not," said Nadal, according to the AS and Marca newspapers. *"The image that this verdict gives our country is not the best."*

If the decision is not overturned, then the world may never know the names of the people who used Fuentes services to gain unfair advantage over their rivals.

It is logical that if tennis players are involved, as Fuentes says they are, that some will be Spanish. Otherwise, why would the Spanish Judicial System not allow the samples to be disclosed? Would they care if they were American, French or German? Fuentes stated, *"I worked with cyclists but also footballers, boxers, tennis players and athletes,"* so who are they? A high-profile player like Nadal, who has amazing fitness levels and can endure the most physically demanding grand slam does become a suspect as some players attest.

Why did Nadal come out so strongly in protest of the judge after the decision when all the rumours were swirling around prior? I have been unable to find any prior comments from him against the exposure of Fuentes samples until the time the courts announced they would be destroyed.

It was April 30, 2013 when the Fuentes blood doping samples were ordered to be destroyed.

Let's hope that in the future the full truth of Operación Puerto and the alleged cover up is exposed, as the public want to know and so do innocent fellow athletes.

Fuentes made the following remarks: *"If I would talk, the Spanish Football team would be stripped of the 2010 World Cup."* FIFA has taken no action to date.

This really does put the Spanish Judiciary under more scrutiny. Hopefully, one day Fuentes will spill the beans if he is able to and not compromised by legal boundaries.

Given the next Olympics may be in Spain, this whole episode has large financial implications for the country. They control the judicial system in their own country and as it is their athletes that are under the spotlight it would be easy to assume that this whole episode is being orchestrated to help them in the Olympic bid. Spain is already embattled financially with record unemployment levels (approximately 26% and approximately 50% for youth) and any sportsman embroiled in the whole fiasco is between a rock and a hard place.

The same rock and a hard place that Armstrong found himself in before he was finally forced to admit his grand illusion. They will now have seen that Lance coming clean has not worked well for him, so if all the suspicions are valid, then it is far better for Fuentes secret list of sportsmen to play along and hope the truth never reaches the light of day. That, unfortunately, for them is not the nature of the truth and time will tell.

Fuentes of course got off lightly to keep his mouth shut and this would have been a low odds outcome for the TAB! Fuentes got only 12 months suspended prison sentence in February 2015.

This wide speculation about Nadal is not likely to go away and it is a tragedy for Rafael if he is in fact not guilty. Perhaps he should volunteer to take a lie detection test by a fully independent body selected by his accusers to finish the speculation once and for all.

The site that first drew my attention to Nadal's potential doping is '*Does Tennis have a steroid problem*' and I recommend you read it as it is incredible and seemingly very well-reasoned. Nadal's amazing success after a long break further causes for questioning the whole case of drugs in tennis. The timing of Rafa's successful returns and the Fuentes case having everything locked down by the judicial system in Spain may all be a coincidence but it might not be either.

"...in 2006, the Spanish doping scandal known as Operación Puerto uncovered widespread blood doping, spearheaded by a Spanish doctor, Eufemiano Fuentes. Initially, this was assumed only to involve cyclists. However, a French newspaper stated that athletes in other sports were also on the list of athletes receiving Fuentes' services, including some top Spanish soccer players and Rafael Nadal.

"Nadal, of course, denied any involvement, and Spanish sports authorities denied any non-cyclists were involved (something proven to be a lie now that Operación Galgo [Greyhound] has opened up). To this day, the full list of athletes' names connected to Operación Puerto has been sealed by a Spanish judge, which is consistent with the

Spanish attitude towards doping spanning back at least to the Barcelona Olympics in 1992 and continuing on to the present."

It was late April 2013 when a Spanish judge ordered the destruction of more than 200 blood bags seized in a raid of a major European doping ring that catered to elite athletes. Judge Julia Santamaria justified the decision to withhold the evidence from anti-doping authorities with Spain's Privacy laws.

Given the very significant amounts of money paid to top athletes, the penalty for Fuentes does indeed seem light but then he had a lot to trade with the authorities, the credibility of Spain and of Spanish Sport along with the bid for the Olympics thrown in the mix. I'm not sure that the scale of offending is that different to Bernie Madoff, the epic US Fraudster who created a giant Ponzi scheme, yet his crimes were clearly identified and the scale known. It would be difficult indeed to unravel the web of financial gain that Fuentes achieved for his clients but no doubt it was substantial or they wouldn't take the risk.

Or would they? Given the pathetic penalties to date, with the exception of Lance, who probably got and will get his just deserts for the remainder of his existence, it would seem a good bet for athletes to dope to the max and take the rewards that come with cheating.

Madoff got sentenced to 150 years and the good doctor got 12 months suspended prison sentence for endangering public health. Maybe that was the problem – the judicial system focused on completely the wrong issue, so that the result ended up being not what it might have been if the truth was allowed to be told.

The penalty in no way reflected the crime being committed – enabling drug cheating on a massive scale. Paradoxically, it is not Fuentes that is really guilty of perpetrating this monstrous cover up as in the excerpt below he offers to reveal the identity of all his clients. Why did the Spanish not allow this to happen?

"Mr Fuentes had offered to reveal his full list of clients but the confirmation that the blood bags will not be passed on to other authorities will rile the World Anti-Doping Authority, who called for those who dope to be named."

The truth about the endemic problem cycling has just continued to explode through the media and on December 7, 2012, the *New York Daily Times* reported that the cyclist Tyler Hamilton who won gold for the US in the 2004 Athens Olympics has requested his name to be withdrawn from the Olympic records.

IOC President Jacque Rogge personally responded to Hamilton.

"I very much appreciate that you have expressed regret for having used performance-enhancing drugs and that you hope that, through your example and future efforts, this will discourage others from using performance-enhancing drugs," Rogge wrote to Hamilton on letterhead bearing the Olympic rings.

The difference between Tyler and Lance is like night and day. One desperately wanted to retain his myth and the other valued his integrity ahead of his medal and did his best to atone for his mistake.

INTEGRITY IS YOUR PERSONAL YARDSTICK OF THE TRUTH AS YOU PERCEIVE IT, AND YOUR MORAL SCORECARD AS VALUED BY YOUR SOCIAL BASE.

From my perspective Tyler has retained his integrity and fully righted his mistake. Everyone in life has this opportunity and it is up to them to identify what they really stand for and constantly check their actions against their beliefs. Initially, Tyler vigorously defended the finding of foreign blood populations and managed to retain his gold, but eight years later, he confessed and asked for his name to be erased from the record books.

THE TRUTH IS A RELENTLESS FORCE THAT DRIVES ALL HUMAN BEHAVIOUR. IT IS UNDENIABLE AND UNSTOPPABLE.

If you think you can hide the truth, ask Lance whether he believes that is now possible?

To top it off for Lance, he was then confronted with a story in a new book *Wheelmen* that claims his one-time fiancé for a brief period sang to Feds about Lance and that she was reportedly with him when he went to receive a blood transfusion.

The *NY Daily times* on October 9, 2013, reported that she was with Lance when he went to have an illicit blood transfusion and later told Federal investigators about what she'd seen according to a new book about the doping conspiracy that propelled Armstrong's cycling teams. Armstrong according to the book didn't try to hide it and tried to normalise it by saying all cyclists were doing the same thing.

Then why say you weren't? There is more to come in this story.

One can't help but feel the conjecture swirling around Nadal indicates he is heading down the same road as Lance did. It's January 2014 and the Australian tennis open final is between Rafael Nadal and a first-time finalist, Swiss beast Stan Wawrinka, known on tour as Stanimal.

Beaten and Booed on 27/1/14.

The Australian open tennis final just finished last night and what an amazing spectacle that turned out to be with Wawrinka dispatching Nadal in the final in four sets, which probably would have been three, if the match had been played under fair rules for both parties.

The extended time Nadal took from the court was inexplicable, and as Wawrinka correctly pursued the time delay from the umpire, so he could understand why Nadal left the court, he was met with a refusal from the umpire. Wawrinka thought he was looking at his feet and then it turns out he went off to have his back treated. Apparently,

Wawrinka was right, and the player is only able to leave the court for privacy reasons, and it was clear when he returned and had massage on the mysterious back injury that it was half way up his back and privacy was not needed.

So why did Nadal leave the court. Stan asked for the reason and insisted that the umpire tell him why and the umpire said he didn't need to. This was not agreed with by Fred Stolle, commentator, who said he would walk off the court and get the Referee, Stephan France, until he got the reason. Fred was a Champion from another era.

Interestingly, the umpire, Carlos Ramos, refused to tell Stan why Nadal left and said he would not.

Stan asked Carlos to get the Tournament Referee repeatedly and is met with *"I'm not doing that"* by the umpire. One must question why is the umpire refusing what seems to be a perfectly reasonable request given the circumstance. This is a Grand Slam Final and not ladies mid-week where a minor indiscretion of the rules won't impact the history of the sport.

Wawrinka repeatedly asked the umpire, Carlos Ramos, what was the medical reason that Nadal had left the court and insisted that in every match it happened. *"Why won't you tell me? Always, always happens, every match,"* that the player knows what is wrong with the competitor.

Eventually, Wayne Mckewen came on to talk to a very animated Stanimal and also provided no answer in what appears to me to be an attempt to hide something, like the truth maybe! Why didn't the referee come on and answer the questions? Why did Wade get the job? Watch the video link on YouTube as it shows everyone's body language. Carlos is exasperated that he can't tell Stan what to do, and I can't tell what Wade is saying, but based on his body language and Stan's comments, he also is not complying with the request.

Carlos Ramos in my opinion deliberately appears to frustrate Stan who is reasonably also asking to see the referee and Stolle agrees. It looks like one-sided umpiring and a foul stench shadows the court but Stan is relentless in pursuing his right. The commentators express concern that Wawrinka will lose his concentration as he was on an amazing role of shot making prowess that not even this drama can eclipse.

The crowd boos the officials as they can sense the injustice unfolding before their eyes. The truth is amazingly powerful and the public sense that what is happening is wrong and rally behind Stan who simply wants to know why Nadal has left the court. An entirely reasonable request that when denied looked like a cover up.

Watch the link below as it is the most amazing high drama on a tennis court I've ever witnessed. Incredibly, it was the quest for the truth by Stan, and denied by officials that created this. I've copied the link below for you, it's a must-see event.

https://www.youtube.com/watch?v=mtfyaG8SRJA.

DENYING THE TRUTH CREATES SUSPICION AND IS THE FUEL BEHIND THE FORCE THAT ULTIMATELY UNRAVELS DECEPTION.

As Fred Stolle so correctly queries while commentating the match – *"Why doesn't Nadal have to play under the same rules as other players?"* – noting that he has often been cited for time violations. The amazing thing I got from his comment was that he apologised and said *"I'm sorry"* when he made it.

Fred you never have to apologise for telling the truth, I'm just glad that we have a tennis commentator with integrity, and also the smarts to make calls during a match that makes sense. The balance of your team of commentators was less than average, and seemed to me to be unable to be objective to the scene unfolding, however, your co-host querying at the end of the drama queried why, if Nadal did have a back problem, did he leave the court as mostly this would be treated courtside. *"Do you think there is a bit more to it than that*?" meaning gamesmanship.

That's how my eyes and ears perceived it. Incredibly, Wawrinka who was just brilliant the way he stood up to Nadal's antics during the match later commented that he thought it was not that nice what happened and that he (Nadal) was a great guy.

It looked to me like Stan rolled his eyes to the heavens when Nadal made an extended speech about how hard he tried, after having been booed when he came back on the court, but the graciousness of both players must be acknowledged after such drama in the final ceremony.

The crowd reaction was clearly a huge surprise to Nadal, as he had taken his shirt off and looked to me like he was expecting a hero's welcome. Instead the crowd perceived it as a deliberate ploy to upset Wawrinka, who was doing what the game is all about, ripping his opponent to pieces with superior firepower. The crowd isn't stupid and they become heavily involved with the match thereafter supporting Stanimal back to some incredible tennis in the third and fourth sets.

IT IS ALMOST IMPOSSIBLE TO DECEIVE A CROWD BY COVERING THE TRUTH IN A LIVE SITUATION. HUMANS SIXTH SENSE WILL SEE THROUGH DECEPTION AND CALL FOR THE RIGHT THING.

I have watched the match many times now and while I have only played tennis to a club champion level, and badminton at national level, I have suffered with back problems in a competitive situation. What surprised me is that prior to him leaning forward to stretch his back, and the whole episode of him leaving the court, he was moving and serving with what appeared to be completely normal speed and agility.

So was the back injury real and when did it happen? I didn't see any cause or symptom and so I am forced to conclude based on what I saw my opinion is that it was gamesmanship feigned to upset what was a royal Wawrinka display that was making Nadal look ordinary on the day. Stan, you played unbelievable tennis that day and that is what I remember most. It was the period you really started believing you could step out from under Federer's shadow and it was great to see.

Wawrinka beat Djokovic and Nadal, the world's number one and two in the same tournament which is an incredible achievement and smashed the dominance of these two, plus Federer and Murray who have dominated the scene for years, in a new-found belief that allows him to achieve at levels previously his mind would not perceive possible.

BELIEVER – Stan Wawrinka winning the
2016 US Open Tennis Final

Even the commentators were wondering if this was gamesmanship. I have no problem with gamesmanship but breaking rules is cheating and anyone who infringes deserves to suffer the consequence as if they had lost.

How awesome, a new champion with a completely forthright approach to the game and the strength to not be intimidated by the officials, or the player and his reputation on the other side of the court. It must be said that the umpire, Carlos Ramos, was completely and deliberately ineffectual in my view and seemed to show disdain at the whistling and booing from the crowd at the end of the video link and as Nadal returned to the court. Take a long hard look at yourself Carlos and see if you think you officiated as fairly as you could have, and should have.

The real truth is that Nadal has never been stood up to like that and the crowd has never seen it and so they rallied behind Stan in what was one of the most courageous tennis matches I have ever seen.

Does the International Tennis Federation want to find out what's going on in its sport and make efforts to clear up the rumours or will one of England's games of gentlemen descend to a state where the audience turns off the TV set and doesn't go to the match? There is a persistent call for the game to be more transparent and have a better doping regime for the benefit of all its players.

Were Nadal's actions real or simply an unsportsmanlike conduct to upset his opponent? Wawrinka, whatever the truth, was impacted as the only set Nadal won was the one where he served poorly and appeared to be struggling with the situation and trying to make sense of it all. Clearly, his concentration was adversely impacted. This is why these guys earn the big bucks, its high drama and the audience was fully involved.

I really wanted to know what the rules are surrounding this remarkable episode, so I consulted the ultimate diviner of wisdom – Google and then downloaded the ATP Tour Rules 2015, and for the sake of this review, I disclose they are not the rules that were governing the tournament at the time and have assumed they have not changed. (Google couldn't find the 2013 rules and the 2015 version came up).

The umpire called that Nadal was taking a medical time out and Stan asked why he was going to consult the physiotherapist. I've copied below what I see as the relevant part of the rules.

The rules allow for an off-court evaluation 'if the player has developed an acute medical condition that necessitates an immediate stop in play'. This case simply does not seem to warrant this as one of the commentator's questions whether Nadal is using tactics to stop the undeniable force on the day – Stanimal!

If there was no accidental injury, as was the case in this instance, the umpire should have followed the procedure below in case B and called the physiotherapist in the changeover. If the player insists, he cannot continue, then the umpire should call the physiotherapist implying again that he will come to the court in the first instance. Again, the procedure does not appear to have been followed.

MEDICAL EVALUATION

During the warm-up or the match, the player may request through the chair umpire for the physiotherapist to evaluate him during the next change over or set break. Only in the case that a player develops an acute medical condition that necessitates an immediate stop in play may the player request through the chair umpire for the physiotherapist to evaluate him immediately.

The purpose of the medical evaluation is to determine if the player has developed a treatable medical condition and, if so, to determine when medical treatment is warranted. Such evaluation should be performed within a reasonable length of time, balancing player safety on the one hand, and continuous play on the other.

At the discretion of the physiotherapist, such evaluation may be performed in conjunction with the tournament doctor, and may be performed off-court.

If the physiotherapist determines that the player has a non-treatable medical condition, then the player will be advised that no medical treatment will be allowed.

MEDICAL TIME-OUT STARTS WHEN?

Case A: When does a medical time-out begin?

Decision A: Medical time-out begins when the physiotherapist arrives and is ready and able to treat the player. Thus, the physiotherapist has completed his examination/diagnosis and the medical time-out starts when the physiotherapist begins treating the player.

Case B: A player asks to see the physiotherapist during the middle of a game although the chair umpire observed no accidental injury.

What should the umpire do?

Decision B: First, tell the player that you will call the physiotherapist and he can see him at the changeover. If the player insists that he cannot continue, then stop play and call the physiotherapist. The physiotherapist will make the decision, upon examining the player, whether a medical time-out is needed.

WHEN TO TAKE A MEDICAL TIME-OUT?

Case: What happens if a player is injured during a match and decides not to take his injury time-out right away? (Before the end of the next change-over)

Decision: A player may call for the physiotherapist at any time. The physiotherapist shall determine whether the medical time-out is to be authorised.

The question as to whether the umpire has to advise the opponent as both Stan and Fred Stolle assert is not covered in this section of the rules, as far as I could ascertain; however, if this is common practice with other umpires, then it seems to have a great deal of validity. What's more it seems entirely fair to the opponent especially when there is no obvious fall and, even more especially, when the opponent makes a remarkable recovery and is able to compete for the remainder of the four sets.

Surely, tennis should be played in the spirit of sport of determining superior human prowess, unassisted by artificial substances and money-making focus that overrides the rules of the sport. Remember the definition at the start of the section giving the meaning of sport:

An activity involving physical exertion and skill that is governed by a set of rules or customs and often undertaken competitively.

Whoever or whatever inspired Stan to stand his ground in such dramatic fashion I don't know, but I completely respect the endeavour as it exposed a dramatic failure in the way the incident was managed.

Is the International Tennis Federation protecting one of their most bankable stars speculated to be the Armstrong of Tennis by Michael Emmett, an ex ATP Tour player and Director of Tennis at all Mayfair Clubs with a journalism degree at the University of Texas?

I believe one day we will know the truth, whatever that may be, and I am not in the camp of the Bloomberg article below, originally published in Bloomberg view, by Jonathon Mahler that espouses it's okay if Nadal is on steroids as it's great for men's tennis. In this article, Mahler says we should be thanking the scientist that has managed to keep Nadal playing and refers to his *"too good to be true comeback"* after his lengthy lay off for knee rehabilitation. Mahler goes further and says, *"Surely, no mere mortal could have accomplished this without pharmaceutical aid."*

Mahler seems to acknowledge that in his opinion Nadal takes steroids and that it's okay if it extends Nadal's career. *"Who wouldn't want to see another 10 years 'artificially' added to Nadal's career?"*

Actually, Mr Mahler, given the choice, I think you would find the answer to your question is most of the paying public. It is ridiculous to suggest that cheating has a place in sport, professional or otherwise.

If tennis is a sport that isn't played by the rules and fair to all competitors, then what is it?

Unfortunately, the original Bloomberg article that was found on the link below now comes up as page not found. I discovered this when reviewing the book on May 8, 2017.

http://www.bloomberg.com/news/2013-09-09/let-s-hope-drugs-prolong-rafael-nadal-s-great-career-.html

Fortunately, after trying searching with Google from a number of angles, I found the article republished in its entirety, it seems by 'Deadspin' on this URL.

http://deadspin.com/lets-hope-drugs-prolong-rafael-nadals-great-career-1279047223

Tennis professional, Michael Emmet, as mentioned earlier and a previous National Champion in Canada, has published his thoughts in the on-court publication as copied below. Michael has first-hand experience and a belief that Nadal will one day be exposed as Lance has been.

"Well, there are just as many Nadal rumours out there. I sat in a locker room a few years back and listened to three coaches discussing the steroids that Nadal was taking. One of the coaches, who was from Columbia, said he saw Nadal ingesting some sort of PEDs prior to a workout session in Monte Carlo. I know this is all hearsay, but enough people in the know have come forward to say they've seen it – I believe this will all come out one day – just like it did for Lance Armstrong.

"My thought is they (Nadal and Armstrong) were both using steroids and engaging in blood doping. Why not, if they figured they could get away with it and gain a tremendous competitive advantage. Obviously, both men were helped immensely by their team of experts during the entire process. This is a huge gamble and a massive undertaking – it's not a venture you go at alone."

The belief that these legends and famous people have in their own mind is that they are invincible and that is what makes them great.

The will they wield that creates their success will also succumb to failure if they are deluding themselves that cheating will be accepted and okay, as long as they are not caught. The power and drive they exude is not only restricted to cheating with drugs as they will use their position of power to manipulate outcomes that suit them, believing that is okay because they are doing it. As we have seen with the late Jimmy Saville, who's legacy has been completely been ruined through sexual abuse of 60 victims ranging in age from 8 to 40, it has now been established that former tennis ace Bob Hewitt has been found guilty of raping young girls.

Multi Grand Slam Champion Hewitt, who was 75 at the time of writing, was convicted of two charges of rape and one of indecent assault. Judge Bert Bam was satisfied that the two women who made the allegations were telling the truth and that Hewitt was very calculating in his approach. Not surprisingly, Hewitt has denied that this occurred but again we have the same situation where the halo of these perpetrators completely clouds their vision and understanding of who they really are and what they really have done.

One victim claimed Hewitt had said rape was enjoyable. The status and power had completely gone to his head so much so that as a coach teaching 10- to 13-year-old girls he thought he could do what he liked and get away with it.

THE TRUTH IS IF YOU CHEAT YOU ARE NOTHING, AND WHILE TIME WILL ASSIST IN THE VERIFICATION PROCESS, THE ULTIMATE DETERMINER OF YOUR LIFE VALUE IS THE TRUTH, BEING THE MOST IMPORTANT DETERMINER OF ALL RECOGNITION OF HUMAN ENDEAVOUR.

While tennis bubbles away with a cloud of suspicion, the drug cheating continues everywhere and the 2012 Olympic Games was no exception with Belarusian shot putter Nadzeya Ostapchuk stripped of her title for taking methenolone.

Valarie Adams, the rightful winner, was right in my view when she stated, *"Once a cheater always a cheater – you should be banned for life."*

"Kick them all out, none of this back after two years stuff."

It's hard to disagree with her especially when evidence suggests that cheats continue to benefit from taking steroids long after they have been convicted and their suspension has been served. It's really ironic that the New Zealand champion speaks as one of three nominees for the athlete of the year award when Justin Gamble is on the top-ten lists for the men, having failed drug tests in 2001 and 2006, and then returned in 2014 to run the fastest 100 m and 200 m that year to November 20.

Ostapchuk slammed the Olympic testing results as *'nonsense'* when she was caught using an anabolic steroid to win her gold medal and really struggled with the concept of returning the gold she did not win.

The real amazing thing in all these instances is that these athletes all develop a belief as to who they are based on their identity built from false achievements. Every day they live this lie and it becomes an intrinsic part of their persona, so much so that they don't recognise the truth. The deep embedded lie has overridden conscious reality.

Lance still thinks he was the greatest because others did it, Ben thinks he would be the fastest today if he had the same training and competition, Andre cleverly kept his image intact and Ostapchuk still competes and thinks now that her reputation is all-important to protect.

"I do not understand where it could come from," she said. *"I'm looking like an idiot to take this in heading for the games and knowing that it is so easy to be tested. Nonsense. I'm being tested every month, every week.*

"I hope for the better. The most important for me is to clear my reputation."

This is a similar catch cry from all those who get caught through a testing programme, or don't get caught as in Lance's case. However, it is all testimony to the theory that the truth is what you believe. All false heroes are so entrenched in their own self-image that they can't see how others now view them, even when they have gone through the discovery of their own grand illusion.

THE TRUTH IS THAT YOU ARE NOT WHO YOU THINK YOU ARE IF YOU HAVE CREATED AN IDENTITY BASED ON ANY FORM OF SUBSTANCE ABUSE THAT GAVE YOU AN UNFAIR ADVANTAGE

IN A PURSUIT TO WIN FAME AND FORTUNE
THROUGH SPORTING SUCCESS.

Recently, there has been numerous events globally that absolutely are tarnishing the very essence of sport and widespread corruption in the London Olympic Games has led to bans on Russia.

On November 8, 2015 the *Daily Mail UK* reported the following about the 2012 Olympic Games showing at least that there is a real determination by WADA (World Anti-Doping Agency) to increasingly act on cleaning up sport.

WADA released a bombshell report where Grigory Rodchenkov, Moscow Lab testing Director ordered the destruction of 1,417 samples three days before an investigation panel arrived on site. The report also revealed that he requested and accepted money to conceal the positive test results. He hit back slamming the report as full of lies and said the witnesses were inadequate. The report found *'widespread inaction'* by the worlds governing athletics body and also Russian Regulators that allowed competitors to take part in the 2012 Olympics with *'suspicious doping profiles'*.

This is a really hot potato, and Dick Pound, the co-author of the report who spent 11 months researching it, said it was just the tip of the iceberg as he squarely targets the Russian Athletics Federation and the IAAF (International Association of Athletics Federations) of *'a collective and inexplicable laissez-fair policy'* allowing athletes to compete.

The report also calls for a lifetime ban on the Olympic 800 m Champion, Maria Simonova – Famosova and the bronze medallist Ekaterina Poistogova plus three other distance runners.

The IAAF considered sanctioning the Russian Federation including possible suspension and, naturally, the Russians have called this political.

It constantly amazes me how innocent the Russians are. They didn't invade the Ukraine and didn't shoot down flight Malaysian flight MH370 with a Russian manufactured missile which crashed in the Ukraine at the peak of the conflict between the Ukraine and pro-Russian separatists, who we all know have nothing to do with Russia, because the Russians told us.

What is really positive is the exposure, and the increasing level of vilification that is attached to cheats since Lance Armstrong was exposed. Now that other sporting bodies have seen that cycling has not been destroyed by the exposure of its greatest hero and biggest fraud, they are free to pursue bringing integrity back to the awesome pursuit of physical excellence, governed by a set of rules that suitably punishes cheats with elimination and loss of any records or achievements as cycling has so courageously done.

Interpol is now conducting an investigation into widespread doping in track and field which can only be positive for all sports as the more the cheats are caught and punished, the less encouraged they will be to chase the money and risk their credibility, which incongruously is also a main driver for their behaviour. The weak penalties and small amount of perpetrators caught only serves to fuel the belief that they can be rich and great and get away with it.

Another global sport that is also in the headlines for the latter half of 2015 for all the wrong reasons is soccer, the beautiful game that is turning ugly. As the architect of the amazing run of years of growth for soccer, a game played by over 250 million people in 150 countries, FIFA president, Mr Sepp Blatter, is under enormous pressure for corruption on an unprecedented scale.

The noxious stench of corruption first really emerged when the desert nation of Qatar was awarded the 2022 World Cup. In May 2015, Swiss Police started the cascade of events that lead to the expulsion of two heads of the game. They arrested some of FIFA's crooks at the Baur Lac Hotel in Zurich. Michel Platini, UEFA boss, and soon after Blatter was suspended for eight years from football for their shady dealings, imposed by the Games Ethics Committee.

Incredibly, Blatter was re-elected president soon after all these public arrests started to occur.

It makes you wonder how deep the web of deception has spread.

In May 27 that year, the US unsealed a 47-count indictment against 14 world soccer figures for money laundering, racketeering and fraud, including FIFA officials. The quantum is some $150 million and at a similar time Swiss Prosecutors announced that they had commenced an investigation into money mismanagement for the awarding of the Qatar World Cup and also the 2018 World Cup to Russia.

Four have already admitted their guilt and are cooperating with the investigation including two sports marketing companies.

You won't believe this but President Putin from Russia thinks Blatter should get the Nobel Peace Prize because he is a *'very respected person'* who had *'done a great deal for the development of world soccer'* and made a *'colossal humanitarian contribution'*.

Can anyone else join the dots here, or is the correlation with the 2018 winner hosting the World Cup, Russia, and Sepp Blatter in my imagination?

In December 2015, Blatter was grilled for eight hours over his payment of £1.3 million to Platini by the Sports Ethics Committee. Blatter claimed he is innocent and his lawyers demanded an immediate withdraw of the ban placed on him. This is consistent behaviour with others that we have already investigated in this book with the possible exception of Ben Johnson, where they have elevated their sense of righteousness to legitimise any level of deceit or dishonesty, in the quest of their dream, or in Sepp's case, goal.

As always, the truth has emerged victor, as Blatter scored the sport's biggest own goal and ended his career in disgrace. A sad end indeed, after 17 years as president and 40 years with the organisation.

The Ethics judges ruled that he had broken FIFA's code of ethics on conflicts of interest, loyalty and offering and receiving gifts.

Blatter and Platini are both likely to be finished in football with Platini's attempt to succeed Blatter at the forthcoming

February Presidential most likely to be in tatters. Both plan to appeal the decision to the Court of Arbitration for sport and Blatter has suggested he will pursue his innocence to the highest court in Switzerland.

Platini has said he will *'fight this to the end'* and seek damages with civil proceedings calling the ethics committees decision *'pure masquerade'*.

"It's been rigged to tarnish my name by bodies I know well, and who for me are bereft of all credibility or legitimacy," Platini said in a statement.

I fear that the problem that the former French national coach and captain has is that it is not he that will be making the decision on his credibility. It will hopefully continue to be reviewed based on evidence, and the rules, so that the sport can move on by digging deep into this horrid fiasco and ridding itself of all corruption and those involved. This includes the players as we have seen in cycling, football, athletics, and likely in tennis that the cancer spreads right through the sport unless governed with an iron fist and a strong set of rules.

An appeal by Blatter and Platini was rejected and the decision by the FIFA Appeal Committee on February 16 2016 remains in force with Blatter banned from all football activity for six years and Platini for four years. Both had the terms reduced in respect of their contribution to the sport. One wonders about the severity of the penalty given the level of offending.

STRONG RULE ENFORCEMENT WITH HARSH PENALTIES BEFITTING THE CRIME WILL IMPROVE CREDIBILITY IN SPORT, NOT REDUCE IT, AND ALLOW THE TRUTH TO FLOURISH FOR THE GOOD OF ALL.

Back in May 2013, Eufemiano Fuentes, the convicted sports doping doctor as covered earlier, threatened to sell his knowledge on his clients and methods and further tarnish soccer's credibility.

Fuentes, considered one of international sport's leading dope doctors, has sent out a list of subjects that – for a price – he is now prepared to talk publicly about. It includes Spanish Champions League football teams, London marathon winners, Olympic medallists and a long list of cyclists he was involved with.

He has also offered to reveal how Tour de France officials failed to detect doping even when they tested those who had been taking performance-enhancing substances.

"How I prepared a team to play in the Champions League," is one category of revelations he is offering, according to an email sent by his lawyers on Friday.

However, following this story through it appears that Fuentes has bought his freedom with his silence as he no longer wishes to make any comments on cycling as reported in a subsequent article in cycling news. Clearly, there are a lot of stories that have been buried for now, but Fuentes remains one of the central figures to these major sports and was most likely silenced by the Spanish Judicial System as part of the evidence-destroying programme ridding the blood samples. Hopefully, the truth behind this will emerge sooner than later.

It is not going to be a short fix for great sports like cycling, football, tennis and athletics to rid themselves of the plague that rots them but confront the issue they must. Cycling has taken a massive step and must keep up the pressure and it's great to see now that football is following suit and also athletics.

The reason they need to front up is that there is new sports ready to take their place to television rights and all the promotional dollars that go with it. One particular sport is growing at an unprecedented rate and is also having its fair share of scandal with doping infringements. I'm talking about UFC and mixed martial arts which are a sport that is brutal in its honesty and takes me back to Gladiatorial times where the fight was to the death.

December 12, 2015 was an epic day for the UFC, as further evidence of this transition to exciting sport that is raw in its honesty emerged. The Brazilian legend Jose Aldo fought the Irish whirlwind Connor McGregor for the world UFC Featherweight title.

You might ask why the UFC, the Ultimate Fighter Championship, is the fastest growing sport in the world but one of the reasons I'm sure is that there is no hiding in the Octagon, everything is exposed, every fear, every confidence and every belief. With a $10.1 million in viewer gates Jose Aldo found out this to his horror when facing the Irishman, who was rightfully crowned as the combined Featherweight World Champion after knocking Aldo out in 13 seconds by a technique that he had envisaged would occur two weeks prior in a press interview. Connor said Aldo would over extend his right hand and that he would respond with his left which is proving to be one of the most effective weapons in the sport. Here is how he explained the power behind his foresight and wisdom.

"If you can see it here (touching his temple) and you have enough courage to speak it, it will happen. I see these shots and I see these sequences and I don't shy away from them. A lot of times people believe in certain things but they keep to themselves, they don't put it out there. If you truly believe in it, if you become vocal with it, you are creating that law of attraction and it will become reality" – *Conner McGregor.*

You can see the full interview on the link below.

http://www.mmafighting.com/2015/12/13/10021252/ufc -194-post-fight-press-conference-video

These are really powerful thoughts that Conner has and the power comes from his complete conviction that what he believes is true. He understands this power and the need to support his destiny with all the hard work and courage it takes to fulfil it, which is why he stands on top of the world, as he also predicted seven years prior.

My belief in the UFC as an organisation has been rocked by the recent disasters that have embroiled the sport in disrepute and the UFC 200 event that was supposed to be such an amazing spectacle for the sport turned out to be a debacle.

Initially, UFC 200 was to be the rematch of McGregor and Nate Diaz who beat McGregor by submission in his first fight, after the confident Irishman jumped up two weight classes. A dispute with the Sports President Dana White blew the eagerly awaited match off the card as McGregor decided he wanted to train and moved to Iceland and missed the press conference for the fight scheduled for July 9, 2016.

Then the head billing was going to be the legendary Jon Bones Jones fighting to get his title back from Daniel Cormier. Jones won the previous fight easily in 5 rounds and subsequent to that Cormier had meritorious wins against Anthony Johnson and Alexander Gustafsson. Jones was fighting his way back after pleading guilty to a hit and run incident.

So the stage was set and this was a suitable replacement for the Diaz McGregor rematch.

But Jones gets caught with out of competition tests for two banned substances testing positive with clomiphene, an anti-estrogenic substance, and letrozole, which works to prevent the synthesis of testosterone into oestrogen. The Nevada State Athletic Commission confirmed the out of competition samples were taken on June 16 and it is likely he will be banned for up to two years.

So Dana White goes back on the search for the headline act for the Gala event and comes up with Brock Lesnar, a previous world titleholder, and Mark Hunt, the New Zealander with an iron fist and a granite head. Finally, July 9 arrives and two titans enter the ring with Lesnar winning a 5 round decision 29-27 across all judges.

But it turns out he didn't win at all, he cheated. On June 28, a sample was collected before the fight on July 9, and Lesnar tested positive for a banned substance. Mark Hunt was justifiably filthy with the handling of the fight and started calling for all of Brock Lesnar's purse to be handed to him, as the only clean fighter. Lesnar pocketed $2.5 million and, clearly, Hunt has right on his side. He has always trumpeted for clean fighting and comes from a country that has an ethic to compete fairly.

He said he thought Lesnar was *'juiced to the gills'* prior to the fight and says this is the third time he has had to fight cheaters. He has never asked for compensation before but is sick of the UFC stating, *"They say they are trying to clean up the sport but it doesn't feel like it."*

"I've told Dana that I want a release from the UFC if they don't sort this out," Hunt said. I congratulate his courage and forthrightness but don't know whether he will get much joy from White, who at the UFC 202 press conference with McGregor and Diaz stood by stony faced as Diaz when questioned whether he was surprised about Jon Jones tested positive shook his head, smiled and said, *"Everybody's on steroids."*

At the start of the interview, McGregor looked at White and said that the main event of the fight and the co-main event of the fight card for UFC 200 were not at the press conference. This was an obvious double standard which hasn't assisted in White being a credible leader in the fight game. Increasingly, he will come under pressure if this pattern of leadership persists.

White later responds in the same press conference to someone questioning him about what he was thinking, after the press had been kept waiting for 30 minutes, about the fight finally going to take place, *"I'm not surprised motherfucker."*

See it on YouTube.

Interestingly, White does an extraordinary flip-flop just prior to UFC 207 allowing a request from Rhonda Rowsey to compete in the event with no media requirement which was the very reason he cancelled McGregor's fight. His reasons were that she was a huge personality in the sport and it is something she asked for, so he allowed it. He also made the following statement in the same article which beggars belief really as McGregor has also done a lot for the sport attracting record pay per view income for UFC 205 in his demolition of

Eddie Alvarez on his way to winning two consecutive titles for the first time in the history of the sport.

"It's definitely not ideal," White stated. ***"It's what she asked for, and like I said, back in the day, Ronda would literally do anything we asked her to do. Anything. And if the guys wouldn't do something, she would pick up the ball and do it herself. So for her to ask for something like this, how can I say no to that? She's done a lot.***

"This is something she asked for. It doesn't open floodgates. It doesn't change anything. If somebody doesn't want to show up for a press conference, I'll pull them from a card again."

DOUBLE STANDARDS ARE NOT THE POLICIES OF EFFECTIVE LEADERS AS IT LEADS TO DISHARMONY IN THE TEAM AND, ULTIMATELY, DISAFFECTION, DISSENT AND IF ALLOWED FOR TOO LONG, DISSOLUTION.

THERE CAN ONLY BE ONE SET OF RULES FOR THE TRUTH TO BE MEASURED FAIRLY.

I fully appreciate that UFC fighting may attract a varied audience but the position taken by White indicated to me that what Hunt is demanding may fall on deaf ears.

It would seem Mr White doesn't like criticism nor to be questioned on his performance and he puts on a brave face but equally it must be very difficult dealing with a firebrand like McGregor who dances to his own tune.

His risk is the growing dissent with the UFC and its management that McGregor referred to as *'running around like headless chickens'* at the very same press conference. Already, White faces open and public derision.

The other unanswered question is how Lesnar got to fight when his test was conducted 11 days before the fight on July 9. If the UFC had advice from the testing body and been able to act prior to the fight with Hunt, then the charade of UFC

200 is beyond reasonable. If Jones had to forfeit, then surely Lesnar should have been in the same boat.

No doubt the lawyers will pour over the fine print as the contract with Lesnar isn't broken if the UFC sanctioned the fight but Hunt is screaming blue murder.

Won't the truth be interesting when it all unfolds? The encouraging thing for me is the tide is turning and the cheats are being exposed. The fact that the Nevada State Athletic Commission dealt with Jones so decisively is positive as he is a major sporting hero, one who I admired immensely until this happened.

On July 29, 2017 the much-heralded rematch of Jon Jones and Daniel Cormier unfolded as one of the most tragic sporting spectacles ever where Jon Jones demolished Cormier in the third round with a brutal display from the sports finest ever exponent at his very best. He was gracious in victory and offered an olive branch to Cormier. It looked like the fairy tale revival of a great athlete from the horrors of his past indiscretions was complete as he was re-crowned World Champion again and acknowledged as the greatest pound for pound UFC fighter ever.

But the drama continues to unfold at the time of this going to the publisher with Jones falling foul of another abuse of an illegal substance on test A by USADA being turinabol. There is conjecture both ways, some say it is a set up or must be from a supplement while others are confident, he has taken steroids even though he had tested clean on random tests for the year prior and then fails on the known test pre fight. Jones in January 2018 passed a polygraph test and has always claimed his innocence in a situation that does not make sense given his clean slate for the year prior to the fight.

It is bizarre that he would pass seven random out of competition tests in 2017 but fail on the day of the weigh in, the night before the big fight. Could someone have spiked Jones diet and if so who would have the motive to do so?

Just as the chemists are getting more sophisticated with their masking of steroid abuse so are the detecting agents, and USADA ultimately determined that Jones was deriving no benefit from taking the steroid turinabol and that the small amounts were residual from previous tests. UFC executive and spokesman in this area Jeff Novitzky confirmed the following:

"Novitzky said USADA shared the findings with experts and conducted an investigation that determined Jones' low levels for the oral turinabol metabolite were merely 'residual' from the Sept. 2017 test Jones failed for the same substance, and that there was 'no evidence of any re-administration'. USADA concluded that the picograms in Jones' system amounted to no performance-enhancing benefit whatsoever."

Jones was cleared and went on to convincingly beat Alexander Gustafsson with a third-round technical knockout from punches and retain his Light heavyweight crown. Many believe Jones is the greatest UFC fighter ever and that is hard to dispute given he has never been beaten (as at June 2019), however, there will always be a shadow over that title due to substance abuse. From a skill viewpoint only it is hard to disagree with his claim to that level of greatness as Jones brings a diversity of attack and defence that has not been able to be dominated.

When asked about his next fight strategy on a TMZ interview with a brutal knockout artist, Thiago Santos, Jones replied, *"The strategy is just to, ahh, just to believe man. I'm big on the power of the mind and I'm a big believer in myself. I've got to continue to work hard. Belief without hard work is you know, just dreaming right."*

When asked how can he be beaten, Jones replied, *"Actually I'm really ticklish, I think that is the way to get me."*

Will Thiago bring a feather and not an iron fist? No, and he also brings a very strong conviction. The longer Jones goes unbeaten, the odds mount against him, but the key to his success is clear. He is excellent at identifying his foes weakness and he believes he has everything he needs to win.

The days of cheating in sport and getting away with it are being turned around by the positive action of crusading administrators who believe that fair play is an intrinsic essence that must be upheld, to allow the true heroes of sport to emerge.

THE TRUTH IS THE POSITIVE FORCE THAT UNITES US ALL AND MORE AND MORE PEOPLE ARE SEEKING IT IN ALL ASPECTS OF OUR DAILY LIVES AS IT CREATES AN INNER PEACE THAT WILL FACILITATE A LONGER HAPPIER LIFE.

Corruption in sport is not confined to doping and bribes for favours as we discovered at the Australian Open again, a sporting event that always creates phenomenal intrigue.

In January of 2016, the tennis world was rocked at the Australian Open by allegations of match fixing. A major website for sports gambling, Pinnacle Sports suspended betting as abnormally large amounts of money poured in just prior to a low-profile mixed doubles match between Lara Arruabarrena and David Marrero against Andrea Hlaváčková and Lukasz Kubot.

The money was heavily on Hlaváčková and Kubot and was easy to detect by Pinnacle as odd. What was not odd was that these two won easily 6-0, 6-3 putting the spotlight on Arruabarrena and Marrero both from Spain. Arruabarrena and Marrero were ranked 33 and 32 in the world in doubles respectively and both rejected the prospect of cheating entirely and Marrero indicated he had an injured knee which affected the performance.

Hlaváčková, at the time of writing (April 25, 2016) is ranked twelfth at doubles and Kubot is a doubles specialist, having won the Australian Doubles Open, in 2014. When I searched this up to balance the article online below, I was surprised, as on paper they should have won anyway but this was not mentioned in the New York Times article, link below, however, it did say they were favourites, and once you get past the sensational headlines, there is a more balanced view that heavy betting alone is not proof of match fixing.

The Open was also then besmirched with the BBC and Buzzfeed reporting that 16 players were repeatedly flagged over suspicions that they had thrown matches but that officials did not discipline them.

Buzzfeed reported that there was indeed a racket in tennis and it wasn't hitting balls. The investigation by the BBC and Buzzfeed was based on leaked documents from within the sport called the fixing files where 16 players, ranked in the top 50, have repeatedly been involved with alleged match fixing after 26,000 matches betting activity and interviews, across three continents. Indications are that gambling syndicates from Russia and Italy are behind it, and have made hundreds of thousands of pounds from the activity.

The response from Nigel Willerton who heads up the Tennis Integrity Unit was that the new integrity code rules regarding match fixing had been established, after the investigation, so lawyers had advised them to take no action.

Willerton insisted that the unit has a *'zero tolerance'* to match fixing which is probably right, but by not acting on the evidence as many suggest they should have does not support the policy. Ben Gunn, a former Police Chief who led the review that recommended the Integrity Unit, said that authorities had missed a perfect opportunity to clean up the sport and Richard Ings, the former Executive Vice President for Rules and Competition at the Association of Tennis Professionals, said that match fixing was a *'regular thing'* in the sport.

The contrast in views from those who were in the sports administration to those that are now is at complete odds.

Tennis administration continues to claim to be lily white but the stain of inaction on reports of this magnitude dents the credibility of the sport immeasurably.

Money, it seems, sets the rules.

But the real Supernova that rocked tennis at Melbourne this year (2016) was the WADA ruling that Maria Sharapova, the women's tours top earner for the last 11 years, was found with the banned substance Meldonium in her system. In early March this year, Sharapova was visibly upset when she announced, *"I made a huge mistake. I let my fans down. I let my sport down. I don't want to end my career this way,"* when Meldonium had come up positive on her drug test at the Australian Open.

Jennifer Capriati, a double Australian Open winner immediately called for Sharapova to be stripped of her titles claiming that she never cheated in her career and didn't have a team of professionals to *"get around the system and wait for science to catch up."* She has a point as Sharapova's comments above ring in my ears; she knows she has done wrong and admits she made a mistake. However, she explains that she failed to read the updated list of banned substances emailed to her on December 22, and nor did her staff, which is difficult to reconcile with a woman that is considered to be the consummate professional.

Nike, the world's largest sporting goods maker, suspended ties with Sharapova while the investigation continued, as did two other major sponsors, Tag Heur and Porsche. Porsche could be considered to have interesting double standards, as they are part of the VW Group that has been found guilty of deceiving consumers with carbon emission data when selling vehicles at an unprecedented scale worldwide.

It looked like Sharapova was gone burger but in a new twist WADA has announced that some athletes have said that they stopped taking it in 2015 and the drug was still showing up in their body, even though they had stopped taking the substance prior to the ban becoming effective. It was used so prolifically that WADA says it detected the drug in 172 athletes since January 1, 2016 and the BBC says that almost 500 athletes tested positive for it at the 2015 European Games.

As at May 23, Sharapova is still suspended and the investigation continues, but the stark reality remains. This drug is supposed to help athletes work harder while training or during competitions by carrying more oxygen than usual to muscles. Meldonium is believed to work through its ability to increase the size of blood vessels and therefore improve blood flow, so isn't Capriati right? Anyone using Meldonium does this knowingly, and uses the drug to gain an unfair advantage over a competitor. Therefore, they are taking an unfair advantage and so the athlete with the best chemist wins with a combined knowledge how to gyp the rules and testing programmes.

Sharapova admits to using Meldonium for a decade, back to 2005, and so in my book, only her Wimbledon victory in 2004 stands as a credible victory, whether the substance was banned at the time or not.

Not many subscribe to the Armstrong theory, that if others also cheat, then it's okay. This was clearly evidenced on his recent visit to New Zealand, to be part of a promotion for a liquor company, where he did not receive a hero's welcome. So why should it be okay in tennis. Hopefully, WADA and the ITF don't blink as they continue their research and determine the most just outcome for the rules at the time. If the rules state you cannot test positive then the timing may be unfortunate for some given the change to the rules, but WADA seemed to be backing down with the following new statements as reported by *Reuters* on April 13.

"Sharapova's lawyer, John Haggerty, said on Wednesday that WADA handled the issue 'poorly' and was now trying to make up for it.

"WADA said there was a lack of clear scientific information on excretion times.

"As a result it is difficult to know whether an athlete may have taken the substance before or after January 1, when it became illegal," WADA said in a statement sent to anti-doping agencies and sports federations.

"In these circumstances, WADA considers that there may be grounds for no fault or negligence on the part of the athlete," it said, adding that *"the presence of less than one microgram of Meldonium in the samples was acceptable."*

It would seem based on the above report that Sharapova's legal team have found a loophole in the process and WADA have not been thorough in their execution. However, on June 8, justice was served in the tennis world with Maria being handed a two-year ban for taking Meldonium leaving her career in shreds and the headlines of the comprehensive 33-page long decision is copied below as it appeared in the *Telegraph* June 8, 2016.

A three-strong independent tribunal savaged her for concealing her use of the drug from everyone outside her inner circle and rejected her claim she had not taken it to enhance her performance. It concluded: "She is the sole author of her own misfortune."

The extraordinary 33-page judgement following a two-day hearing in London last month revealed:

- *Sharapova failed not one, but two drugs tests for Meldonium, the first after her Australian Open defeat by arch-nemesis Serena Williams, and the second out of competition a week later.*
- *She took the drug, which is also known as Mildronate, six times in a single week at Wimbledon last year before it was banned by the World Anti-Doping Agency and five times in a week in Melbourne.*
- *She was responsible for five of the 24 positive Meldonium tests in tennis last year. She continued to take the drug years after ending her relationship with the doctor who had first prescribed it.*

The report further revealed that she had never disclosed her 10 years of use of Meldonium and failed to have her ban reduced by claiming the ban would disproportionately affect her and cause a substantial loss of earnings and sponsorship and irreparable damage to her reputation.

The review panel advised that if Maria had not concealed her use of Mildronate from the authorities and members of her own support team then the contravention would have been avoided. In response, Sharapova said she intended to fight what she thought was a harsh suspension to get back on the court as soon as possible.

Maria was staring evidence in the face and couldn't believe or accept her wrongdoing which is symptomatic of cheats at the highest level. The truth can only be what you believe if it is based on the five pillars of what determines the truth as explained in the Relationships section. The five pillars are love, respect, faith, freedom and honour and are covered later but my view is that Maria is caught up in her own self-delusion, that so many drug cheats are, and what she justifies to herself as being true is a fantasy based on all the evidence provided by the independent panel that assessed the facts, the crime and the penalty.

Maria thinks it is too harsh but my view is that the penalty is lenient even if she will probably be at the tail end of her career when she is again eligible to play. By her own admission she made a mistake, a costly one, and there is no way to reinterpret the facts later to suit a belief that has clearly been determined to be wrong.

Later in this section, I conclude with my thoughts on what is required to work through the complete eradication of cheating of any type in all sports.

The job WADA and the Sports Integrity Initiative has ahead in taking on a world of corrupt athletes in a plethora of sports is not an easy one as the abuse is really widespread. In the year 2015, prior to the banning of Meldonium, more than 3600 athletes tested positive being 6.2% of the 58,760 samples collected both in and out of competition. The efforts of WADA and the Sports Integrity Initiative must be applauded. 58,760 samples in one year is a massive undertaking.

Even though WADA was only formed in 1999, it has progressed into a well-recognised international agency, responsible first for harmonising all the many variegated rules and regulations from sport and countries into a global code uniting sport with governments in a unique partnership, that has a relatively modest collection of annual dues.

Director general of WADA, David Howman, advises that WADA has invested more than US $70 million in scientific research and developed partnerships with organisations like Interpol, the International Federation of Pharmaceutical Manufacturers and the Biotechnology Industry Organisation in their quest for true sport. However, he says that science alone cannot eradicate cheating or even very often detect it.

Howman believes the clever cheating athlete is getting better at cheating by being more extensively funded and more sophisticated. The money a top footballer can earn annually is more than WADA's annual budget, so while detection methods have improved in the last decade, the desire for financial gain and personal glory overrides the risk and penalty for many at the pinnacle of their chosen sport.

Tyler Hamilton wrote in his book that he and his teammates had a 99% chance of avoiding detection as long as they followed the rules set out by their support crew. He stated in the book, *"The test for EPO is a good example of how big an advantage (Michele) Ferrari (physician and trainer) was to us. It took the drug-testing authorities several years and millions of dollars to develop a test to detect EPO in urine and blood. It took Ferrari about five minutes to evade it. His solution was dazzlingly simple…"*

That is pretty good odds and probably better than most other illicit pursuits – 99% success – wow!

What is really fascinating is that non-analytical cases are emerging where the truth is being determined without the need for proof from testing. This ultimately undid Lance Armstrong and Marion Jones, US Olympic sprinter, as both were tested many times in their career and never found to have an adverse analytical finding yet both cheated throughout.

Jones stated in her book, that she had not taken drugs and it was only through an investigation process which led to her lying to a Grand Jury and, ultimately, a charge of perjury against her that she confessed and went to prison.

Armstrong bullied and threatened anyone who dared challenge his deception but was ultimately forced to confess his guilt as the combined evidence bought by US Officials was not refutable and has a potential cost to the former cyclist of US $100 million.

Hopefully, other cheats are noting the severity of these penalties and downstream impacts as only through severe corrective action will behaviour change.

The huge issues that WADA faces includes, underworld drug trafficking on the increase, more black market pharmaceutical products available, more sophisticated cheating at the high-end of sport with athletes surrounding themselves with powerful entourages, legal scientific and research costs and the trickle down impact where it is accepted in some countries that doping is okay if you don't get caught.

"Sport has no real power or jurisdiction, Governments do," Howman states.

Rafael Nadal now seems to be heading down a similar track to Marion Jones and Armstrong as on April 25, 2016, he confirmed he is suing the former French Sports Minister, Roselyne Bachelot, for alleging he had absented himself from the Tour in 2012, to hide the use of performance-enhancing drugs and was a positive doping control.

"I hereby make public the defamation lawsuit against Roselyne Bachelot, that I have filed today April 25th 2016 before the Paris law courts." – Rafael Nadal

In *Agencia EFE*, he also commented that *"Nobody can say something like that without information."*

Bachelot's comments that sparked the case, *"We know that Nadal's famous seven-month injury was without a doubt due to a positive [drug test]."*

With these comments posted by Eric Silvestro, Digital Writing RTL, on March 11, 2016, the flame of intrigue over Nadal was again ignited. The original French translation is copied below for accuracy.

Bachelot directly challenged Rafael Nadal by stating:

"The authorities keep voluntarily under the coat the positive controls of the players; it is a secret of Punch. There was a very long stop of Rafael Nadal between July 2012 and January 2013, which aroused heavy suspicion."

"Elle a mis directement en cause Rafael Nadal en déclarant: "Les autorités gardent volontairement sous le manteau les contrôles positifs des joueurs, c'est un secret de polichinelle. Il y a eu un arrêt très long de Rafael Nadal entre juillet 2012 et janvier 2013, ce qui a suscité de lourds soupçons." (Original text, before translation)

The case of the unusual but clever Mr Eufemiano Fuentes in June 2016 took another bizarre twist with the definitive legal verdict on Operacion Puerto being decreed that the 211 blood bags at the centre of the 2006 anti-doping probe will not be destroyed as had previously been ordered by the court ruling in April 2013. Mr Fuentes has also been cleared of all charges.

The quest for the truth will not go away and those guilty of the crimes should do their time.

Previous articles have referred to 200 bags or more than 200 bags of blood and this is the first time I have seen a definitive number. Does this include all the bags discovered?

In cycling news, in one of his first interviews after he was cleared of all charges, Fuentes was asked by Spanish radio station COPE if *'major names'* could appear on the list of bags seized. Fuentes responded, *"It could be, it could be,"* adding, *"but I'm not going to give you clues or names. If they are going to be found out, it's a question of waiting to find out."*

Legally, the process of naming and shaming the athletes that can potentially be exposed by the anti-doping authorities and whether this may constitute slander, as the statute of limitations has now passed, has already been raised in Spain. WADA's revised 2015 statute allows for ten years to punish athletes guilty of anti-doping effective January 1 that year. For

Operacion Puerto, it is understood the eight-year statute will apply which has long since lapsed as the Operacion commenced in May 2006 when the first arrests were made.

The judge has ruled that athletes implicated can be identified.

The questions I have are as follows:

1. Why did the Spanish Judicial System take so long to release the samples and only do so after the statute of limitations has lapsed? Surely, WADA must now amend this rule and leave it open indefinitely. There is no time frame on the truth as previously advised in this book and the interest level and decency to spectators, the media and most importantly other clean athletes dictates that the villains must be held to account.

2. Will the samples that the judge ruled will be handed over to the sports authorities for analysis be able to passed on to the appropriate sports bodies for appropriate discipline. The UCI (Union Cycliste Internationale) will partner with WADA, the Spanish Cycling Federation (FREC) and the Italian National Olympic Committee to analyse the DNA to see who it belonged to and *"where applicable, pursue anti-doping rule violations"* says UCI President Brian Cookson who celebrated the decision. From these comments, there is little doubt that cycling has strong and just leadership that is determined to clean up the sport. I salute your endeavour, Sir.

3. Why didn't the ITF appeal the initial Spanish Judiciary decision? Something to hide perhaps that is better off buried. Nadal's reaction to the news that the most affected athletes were Spanish was – *"I find it unfair to not give the names of cheats, whether they are Spanish or not."*

4. Does the fact that the statute has expired legally protect athletes, even though the judge has been clear

that the athletes can be identified and is this legal strategy to try and maintain integrity?

5. What has Fuentes had to compromise to get his complete exoneration? Fuentes emphasised, *"If there is no crime, and there is none for either myself or the sports people involved,"* at least not according to Spanish Public health laws 2006, which were those applied to Puerto, *"Then I have to say I am professionally bound (not to comment further)."* Sounds like I am not going to get to read his book which I was so looking forward to.

6. Can WADA and the UCI take legal action with the samples they now have the rights to beyond the Spanish judicial system so that fair and equitable justice for all concerned can be achieved? Spain is so tainted with this episode the full truth may only be able to be determined in other countries not compromised by the sports people at the centre of the doping scandal.

It all smacks of an attempt to keep the history books intact due to the statute of limitations, even though there is likely to be some serious egg on face in sports other than cycling including Champions League footballers, tennis players, athletes and boxers.

I have searched various websites including the famous *"Tennis Has a Steroid Problem"* and detail some quotes below from leading tennis players which are fascinating.

"I believe in my sport. That's the most important thing," Nadal told the media in Madrid. *"I believe that my rivals are clean. I believe that the sport is clean and I believe in our anti-doping programme, no, and it's an independent one."* Rafael Nadal, May 1 2016 – Tennis Now

"I think we all agree that we all want the sport clean and of course as transparent as possible." Djokovic told the media in Madrid. *"I think we all agree that we want to be playing the sport on an equal level in competition terms. The crowd when they come to watch us perform on the biggest*

tournaments, they want to know it's played under fair conditions." Novak Djokovic, May 1 2016 – Tennis Now

"To say today that tennis is clean, you have to be living in a dream world." Nicolas Escude – French Davis Cup Player 2002. Tennis has a steroid problem blog.

"If I'm guilty of drug taking then so are half of all the world's top tennis players." Greg Rusedski January 10, 2004, *Daily Mail London.* Rusedski in his defence said that 47 of the top 120 players tested showed elevated levels of nandrolone. He stated that all the samples had the same *'unique analytical fingerprint'* which proved the drugs had come from the same source which *"was believed to be the tablets and drinks distributed by the coaches working for the sport's governing body, the ATP, the very organisation which will be prosecuting the game against him."*

"Tennis is manipulated and drugged. And what has been done about it this year? Nothing." Daniel Köllerer September 27, 2013. Tennis Professional – The Ultimate tennis blog.

"It's bizarre, I can't run home from dinner and get tested, it's very invasive." Serena Williams February 12, 2009. *Telegraph* staff and Agencies.

"The International Tennis Federation should take measures," Nadal said. *"I don't have the impression that it's good to put so much pressure on us. They harass us. If I lose tomorrow, I'll go back to Mallorca and who will know where I am if I have no access to the internet? Now, if they knock at my door in Mallorca, they're going to give me a warning. It's happened to Carlos (Moya) before. They sent him a warning and this is most unfair,"* he said. Rafael Nadal May 30, 2009. *Reuters.*

*Espn.*go.com/sports/tennis/news/story?id=4215398

"As long as we don't have proof that the game is not clean, then it is clean." Djokovic April 19, 2016. *Express.*

I don't buy the last one by Djokovic at all, as there are just way too many instances of players being caught and it probably only scratches the surface. Simply go to the *Tennis Has a Steroid Problem* blog and click on Doping Cases.

Greats like Mats Wilander, Petr Korda and Martina Hingis are listed amongst a host of other professionals with the date, tournament and substance abused.

Former World number one Marcello Rios had this to say:

"I know that if nandrolone were found on Agassi, they would not disclose it. He is a very prominent, very popular player and if he were to fail, the world of tennis would fall with him. The ATP would not say it. They are such a large dependent organisation that it would be a problem if Agassi or Sampras tested positive. (We) the South Americans have discussed it repeatedly. It is a complicated subject. I do not have a problem in saying it: we always said, (we ask ourselves) who publicly certifies the doping tests of Agassi or Sampras?"

Marcelo Rios – Taken from the book Marcelo Rios: *The Man We Barely* Knew.

TIME WILL TELL THE TRUTH IRRESPECTIVE OF THE LEGAL PROCESS.

The Ultimate Tennis Blog had this posted also in September 2013 which is from Daniel Köllerer who is a former professional tennis player from Austria who turned professional in 2002 and was given a lifetime ban in 2011 for match fixing.

"Tennis is manipulated and drugged." And what has been done about it this year? Nothing. Except in my case. I've paid for everyone. Now they've stopped Viktor Troicki and Marin Čilić. But, why?
"Let's take Nadal. It's not possible that he tests negative. After 7 months out of the courts due to injury, he came back and won 10 out of 13 tournaments. That is impossible. Impossible! Imagine what it would mean for tennis if it broke the news that he tested positive."

Whether Rafael Nadal turns out to be the Lance Armstrong of tennis or not will be determined in time and the rumours and conjecture just won't go away. The recent comments made by Roselyne Bachelot add fuel to the fire. Whether it can be proved and whether the murky waters of Operacion Puerto will ever be cleansed remains a mystery, however, the DNA testing will be interesting indeed and I am sure there will be many athletes with samples that are going to be screened that are now deeply concerned about what comes next.

On November 16, 2017 the courts awarded Nadal €10,000 in damages against Bachelot who was found guilty of defamation. Nadal has pledged the funds to charity as Bachelot failed to prove her statements were true.

Nadal had the following comments after his successful case:

"When I filed the lawsuit against Mrs Bachelot, I intended not only to defend my integrity and my image as an athlete, but also the values I have defended all my career. I also wish to stop any public figure from making insulting or false allegations against an athlete using the media, without any evidence or foundation, and to go unpunished."

Whether this will put an end to the rumours is a moot point as no doubt some will believe the absence of evidence does not in itself prove innocence and ended up being the final determination with Armstrong. The problem for Nadal is that there is such wide speculation that even if he is completely innocent his reputation is besmirched by the accusations.

LIES TRAVEL FASTER THAN THE TRUTH BUT THE TRUTH ALWAYS WILL FINISH FIRST.

When you consider that the Olympic Games was inspired by the Ancient Games when Frenchman Baron de Coubertin wanted to create an event, where the youth of the world come to compete against each other without resorting to weapons, it is most probable he never envisaged that the evil side of human nature would gain such traction that cheats could get to dominate a sport like Armstrong and others did.

As the truth is again on the ascendancy in the pendulum of human morals, the world turns full circle and surely dishonesty will be eradicated and more and more athletes disgraced.

My belief is that WADA, or a similar organisation, should have the complete authorised autonomy to eliminate any drug cheat from any sport at any time if they are convinced of malpractice against the governing bodies rules. This needs to be over and above the power of each sport's ruling body like the International Tennis Federation, and the Union Cyclist Internationale and FIFA, the International Federation of Association Football, so that politics and greed cannot be allowed to fail the duty of the administrators to create an even playing field for all athletes in every sport.

WADA needs a much greater commitment from the heads of state, the heads of all International Sports played competitively and the minds of the paying public who can vote with their wallets and support clean sports and athletes. The commitment needs to be so great that WADA has the unfettered authority to ban any athlete for any period of time providing this penalty base is applied consistently across all sport, or sanction any administration, without fear of any possible reparation of the penalty they impose, at their sole discretion. The rules governing WADA (or other suitable body) and its authority need to be clearly determined and ratified.

The two-year ban is simply inadequate and I am in favour of lifetime bans for offenders and the stripping of all titles, without the need to verify whether they were cheating at a particular event or otherwise, if they have been caught using banned substances for individual advantage. The sponsors, if they have not been aware of the athlete's drug abuse, should have access to a complete return of all sponsorship funding, with interest, at the countries current business loan rate. If the penalties are harsh enough, the offending athlete's cavalier attitudes will be diminished as they watch their fellow's careers end in disgrace.

All professional athletes from all sports should be forced to sign contracts like this enforced by WADA or this new Global Body. If they don't want to, we will know who the cheats are, and will have made giant steps in cleaning up sport.

Anyone avoiding drug tests becomes immediately under the suspicion cloud, don't they? Why not have tests if you have nothing to hide?

Countries that do not get on board should simply have their athletes banned from international sport. End of story.

Fully compliant sports accepting the rules would be able to advertise to the public that they are clean, just as a food manufacturer can advertise it is gluten or sugar free. The public can then determine what sports to support adding weight to the movement.

Unfortunately, it should not end there as if there are issues with the administrators, as has been established in football; these people will also need to be able to be removed from their position. WADA or a similar body again should be granted unfettered powers, having gone through a suitable and fair process, to completely remove those found gaining from or facilitating anything that does not determine a completely fair contest.

Had this power existed, the debacle that occurred prior to the 2016 Olympic Games which resulted in the International Olympic Committee (IOC), 12 days out from the start of the Games, deciding not to accept the entry of any Russian athlete to the Olympic Games Rio 2016 unless the athlete could meet the conditions established which included the athlete being required to have to provide evidence to the full satisfaction of his or her International Federation that they were clean, may have been avoided. The absence of positive national doping tests in itself was not deemed sufficient for entry approval.

The IOC, which is an independent organisation made up of volunteers distributes 90% of its income back to Olympic sports and made this decision guided by a fundamental rule of the Olympic Charter to protect clean athletes and the integrity of sport.

The reaction from the individual sporting bodies varied considerably with athletics only allowing one of the entries to proceed from the 68 received and the IAAF allowed the whistle-blower, Yuliya Stepanova, to compete under a neutral flag along with long-jumper Darya Klishina, who is based in Florida. Stepanova was subsequently prohibited however by the IOC for having served a doping ban. The IOC acknowledged her contribution to cleaning up sport, but this did not prevent the ethics committee from concluding that she herself did not have a clean sheet.

In June, the IAAF president, Lord Coe, said, *"Russian athletes could not credibly return to international competition without undermining the confidence of their competitors and the public."* This was a massive step and one that was widely debated however given the diabolic shambles that occurred in London was, in my opinion, the right one.

Rowing banned 22 of 28 and cycling 11 of 17 where other sports like tennis, fencing, gymnastics, handball, shooting and volleyball allowed full participation.

The doctor at the head of the Russian doping scandal, Dr Grigory Rodchenkov, maintained that WADA knows nothing of the cheating that he spearheaded in the Sochi Olympic Games. He said in the illuminating documentary Icarus, *"I know I could change the past by telling the truth. But would you like telling the truth you would be annihilated?"*

These are very powerful words from a man that faced up to his deception, when he had his back against the wall, and now is reportedly somewhere in hiding in the US.

In January 2018, the Court of Arbitration of Sport upheld appeals from 28 of 39 Russians athletes that were given lifetime bans for doping violations on the basis that there was insufficient evidence and their results from the Sochi Games were reinstated.

Following the Olympic Games in Brazil, 2016, Newton's law that each action has an equal and opposite reaction proved alive and kicking, other than in physical objects, when assumed Russian hackers going by the name of 'Fancy Bears' pushed back on WADA's recommendation to ban all Russian athletes by releasing information from hacking WADA databases.

Interestingly, Fancy Bears mission is *"fair play and clean sport."*

https://fancybear.net/

WADA confirmed Russian hackers broke into its database and posted some athletes' confidential medical data online revealing records of 'Therapeutic Use Exemptions (TUE)' which allow athletes to use substances that are banned if there is a verified medical need. The *Daily Mail Australia* on September 16, 2016 reported that *"WADA confirmed Russian hackers broke into its database and posted some athletes' confidential medical data online."*

Fancy Bears released documents on the following athletes; Serena and Venus Williams – tennis greats, Simone Biles – maybe the greatest gymnast ever, Mahé Drysdale – Double Gold Olympic Rowing Champion, Mo Farrah – double 5000 and 10,000 m Olympic Gold medallist and Rafael Nadal – 19 Grand Slam tennis titles and Olympic Gold medal in 2008 among many others revealed by the hackers and having taken banned substances. Enter the web link to Fancy Bears above and see for yourself.

The system for 'Therapeutic Use Exemptions' has been called into question since the Fancy Bears brought it to public attention and it was not something I had ever heard of before, as an avid follower and participator in sport.

Richard McLaren a law professor at Western University Ontario Canada and author of the report on Russia'state-runn doping programme said the TUE system was open to abuse by athletes to allow them to take banned substances.

"One would have to conduct investigations on specific sports as to whether or not too many TUEs are being used with respect to particular substances."

"One of the common TUEs is for ADHD medication – there may be abuse there," he added.

"That's one area that probably needs to be looked at – how frequently are [certain medicines] being used in particular sports?"

In response to being exposed, this is what Simone Biles had to say, *"Having ADHD and taking medicine for it is nothing to be ashamed of, nothing that I'm afraid to let people know."* If so, why wasn't this made public prior to it being exposed by the Fancy Bears, whose methods may not be legal or orthodox, but have honest endeavour?

Venus Williams suffers from an autoimmune disorder known as Sjogren's Syndrome and she is permitted to use the otherwise banned drugs prednisone, prednisolone, triamcinolone and formoterol while on tour.

The documents Fancy Bears says it hacked from WADA's Anti-Doping Administration and Management System (ADAMS) database contain information that Serena Williams, one of the world's greatest ever tennis players, was taking a number of banned substances.

Serena was permitted to take oxycodone – an opioid used to treat moderate to severe pain, hydromorphone – an opioid morphine derivative for pain, prednisone – a powerful anti-inflammatory that appears to substantially improve running performance where one runner reported in Letsrun.com that they had used it a few times and felt like they could run through a brick wall, and methylprednisolone in 2010, 2014 and 2015, despite the substances being placed on WADA's list of banned substances.

USADA, the US Anti-Doping Authority announced on September 9, 2014, that Wallace Spearmon Jr, of Fayetteville, Ark, an athlete in the sport of track and field, has tested positive for a prohibited substance and accepted a three-month sanction for his rule violation.

However, the documents released also showed that Williams had been given special permission to take some of the drugs. The authorisation was given by Dr Stuart Miller from the International Tennis Federation (ITF).

No matter how hard I searched on Google I could not find a reply from Serena to the release by Fancy Bears so that her side of the story could be told, but I did find the following on *Quora*, a search for questions, peoples and topics that I was blissfully unaware of. The site is revealing on Serena's history as follows:

Several tennis players have admitted to use of PEDs and recreational drugs. (E.g. John McEnroe – steroids, Richard Gasquet – cocaine). According to an anonymous poll conducted by ESPN, over 22% of the players said they knew a player who was on PED.

Against this backdrop, several top players including Serena have come under the lens. Serena has faced allegations of drug use throughout her career and for good reason.

1. *It was alleged that she managed to evade drug testers (for OC) entirely for two years in 2010 and 2011. She covered up failed ICs by citing phantom injuries. She also famously locked herself in a panic room and called 911 when an out-of-competition tester called on her in October 2011. She never provided a sample afterwards and the tennis authorities did not answer why.*

2. *Serena was one of the players (including Venus Williams, Jennifer Capriati and Lindsey Davenport) who protested against the WTA's new drug testing rules in 2000 which led to the cancellation of WTA's off-season testing program too. She has protested vociferously against any attempts made by the WTA/ITF to make testing more rigorous and stringent. She once reportedly declared that "Women don't need to be tested because women don't take steroids."*

Perhaps this is why she is silent now as after clearly stating, *"Women don't take steroids"*, she has been found out by the release of the WADA records by Fancy Bears that she in fact does take them and while competing in a women's tournament. Methylprednisolone is a steroid.

This site, *Quora*, goes further by concluding that it is highly likely that Serena is using steroids and then in a further update on September 15, 2016, points out that WADA data from Fancy Bears is *'pertinent'* and *"that some commentators were quick to point out that some of the TUEs (Therapeutic Use Exemptions) given to Serena Williams were backdated, which means that they were authorised much after the medication was taken, with the complicity of ITF."*

It should come as no real surprise that given the allegations swirling around Nadal that his TUEs came in for a lot of attention when it was revealed that *"he received intramuscular injections of Tetracosactide, which stimulates the production of corticosteroids and has been named in several doping cases involving cyclists. The Spaniard was injured at the time the certificate was retrospectively applied for in August 2012,"* in an article by the *Guardian* referring to Fancy Bears hacking leaks.

On March 11, 2016, it was reported in the *LA Times*, before Nadal advised he would sue Roselyne Bachelot over doping allegations that Nadal said, *"I am a completely clean guy. I work so much during all my career, and when I get an injury, I get an injury. I never take nothing to be back quicker."*

On Monday night September 19 that same year, Nadal told Spanish media the following when attempting to explain the damming evidence from the Fancy Bears WADA revelation: *"When you ask permission to take something for therapeutic reasons and they give it to you, you're not taking anything prohibited."*

"It's not news, it's just inflammatory."

The two statements to me seem to be completely at odds to me. On the one hand, Nadal says he has never taken anything to assist in recovery from injury quicker, but on the other, he says that if he has taken something for therapeutic reasons and it has been given to you and approved then it is okay.

Stephen Wilson of *AP News* reported on April 26 that Nadal was fed up with being accused of doping and wants his drug tests made public and had written to the ITF accordingly. In a letter obtained by the Associated Press to the ITF, Nadal stated, *"It can't be free anymore in our tennis world to speak and to accuse without evidence."* Nadal's letter was sent to the ITF President David Haggerty the same day he filed a suit against Roselyn Bachelot.

The ITF in turn confirmed it had received the letter from Mr Nadal and that he had never failed any tests under the Tennis Anti-Doping Programme and confirmed this in a statement to the Associated Press.

The very same article also advised that, *"The ITF said, Nadal, like other players, has access to his anti-doping records through the World Anti-Doping Agency's database and is free to make them available."*

This seems clear then that Nadal has and controls the rights to make his drug records public and need not call for the ITF to do so as he holds those rights in his own hands.

Nadal went on to say that some of the media, sponsors and fans had no faith in the tennis anti-doping system and we have seen evidence of that earlier in this section.

Is there any reason why Nadal and Serena didn't advise people before the revelation that they were in fact using performance-enhancing drugs before Fancy Bears exposed them and how is the TUE system managed?

Nadal said he had never taken anything to improve his performance but took what doctors advised him was the best medication to care for his troublesome knee.

As part of attempting to present the information fairly and in an unbiased way, I contacted WADA to see if I could use the information on Nadal that was posted on the Fancy Bears website as an example of a TUE and publish it in this book. WADA advised that they were not in a position to authorise the publication and did not support it. In a carefully worded email, they advised that the information by Fancy Bears are either illegally obtained or forged and that publishing them may well breach the privacy rights of the athlete.

This response lead me to search for more public records and on June 6, 2017, I found the AP news article referred to above which put context to the question circling in my mind, why would Nadal not want his record to be made public when he is asking the ITF to do so? I wondered was it the ITF controlling the intellectual property or was it Mr Nadal?

WADA's reply to me and the ITF reply to AP news make it clear this right is in Nadal's hands so I don't understand why he didn't release the information that he says he wants transparency around and only did so after Fancy Bears exposed the whole TUE programme which up until then had been kept mysteriously quiet by all concerned.

On further investigation, I found Tennis.com had already published the TUEs for Nadal, after the Fancy Bears revelation, and reported that Nadal had already confirmed the documents were authentic when speaking to Spanish reporters. A copy of the TUEs in question can be seen be viewed by searching Fancy Bears or

http://www.tennis.com/pro-game/2016/09/rafael-nadal-wada-russian-hackers-rio-tues-tennis-performance-enhancing-drugs/61215/

WADA subsequently confirmed to me they were aware that Nadal had acknowledged the Fancy Bears release was authentic.

We know the TUEs were illegally obtained and we also know that Venus Williams and Simone Biles have acknowledged them as being correct and explained the reason why they were used giving validity to the quality of the documents. The documents come on the official ADAMS format as detailed on WADA's website as *"a free and highly secure Web-based database management system that supports the coordination of anti-doping activities worldwide – from athletes providing whereabouts information, to anti-doping organisations (ADOs) ordering tests, to laboratories reporting results, to ADOs managing results."*

It must have been very embarrassing for WADA to have had Fancy Bears hack their website, given the web security claims, but it is part of the world we live in where the truth pendulum is again swinging to the fore. Possibly, some of the information leaked by Fancy Bears is not correct but when the information is released by a well-established reliable source like the *Guardian*, a British daily newspaper since 1821, it must have some substantial validity. I have been unable to find evidence of anyone refuting the validity of the documents published when athletes have been referring to them.

THE TRUTH DOES NOT WAIVER FROM ITS ORIGINAL POSITION, OR CONTRADICT ITSELF, UNLESS NEW EVIDENCE REFUTES PREVIOUS STATEMENTS. IF THERE IS NO NEW EVIDENCE, THEN THERE IS NO NEED FOR THE TRUTH TO CHANGE COURSE. IN THIS WAY, THE TRUTH IS CONSISTENT.

Nadal is not the only one under the spotlight.

Mo Farrah also has mystery swirling around his response to his use of TUEs where he initially indicated that he had done so on one occasion but later indicated it was twice. Quite a significant error for such a hot topic but Mo continues to protest his innocence.

Bradley Wiggins is another prominent Tour de France winner who was basking in the glory of becoming the country's most decorated Olympian at another glittering games for Team GB's cyclists only to have to fight for his reputation from even his most loyal supporters over his record on PED's as a result of the WADA leaks from the Fancy Bears hacking group.

The Guardian on September 19 reported, *"Wiggins has been forced to deny that the controversial Belgian doctor Geert Leinders was involved in his obtaining so-called therapeutic use exemptions (TUE), after details of the TUEs granted to both him and fellow Tour de France winner, Chris Froome, were leaked late on Wednesday night. The leak detailed three TUEs obtained by Wiggins for the treatment of asthma and allergies."*

Mahé Drysdale, the awesome Kiwi rower sheds some light on the nature of whether TUEs are confidential in his following comments.

"I'm disappointed that our confidentiality has been hacked, it's illegal what they've done. But on the other hand, I think it's a good conversation starter because my feelings on it are if you apply for a TUE, then it should be public. Have some transparency there. My personal opinion is if you're going to use a substance that others can't use you should be able to justify and be happy for it to be out in the public domain," Drysdale said.

If the process of using TUEs is in fact as it is intended, it may be that does to some extent exonerate the users from the adverse publicity the exposure has created. I agree with Mahé and Rafael entirely that this process, and any doping test, should be completely transparent as this will assist in eliminating improper use which in so many instances could be interpreted to be not for the intended rationale.

I decided to contact Mahé directly as he lives in New Zealand and asked if it were possible to interview him and use his TUE in my book as an example, given he was happy to be so open and transparent, and explain why he used TUEs in the above article in the NZ Herald.

The opportunity was declined by Mahé via Fuse Group, a consulting management company acting on his behalf.

Given Drysdale had stated they want this information to be transparent and public I was surprised by the response.

I believe the hacking work of Fancy Bears to be illegal but nothing I can find indicates they have done anything to falsify the 'Therapeutic Use Exemptions' they have exposed.

There is certainly a connection between top sports people and those with therapeutic exemptions. This seems odd to me as the natural order of humanity and the animal kingdom is that the strong prevail, yet we have the situation that many of the world's greatest sports stars are competing with illnesses that require strong medication, or so we would be lead to believe.

Whether there is any further exposure for some of these athletes when the release of Operacion Puerto occurs, will probably be haunting those on that list, also and it will be interesting to see if any are the same as those released by the Russian hackers. On August 22, 2017, *the Guardian* revealed that the Football Association and FIFA had condemned in the strongest terms the theft of a small cache of emails hacked by Fancy Bears that claimed 25 players had been allowed to use TUEs in the 2010 World Cup including the former Premier League players Dirk Kuyt, Juan Sebastián Verón and Carlos Tevez for the prescribed use of corticosteroids, a class of steroid hormone. These were given to help the athlete breathe better but could also be performance-enhancing.

The Guardian had not been able to verify the leaks but the condemnation does give them some validity and the use of TUEs does not in itself suggest any of the sports people have done anything wrong as it is not illegal. The FA said in a statement, ***"The details of ongoing cases cannot be discussed or disclosed until due legal process has been completed."***

The latest on Operacion Puerto is that in June 2017 the Provincial Court of Madrid clarified the following in response to a request from Fuentes that the blood bags be returned to him to protect the privacy of the doctor-patient relationship. ***"It said that the blood bags were only passed over to the authorities to verify if they belonged to athletes with open cases, rather than begin disciplinary proceedings."***

The court declined the return of the samples to Fuentes and said that as there were no open cases, the identities of the athletes could not be made public. This is setback in the quest for the truth but the problem for all concerned is that more people now know the identities and the emergence of the real truth is more likely to occur despite incredible efforts to cover up the whole episode.

Earlier in the year, it was reported that WADA was struggling with the legal process to release the athletes concerned as they had now identified them.

WADA Director General, David Howman, had this to say before the Courts ruling:

"So many people all over the world want to know the name of those involved. However, there are legal problems to deal with.

"We will see how it is resolved. Operation Puerto needs to be closed, to know what there was inside it, to avoid it happening again in the future. It is evident that this saga of more than a decade is not going to produce an ideal outcome, but it is not in my hands. I respect the decisions of the judges, of WADA, and of the involved parties, although it is difficult to accept them."

The final determination by the Spanish Authority does smack of a cover up as why did the whole scenario get this far if the original determination was clear in the first place? Probably, it wasn't and this is why the letter of clarification was required.

Why did WADA go to all the trouble of identifying the athletes to now learn that couldn't achieve the goal of exposing them? Was the threat of legal action so strong that WADA had to find a way out?

I wonder how much the public would fund the court case to support WADA to complete the exposure of the cheating athletes, as it is in the interests of the truth and fairness for sport, their overriding mission. I know I would contribute and based on what I read on blog sites there are many others that feel very passionate about the truth being uncovered.

This isn't the first time that the law is impeding the revelation of the truth as you will read in the Truth of Business section even though it is clear there is wrongdoing. The quest for the truth should override laws that hide it as the privacy laws are being manipulated to do in this instance. If the legislation is wrong, a court should determine that as part of the legal process and not have a charade where rules are used to protect wrongdoing. The overriding law should be that the judicial process should seek the truth.

How epic would that be?

The only conclusion that can be drawn about the truth of sport is that for many it has become a blind obsession for power and money and that greed has replaced the hunger of earnest human desire for fulfilment of one's aspirations. The pure heart of endeavour that fuelled great Olympic athletes and sporting heroes of the past has become a drug-infected oxygen pump sugar coated in dollar bills.

However, I believe the gradual decline of sporting integrity throughout history has turned the tide and will reverse itself and progress again to the state where honour will be the dominant pursuit of all athletes, fair play the only option for the administration and an adoring public able to cherish the real victor of the day.

I believe this is attainable and that all mankind should support this faith, and come forward and eliminate the scourge that demeans our esteem as humans. The 2016 Olympics, Lance Armstrong's and Marion Jones trial are all watershed moments in this transition as was the 2017 World Athletic Championships when gold medal winner and previously twice suspended drug cheat Justin Gatlin was booed over his victory in the 100-metre sprint.

The dilemma now for those athletes who have been abusing and their sport's administrators is how to unfold the truth. Hopefully, they will all have the courage displayed by Lord Coe and his lead at the Olympics in 2016.

On June 3, 2016 the man named as the Sportsman of the 20th Century, Muhammad Ali, passed and I could not help but feel humbled and awestruck by the outpouring of grief and recognition for this most beautiful human. Lennox Lewis, another world boxing Champion, summed it up for me on the radio when I was driving home when he said, *"Ali taught us to not be afraid of the truth."*

The Truth of Business

Different truths emerge in business all the time and these often end up in court where the masters of truth, lawyers, determine the outcomes based on how long they can drag out proceedings to maximise their fees. In fact, don't they create the issue in the first place by poorly drafted contracts?

Worse still you may end up with massive fines, or even behind bars, if you fail to pursue fair and legal practices in your business dealings.

Misunderstandings are often the route core of failed business relationships and often this can be caused by two parties coming from entirely different cultures and belief systems. An example of this from my own personal experience is that some Australians can have a different version of the truth to New Zealanders. An Australian company that held the licence to a brand we were using in New Zealand, in a past business life put it like this: Relationships are based on a win/win basis as long as they come first.

This was different to our culture which was that both parties should work together to share in the benefits. It is after all the only sustainable platform for a long-term relationship. If one sees the other as a means to an end, that is what will occur, there will be an end as the party that is being taken advantage of will seek other arrangements and ultimately the association blow apart.

In this circumstance, the Australian Company intended to gain control of our business by a number of means including influencing board members, attempting to force us to adopt there IT platform even though I had established that this was a major downside risk and cost and even going to the extent of attempting to cancel our licence agreement. This was vigorously and successfully defended but clearly indicated how business relationships can easily sour when greed blinds the original endeavour.

Ultimately, they failed in this pursuit, and as General Manager, Company Secretary and MD of our subsidiary, we took some solace in ultimately acquiring their brand from the receivers that wound up the Australian principal. Their ideals had become so misaligned with their supplier, customer and membership base that the business imploded. This outcome, I believe, is inevitable with all attempts to deceive customers, close partners and suppliers and this is dealt with in some detail further through this section.

Believing someone, without ascertaining facts, can be fraught with danger because it means you trust that person, and while trust is necessary in business dealings, it's best to have that trust supported by a contract that legally defines the basis of your relationship, irrespective of how well you think you know someone.

The key thing is to understand your partner's plans and future ideals as best you can before you go into business with them and confront a competitor in the market that turns your plans upside down. Take time to get to understand what motivates them as this is something you will learn anyway as you roll down the road together. Its best you know first what challenges you may confront before you undertake them in the blind excitement of a new idea.

In the Business Truth section, I will endeavour to share some hard-won business truths I have uncovered during my years in various leadership roles. Two of the most important aspects of any successful venture is not only seeing the goal but also understanding how you will achieve it.

You need to lay strong foundations and a clear direction in any relationship during the honeymoon stage and agree, as best you can, on where you are going together or you are headed for troubles that will test your wits to the extent you feel like you are living a nightmare.

IF THERE ARE NO RULES THEN THERE IS NO DISCERNIBLE TRUTH TO DEFINE THE RELATIONSHIP.

Getting a collective belief of future direction in your company is pivotal to its future – everyone needs to know and believe where you and they will be in 5, 10 or even 50 years. A classic example of long-term vision driving a successful business is Elon Musk with SpaceX and Tesla wanting a sustainable world and the establishment of life on Mars. That is some vision and achievements on this path have been astonishing.

Believing optimistically always creates better outcomes than a pessimistic view but, in good partnerships, it is very useful to have a combination of both, the rampaging bull spirit tempered by the sage of reason. Reasoning outcomes is essential and should not be seen as negative but rather a better way to plan for the many surprises that competitor and variable market conditions will hurl at you.

This should be done by developing data and robustly prepared business plans. These plans should prove and quantify your belief in the numbers that should then be critiqued by an independent financial advisor or analyst. This financial advisor should have a proven pragmatic business history of success, otherwise don't bother. Be aware that if this advisor is to be contracted ongoing their advice may well have an element of self-interest.

Bad financial advice can seriously adverse a company so you need to understand that advice and critique it. My advice is don't let finance people run your company, only let them count the money and prepare forecasts, unless they have a proven track record in successful business management. At the end of the day, if you own the business, the buck stops with you, so you need to make sure you have the right people in place and the right contracts to facilitate your ideals. Always be positive and pursue your belief no matter what.

The best example I can provide of positive and negative belief systems is what happens on the US Stock Market when greed is driving a bull market and it turns to a bear market. The change can be sudden and dramatic and billions of dollars lost because more people have adopted a negative view than a positive one for the future – usually based on an event that potentially changes dynamics around the globe as a result of a looming war in the Middle East, or a major liquidity squeeze like what occurred in the Global Financial Crisis of 2008 and 2009.

Fortunately, hope is a more powerful motivator than fear, because that is probably the only thing that is keeping the business world ticking over since the Global Financial crisis. There is a lot of conjecture as to which is the biggest motivator and I cover this below with some interesting extracts on the matter.

The reason I believe this and know it to be true is that there is more debt in the global financial system than there is money so hope must be stronger than fear. The fallacy in this theory is that it assumes that everyone knows that the debt levels are higher than equity and the world is technically bankrupt.

If everyone did understand that there is more debt than money, I am not sure my theory espoused above would hold water. However, most people believe the financial system is sound, whether it is based on ignorance or otherwise, and this is the bottom line that supports hope being more powerful than fear.

Who wants to believe that the global financial system will collapse?

Another powerful example on the power hope has over fear is how it operates on an individual and mass level like in the US election when Obama pinned his star to the positivity of this belief.

The downside of pedalling hope as a vote catcher is that there is always the reality to deal with in the future when expectation needs to be met by achievements that the hope was centred on.

All the money in the world doesn't come close to being able to pay off the world's debt which is in the order of $150 trillion US dollars in 2016 and possibly at a level that it is not humanly possible to pay it off.

Some people believe that the financial system is doomed and a look at the facts does make that view one with a decent amount of credibility.

Since the Global Financial Crisis (GFC) global debt has grown by $57 trillion dollars (2015) and no major economy has reduced its debt to GDP ratio. In the US alone, if you took every dollar out of the banks and multiplied it by six, there would be not enough to pay off all the debt.

The estimated global debt is approximately three times the Global GDP and the worrying sign is that the increased debt levels are having an increasingly anaemic impact on growth.

On top of this toxic recipe, the total notional value of all known derivatives around the globe is estimated to be somewhere between 600 and 1500 trillion dollars, so we all exist in a gigantic bubble never seen before in history that will be the largest financial disaster ever when/if it bursts.

The essence of what drives hope and fear is fascinating as they both have the ability to promote growth within us. They are mighty influencers and only effectively controlled by strong leadership in either direction depending on the leader's motive.

Hope creates space in the mind and heart where fear more often than not restricts it. You tense up when something threatens you and your mind and your energy focuses on doing whatever you need to that will get you out of danger. Yet when you feel hopeful, the opposite occurs and you relax and you feel generous and open and ideas expand and flourish in this environment.

Fear on a national level can drive sexism, racism and hate and some would say the ISIS movement is driving global racism against Muslims and driving nationalism in many quarters of the world including the US. Hope, on the other hand, on a national level can put a country or culture in danger as resulting complacency can be divorced from real dangers that may exist.

Recent election campaigns in the United States are fascinating examples how these two powerful motivators can be utilised. In 2008, Obama inspired the public with his message of *'hope and change'* and it is a strategy that proved very successfully and one that he delivered with strong oratory skills.

"A leaders' job isn't to educate the public," Jon Favreau, an Obama speechwriter during the 2008 campaign, once told The Boston Globe, *"It's to inspire and persuade them."*

Obama did inspire people to want the same things in their country that they want in their personal life and he became the first Black president in US history. However, there are divided views on his achievement levels.

When the best part of fear and hope is combined, we get the optimal result and the best position we can. The most positive part of fear is that it makes us value what we are afraid to lose, and the best part of hope is that when we know what we are afraid of losing, we set about implementing ways to maintain and cherish what we love. When hope is the greater force, we succeed and we achieve what we believe. Hope is the core essence of progress.

YOU CAN ACHIEVE WHAT YOU BELIEVE.

The 2016 US Election was fascinating as Trump's strategy to make America great again got the balance right. Fear that the economy was a disaster, that immigration policies were ruining societal values and eroding jobs while creating the vision of hope that the country can again lead the modern world.

Emotive drivers are hard to measure but unbelievably powerful.

I digress from business into this macro-view because these motivators are part of what drives and makes your business thrive or dive and you need to understand them.

So the take-outs so far from Business Truth is:

1. You need to have a plan that the partners agree on.
2. You need time to define it legally, so that it as best possible reflects both parties' desired outcomes from the venture, if more than one is involved.
3. You need to balance the positive view with hard data and analysis that is caused and affected by a proven and capable financial analyst, so you can determine what you plan to do is achievable.
4. You need to believe that you will succeed and instil hope in your team, as it is the enthusiasm you instil in your team that will significantly determine your success or failure.

When you have established the above, it is imperative you find a good leader. As a business owner, this is often the hardest thing to recognise, that you as owner don't have the ability to run your own business and this is particularly common in small to medium family businesses that grow beyond their skill sets and knowledge base.

The first thing is to recognise that this is what your business needs and then go about finding that person that can make your business achieve the dream that started it in the first place.

You have to determine the skill sets and attributes and you will never guess what I am going to say is the most important attribute on the list. If you guessed that he or she has unquestionable integrity then you are right.

If you reason through the logic that has been applied to the relationship foundation stones above and what will make your business work, you can see that to be successful, the base element is the business must be based on the truth.

A clearly defined vision and plan that has been critiqued externally as being realistic, a shareholder agreement that determines what both parties want, and a positive hope for the future will ignite the business and, with the right leader, it's potential be realised.

I can absolutely assure you success will not come your way unless your leader has the virtue and integrity to have the troops believe the vision he or she espouses. He must never be caught out misleading investors, breaking rules that bind the organisation, being promiscuous or playing favourites. These are not traits of successful leaders.

The point here is that if you want your team to believe in the company's future, and be united in that quest, your leader must be able to be trusted and believed or the team will pull in different directions. It is hard enough keeping a team focused on a commonality of interest, even when you have an unblemished record, so imagine how impossible it is when it becomes known that your leader is a fraud. That is when hope accedes to fear and negativity takes hold as the binding essence of good, being the truth, has been destabilised.

Your leader must have integrity – that is the essential unavoidable reality if you want to develop a long-term sustainable business. There are very few leaders that can survive blemishes on their integrity when proven.

Leadership is defined by Wikipedia below which I believe is an excellent explanation of what leadership is: it's how the leader is able to achieve this that is important.

Leadership has been described as *'a process of social influence in which one person can enlist the aid and support of others in the accomplishment of a common task,' and 'organising a group of people to achieve a common goal.'*

The leader must be a good communicator so that he can share the goal for the company and have every one come along for the ride. I list below the main qualities I see as essential for a leader:

1. Integrity – must always be true to the company and its peoples expected values.
2. Strength – must be able to make hard decisions for the greater good and not waver under attack. Must appear fearless.
3. Energy – must show the drive and commitment to the vision which may be developed by others. Must be able to act quickly and decisively.

4. Intelligent empathy – must be able to understand and react to all levels of people in the organisation.
5. Team builder – must be able to create enthusiasm through involvement.
6. Creative – great leaders are often visionary and see the future clearly and know how to develop the opportunities they see.

There is no absolute set formula for this and there are exceptions to the rules above. Sometimes a great visionary can inspire a company to amazing achievements, but in the end that will not be enough on its own, as usually the company will grow to a level where it needs a sustainable inspiration formula established within the business as no one person has a mortgage on all the great ideas.

General Norman Schwarzkopf who became Commander in Chief of the US Central Command was an inspiring leader who I once had the privilege of seeing live and he closed his speech with a story on when he was walking down the corridors of power in The White House having just assumed control and asked his predecessor, *"What do I do?"*

The answer fired back as the ex-leader headed to the Middle East to solve a crisis was, *"Do the right thing."* What a pearl of wisdom this is that we should all benchmark ourselves from.

Schwarzkopf's 14 rules of leadership are summarised below and are viewed from a military sense, but as I have said, the similarity between business and war is remarkable in its strategic drivers.

Leaders lead people not processes, have the courage to do the right thing, do not seek reward as leadership is enough reward, encourage others to have their say, set high standards and recognise and reward success, and take charge when they need to.

Having the moral courage to do the right thing is something that is essential in leaders.

Great leaders know this instinctively and establish ways to get those ideas developed from inside and outside of the company and how to utilise them for the company's benefit ongoing.

Arguably, the most brilliant CEO of them all was Steve Jobs who created Apple into the technology giant that was the darling of the stock market through an incredible barrage of innovation that inspired the world into adopting smart technology.

Tim Cook's (replacement CEO) unenviable challenge is to maintain that innovative spirit and drive, and in my opinion, he is losing the battle with his argument for incrementalism or view that innovation is not change, it is making things better. The making things better theory may be the internal understanding of innovation at Apple but this is where I believe there is a disconnect with the public. They see Apple as a ground-breaking innovator that is not afraid to turn markets on its head, in fact, that is what they have come to expect and their expectations are not being met which has seen a reversal of fortunes for the Apple share price.

In May 2015, Samsung launched the inspirational 6S phone as a swipe back at the wildly successful Apple iPhone 6. Interestingly, Apple's launch of the big screen iPhone 6 has impacted Samsung sales as clearly Steve Jobs was wrong in his belief that consumers didn't want the big screen. Samsung has responded by making a beautiful phone with the S6 having a high-quality case and a beauty that in my opinion more than rivals the iPhone. The curved glass edge is brilliant and the fast-action camera feature, along with the highest-quality screen ever, are big features.

The brands are now starting to narrow their differences and homogenise into a similar market position, and with Apple being successful in China, they appear to be clawing back substantial share from Samsung's dominant global sales position. In the last quarter of 2014, Apple outsold Samsung by selling 74.8 million smartphones versus 73 million smartphones which is a major reversal and a comparative 25 million gain to Apple mostly on the back of a massive increase in China.

Nobody said it would be easy following a genius like Steve Jobs and Tim Cook has massive boots to fill. Only time will tell a story of inspiration versus tenacity.

Dial forward to mid-2016 and we see a very interesting story emerging which illustrates my point entirely. Apple's share price is now firmly below $100 and was the second worst performer on the Nasdaq Stock Exchange falling by 30% in value to July 2016. The price on July 15, 2016 was $98.78 USD down from $130 a year prior.

Some blame the demise on falling mobile sales, and in the last quarter to March 2016, Samsung has recorded record profitability while in the same quarter Apple was expected to reduce iPhone production by approximately 30% according to *The Guardian*, post of January 6, 2016. Smartphone saturation outside China was stated as a key reason.

Samsung gains in the IT and mobile division were largely due to the successful launch of the Galaxy S7 with improved cost savings and streamlining of mid to low end smartphone line-ups.

Samsung has its own difficulties with the meltdown of the revolutionary Note7 resulting in two consecutive recalls. The drive for new innovation is no fiercer than in this category where the customer craves new technology for more reality in games and more social content.

However, the real reason for the price tank is Tim Cook's leadership style according to Michael Yoshikami's post on May 24, 2106 with CNBC. He asks the question whether Tim Cook's low-key leadership style is hurting the share price citing his low-key style compared to Steve Jobs ability to whip the market into frenzy even when the company was not in product launch mode. There is no doubt that he was the inspiration, the vision and the drive that made the company successful and I believe that Michael is right.

That magic has gone. The belief that Apple was simply the best product on the planet even when it was staring down way more formidable specifications from other brands like Samsung or HTC. There are cartoons on YouTube where sales people try to reason why a die-hard Apple consumer should buy a smartphone, but the belief that the brand was the best defied the facts and customers flocked to the brand. I really recommend you check the link out below as it perfectly illustrates the magic the brand had which was almost entirely due to Steve Jobs' driving force.

https://www.youtube.com/watch?v=FL7yD-0pqZg
16,778,228 views

Nothing more clearly illustrates the truth is what you believe, not the facts than this video. It is utterly brilliant.

Yoshikami asks if Elon Musk, the CEO of Tesla, was running Apple right now whether the share price would be where it is. It is a fair question given his ability to do what Musk has done in the automotive industry. He also goes on in the article to say that the strong balance sheet and cash flow of Apple will ultimately make the current share price look low and with Warren Buffet having recently bought shares that is probably most certainly true. However, if Tim Cook stays in the role, then an exciting new raft of product needs to be released under his direction or someone else needs to take up that challenge and execute it decisively in the market place.

On May 4, 2016, *Forbes* posted that **"Samsung topples Apple as Galaxy S7 defeats iPhone."**

Samsung has regained the top spot in the important US market that it lost 11 months ago and now has 28.8% share as opposed to Apple's 23%. The battle will rage on but no doubt leadership will play a pivotal role in determining the outcome. Samsung's leaders face a critical time with recall of Note7 and to date seem to have isolated and handled the fall out well, albeit at huge cost.

At times like this, brand image and credibility is everything and no cost will be spared to make it right for the product failure.

Dial further forward to the first quarter of 2017, and we see that the goodwill Samsung has in its brand and its innovation drive are not rocked by the problems with the Note7 showing that when you face adversity it is the putting the situation right that matters to maintain customer loyalty. Samsung has soared to 26.1% from 18.5% the previous quarter and Apple is down to 16.9% from 20.3%. The Chinese brands of Huawei and Oppo continually chip away at market share so both the leading brands jostle for the high ground, and in June 2017, Samsung's S8 is selling at higher prices than Apple's i7. The next quarter will show strong results for Samsung I believe and Apple needs something special with its new i8 launch later in the year to arrest the fickle fortunes as new models come to market.

Leaders are vital in creating growth and disciplines in companies to develop them to their full potential. Whether the company has stalled due to lack of capital, increased new competition, shifting consumer buying trends like online or lack of investment in product, a strong leader can turn the company around, create a new direction, build new teams and develop new markets, and find new sources of capital or credit.

Many do this instinctively; it is born in them and no amount of study makes a leader in my view. Great leaders create what they believe, and the drive and energy they can bring to a cause devours everything in their way.

Probably, the greatest leader in history, Genghis Khan, the rampaging Mongolian who amalgamated all Mongol tribes together to succumb the omnipresent Jin Dynasty is evidence of this.

Having just read Conn Iggulden's *Lord of the Bow* on the great conqueror, I couldn't help but compare my theory on leadership with what he told his sons before sending them to war and how nothing changes over time when it comes to leadership. I have bracketed references to the qualities I believe a leader should have and note them below in the excerpt from this novel.

When he sent his sons to war, they were treated no favours for being his son and had to earn the right for succession. He told his sons,

"If they are to be raised to officers, they will have shown themselves in battle to be quick thinking, skilled and brave

beyond the men around you. No one wants to be led by a fool, even if he is my son – (intelligent).

"However, you are my sons and I expect the blood to run true in each of you – (integrity). The other warriors will be thinking of the next battle or the last. You will be thinking of the nation you could lead – (creative visionary). I expect you to find men you can trust and bind them to you – (team). I expect you to push yourself harder and more ruthlessly than anyone else ever could – (energy). When you are frightened, hide it. No one else will know and whatever causes it will pass. How you held yourself will be remembered – (integrity and strength).

"When you are tired, never speak of it and others will think you are made of iron. Do not allow another warrior to mock you, even in jest. It is something men do to see who has the strength to stand against them – (strength). Show them you will not be cowed and if it means you must fight then that is what you must do.

"His son asked, 'What if it is an officer who mocks us?'

"Genghis replied sharply, 'I have seen men try to deflect such things with a smile, or dipping their head, or even capering to make the others laugh even harder. If you do that, you will never command. Take the orders you are given, but keep your dignity' – (integrity).

"If you have to fight, even if it is a friend, put him down as fast and hard as you can. Kill him if you have to, or spare him – but beware of putting a man in your debt. Of all things that causes resentment. Any warrior who raises his fist to you must know he is gambling with his life and that he will lose – (strength)."

Genghis Khan ruled with an iron fist and often talked about his word being iron. He would always honour his commitment whatever it was, to destroy a kingdom or to grant freedom. The truth and integrity was the basis of his rule and his disciples followed it with enthusiasm and respect.

Genghis Khan is arguably the greatest leader in history given he conquered more of the known world than anyone before or after his epic reign of power. He ruled a self-made empire of 12 million square miles which lasted in parts for seven centuries. Surely, there are lessons in this incredible domination.

Genghis Khan (Photo credit: Wikipedia)

His vision united disparate tribes in a common cause and he encouraged learning and gave women increased rights, abolished torture, embraced religious freedom and ran his kingdom based on talent and ability, not class, wealth or privilege.

Khan focused on creating peace in lands with people he conquered and died an old man unlike other aggressive conquerors that died violent deaths in their young years. His goal was to unite the whole world into one empire and to this end he succeeded like no other because his quest and actions had honourable intent.

He died an old man surrounded by his loving and loyal family, testimony indeed to his greatness. The Mongols took no honour in fighting; only winning and they would do whatever was required to get victory.

The great Khan believed there was no good in anything until it was finished. Think about that for a minute and how that applies to the endless ideas and dreams you didn't pursue. Every time you don't create something and chase the dream or idea that comes to you, nothing happens. If that isn't tragic and cause to get up and go, I don't know what is.

DO NOTHING AND NOTHING HAPPENS, ALL BEGINNINGS START WITH THE BELIEF AN IDEA CAN EVENTUATE.

He also could not be happy until his people were happy and did not indulge himself in anything more than what his people had. Compare that with the corrupt leadership that exists today and we know why there is so much disharmony today. He was not the bloodthirsty ruthless leader many portrayed him to be, how could he be with a vision that pure?

Khan was self-reliant and believed no friend was better than his own wise heart.

Also he believed in being humble and being close to and understanding his people.

"The mastery of pride, which was something more difficult, he explained, to subdue than a wild lion. He warned them that, 'If you can't swallow your pride, you can't lead.'

"People conquered on different sides of the lake should be ruled on different sides of the lake."

Khan was born poor and illiterate in a world of conflict and strife and he moulded his life quest by adapting continuously to the ever-changing challenges that he confronted resulting in a legacy the world will never experience again. His iron will, unshakeable belief and ruthless reputation preceded him and was used to engender and precipitate cooperation that otherwise may have been supremacy through bloody battle.

And so it must be in a successful modern business. There must be somewhere that the buck stops and decisions are made, visions created and followed, when and how they need to be.

A culture develops from this discipline and it need not be that this environment can't be fun; in fact, it's better if it is.

The respect and joy that comes from success and recognition to those who have contributed to that success is the most powerful motivator there is. I recommend you read *Lord of the Bows*; it is not only thoroughly enjoyable, it is a valuable insight into the dynamics that play in awesome leadership on a scale never seen before.

The whole culture of the Mongol people was centred on its leader and his standards that were high by any measure. When you consider the world we live in now, it is frightful how standards have been diluted over the years mostly through poor leadership.

Governments in the Western world are largely to blame for soft policies that cater to minorities and do not have any vision to inspire the people to a common goal or set of goals. They also fail miserably to communicate their vision to the people they are responsible to and many put self-interest and maintenance of power ahead of the good of their people.

Your leader has to identify the strengths, weaknesses opportunities and risks in the business and do this totally objectively and honestly. Often owners are too close to staff as they have been with them for a long time or they haven't had enough experience to assess their abilities for the role they are required to carry out.

Company structures can spiral out of control based on bad advice adding unnecessary cost and inefficiency. So not only must the leader have the ability to determine the best structure to suit the company's business objectives, he must also be able to understand the roles required to meet those objectives and put the best people in place to achieve them.

Leaders do not try and employ staff with lesser abilities than themselves, so that they do not feel threatened, they get the best people they can to achieve the purpose within the pay parameters determined within the budget. That would be not in the company's best interests and putting your own situation first.

Have a look around the company you work in and watch how many managers employ staff to protect their position.

Never mislead your staff as to the status of the company especially when it is trading in adverse times and in duress. We can learn from the mistakes that have been made and they create the opportunity to improve.

"Our bravest and best lessons are not learned through success, but through misadventure." – *Amos Bronson Alcott*

The company I am employed in as CEO while writing this book underwent a restructure that was necessary to build the confidence of the existing financier in a new business plan. The business was diverse and made up of far too many entities than was really necessary to efficiently and effectively manage the business. The business had grown to a stage where corrective action, a new business plan and complete restructure was required to allow the business to meet its full potential as the basic margin opportunity and market imperative was sound.

This business comprises an importation company that wholesales exclusively to the group's own retail network controlled by the group's franchise company.

The retail network of stores is approximately 50% owned by the family that owns the import/wholesale company and franchisor Company with the balance of the retail stores owned by individual franchisees. A disconnect had built up between the franchisor and the franchisee for a variety of reasons, that I won't dwell on here in detail, where franchisees that weren't owned by the franchisor felt disenchanted and did not support promotional activities necessary for the group to flourish, and like most issues in business, there was fault on both sides.

The franchise agreement was not being enforced and the franchisees had taken an influential role with franchisor management that was causing a rift so wide that the business had reached an impasse and promotions were not happening due to disagreements primarily on margin and stock supply. The role of the franchisor and franchisee had become blurred and no one fully understood what role they needed to play and how the businesses could best interact with each other to maximise profitability.

To be the instigator of a new truth, a new direction, does not always make you popular but leaders know that they are not there to be popular; they are there to do what's right.

As I mentioned previously, it's really important to do a SWOT analysis on your business and be brutally honest with yourself and listen to what each company in the supply chain is saying and put plans in place to rectify it.

The medicine does not always taste that good for those it is being administered to, but be sure of the formula, and never flinch from the strategy as only through absolute transparent consistency, and good communication of plans, will the barriers be broken down and the company flourish. It is critical to carry out the plans and regularly inform all parties of the progress as this is what keeps everyone focused on the goal.

When doing the SWOT analysis, I always have a very close look at the competition and get right inside their minds to understand the strategies they deploy to take their business to market. In a retail supply chain like ours, this means having a full understanding of the strengths and weaknesses of the suppliers to the opposition retailers.

In this instance, the competitors were very effectively spinning a story that they sold better quality products than ours and as we were positioned as a bulk retail outlet that bought in our own product and sold under mostly our own brands at low prices. We also had some issues with some suppliers from India, not all, that produced product not to the specification of the order that lent credibility to their statements. And dented ours!

This had to stop as credibility is paramount in business and I believe is the single most important factor to continuously focus on. Never do anything that your staff, customers, suppliers or franchisees will be able to prove is a deliberate distortion of the truth as once you have lost your credibility reversing it is a monumental challenge.

Our plan was to expose and undermine the opposition's business strategy by stealing their thunder and making their market position innocuous.

We did this in several ways:

1. We approached many of their main suppliers that had established credible brands and convinced them to supply us as we had developed the strongest promotional calendar, were the biggest group and had a well-established database. This was a progressive exercise and continues to this day, but in the first two years, we opened up many new supply lines, some in competition with our own brands, and migrated sales to us and grew the suppliers market presence making it a true win-win relationship. We planned this introduction carefully and had no discernible cannibalisation of our own brands.

2. We got tough on suppliers that would not meet our quality controls and dropped them if they couldn't produce to our standards. Buyers weren't only empowered to do this, they were encouraged to as you are only ever as strong as your weakest link. Never allow a supplier to get away with delivering product not on specification or of a quality that does not meet regulatory body requirements. The customer doesn't care that you didn't make it, you are the agent selling it and therefore responsible for it. You must fulfil your promise and meet the expectation of the customer – always!

3. We changed our logo, which had been poorly developed due to the colours being not distinctive and the font not as clean and slick as it could be. When this was done, we developed a new store identity to suit our new clean vibrant image which proudly extolled the new brands on the outside of the store. While we were at it, we realigned the store size, rent and salary ratios to revenue and renegotiated leases with landlords to our new business model. This did two main things – it made the store much more profitable and funnelled cash into the business to feed stock purchases to create growth. Importantly, it told the staff and the customers we were changing and was visible proof of our new market position. Our new promise of selling better quality products was reflected in our in-store presentation and in the quality of our marketing as it is most important that you deliver your promise to the customer on all levels.

4. We changed our managers in our poor performing stores and let the new managers develop the store by giving them clear direction, targets and rewards and more information to measure the business with. It is incredible the difference putting the right people in the right roles, with the right artillery will make to your business. People are always your number one asset so treat your talented loyal staff well, and develop a culture that encourages their success and the vibe will spill over to your customers. The till will ring and profits will flow like never before. Some staff resisted change and were entrenched with the old ways and as the business progressed the new culture made their position difficult. Ultimately, they change or leave, as in all things you either change or you die.

5. We restructured the organisation and liquidated companies that were adding unnecessary complication, and cost, to the business and then amalgamated the retail stores all into one company

that is now a really successful business. Reporting is accurate and timely as we also disestablished the old finance team and enlisted an external professional organisation, to provide reporting we required. This meant we could much more effectively forecast our financial requirements and remove the internal void between purchasing and finance.

6. We refinanced the business in accordance with the new agreed business plan and religiously followed the plan. This took serious drive and commitment by all. We travelled faster than the opposition.

PATIENCE IS FOR SLOW PEOPLE.

The results have been phenomenal and, in two hectic years, we saw the retail network profitability improve substantially and were getting sales growth of 35 to 40% over last year in some stores each month. One store we relocated has had months this year where it has grown by 85% and 60% on the prior year. This is after reducing the rent and rates by nearly half and moving into a new smaller site better suited to the business so the store feels full of stock. This has been an important part of the psyche that turns customers on. Who wants to shop in a store that feels half-empty? The stock levels have increased and the shop size reduced. This has caused some logistic issues but the bottom line is worth the pain.

Don't under estimate how critical it is to tell your story to the market and deliver it.

HOW WELL YOU TELL AND DELIVER YOUR STORY IS THE ULTIMATE TRUTH THAT DETERMINES YOUR SUCCESS OR FAILURE.

This may well be the issue with Apple as outlined earlier, the new CEO isn't delivering a message that the customer is used to hearing. The compelling inspiration that established the brand is fading.

Another really key ingredient in delivering your plan is to have a General with Genghis Khan like qualities that can always out pace, and outlast the opposition, as described in clause 3 of leadership qualities above. If your leader is driving his team and has good disciplines in place to make the management team act out the strategy and drives the business at a faster pace than the opposition, then the opposition will be overrun.

There is nothing surer.

Fast decisive coordinated operations will always defeat divided slow acting businesses. The leader must set the pace and the standard. The weaker players in the team may revolt and stand against the new direction a leader may take, as will stronger members of the team who have selfish interests at heart even though they know the new direction is right for the company.

None of this will prevent the strong CEO from taking the business forward in a relentless concentrated push on with the business plan. Sometimes there may be a decision that is wrong, but a continued push in the same direction will dwarf these bumps on the road as the goals are forever in his sight, and get closer daily, as every moment of truth is aimed at achieving the desired outcome.

CONSISTENCY OF BELIEF WILL ALWAYS PAY OFF IN CREATING THE DESIRED TRUTH. HONESTY AND COMMITMENT IS NOT A POPULARITY CONTEST.

Always you need to be consistent; it is a key ingredient of the truth.

Recently, we have seen one of the great leaders on the US investment scene defraud his investors of a cool $65 billion over two decades. Bernie Madoff helped found the Nasdaq Exchange, and so was a highly credible player, but he developed a giant Ponzi scheme and made off with the cash.

He was so credible that celebrities like Stephen Spielberg, Kevin Bacon, Zsa Zsa Gabor and fat-cat billionaires, banks, charities and even humble investors were all taken in. When he finally fessed up to his giant Ponzi scheme, the largest in history, he was sentenced to 150 years in prison.

Madoff was made by the Securities Commission to provide proof of his holdings and had an obviously incredible ability to hoodwink investors for his own selfish gains. He was so self-motivated, with a complete lack of consideration, that his actions caused his son to commit suicide on the second anniversary of his father's confession after relentless attacks on him that he was involved in his father's grand illusion.

Madoff said he acted alone, but since his confession, seven others have been arrested.

So what did Bernie believe and how did he make these other clever people believe in him. He used his latent credibility and obvious success to have these people set aside the normal sensibility that says:

IF SOMETHING IS TOO GOOD TO BE TRUE, IT PROBABLY IS.

Consistently delivering returns that belied the broader markets would normally cause someone to do a double take but the fraud grew to a gargantuan $65 billion before the game was up.

It was all a complete sham from the outset and is a classic example of how much harm that can come from lies and deception. The penalty of 150 years for Bernie is about right but it's just a shame he won't get to serve them all or pay back all the people he deceived. The innocent had to suffer for the lies and pleasure of a few.

Like the great drug cheats in sport, see Sports Truth, Bernie just believed his own media and got completely caught up in the belief that he was infallible. Just like Lance Armstrong, Bernie also has had the unbelievable shame of having to deal with confronting his son over the image of a hero he had created when he really was just rivalling Lance for the title as the biggest liar on the planet.

Unfortunately, the lies cost the life of Bernie's son Mark.

Bernie consistently insisted he acted alone despite 15 people being convicted from the fraud and a major bank paying a multibillion-dollar penalty. Madoff has lost both his sons, one to suicide and the other to cancer. I have always thought that the worst possible event that can occur in anyone's life is to see their children die. It is just not the natural order we all live by, and the love we pour into our children would be transformed into a flash of memories from a life source that most of us cherish beyond all else.

Madoff's comments below give strong credence to Karma.

"As difficult as it is for me to live with the pain, I have inflicted on so many, there is nothing to compare with the degree of pain I endure with the loss of my sons Mark and Andy.

"I live with the knowledge that they never forgave me for betraying their love and trust. As much as I tried to reach out to them in an attempt to explain the circumstances that caused my betrayal, they could not find it possible to forgive me. I do understand their unwillingness. The fact that I was trying to protect our family by sheltering them from any knowledge or involvement in my wrongdoing still fails to allow me to forgive myself."

Irving Picard, the court-appointed trustee seeking to recover funds for victims, had sued both of Madoff's sons claiming they knew or should have known about the fraud and the action was continuing at the time of writing. Both had claimed they could not have known about the fraud, since it occurred in a part of the business, they had no involvement in. The horrible stress that must come with a situation like this ended up claiming their lives through a web of deceit their father wove.

DECEIVER: Bernard Madoff walks out of federal court after a
bail hearing in New York on Jan 5, 2009.

(Getty Images)

In more recent emails, Madoff pointed to the decision by
a British court dismissing claims against his sons.

*"I would remind everyone that the trustee's civil
litigation against my sons as directors of Madoff Securities
International in London was not only DISMISSED, the
judge lambasted the trustee for his baseless claims and
unnecessary harassment of my sons,"* Madoff wrote.

No doubt Bernie will have to live the retched existence he
so deserves for the rest of his life and the clear message is that
if you don't tell lies in the first place, you won't have to spend
your existence defending the indefensible.

Why would anyone believe anything Bernie has to say
now? The complete basis of his ability to interact with anyone
on a meaningful basis has been lost with his credibility in
shreds.

YOUR GREATEST ASSET IS YOUR INTEGRITY.
NEVER SACRIFICE IT IN THE QUEST FOR MONEY OR
ANY MATERIAL GAIN, AS THE LOSS OF YOUR
HONOUR IS NOT RECOVERABLE.

I was interviewing a young lady recently for a role in one of our stores, and I was querying her regarding her school experience, when amazingly she asked me whether she should tell the truth. Really! Applying for a job and asking at an interview whether you should tell the truth.

She obviously had no understanding of its importance, and therefore had no place in our organisation. You must uphold your beliefs and standards in every facet of your business.

The result of all Bernie's lies and deception – mayhem in people's lives as their life savings are spurned, anger in retaliation and a breakdown of the family unit that leads to your son's death.

Can you even begin to imagine what it would be like to kill your son or be responsible for it?

Downstream impacts include a massive loss of credibility to the institutions that were involved; the J P Morgan Chase Bank paid a whopping 2.5 billion dollars in penalties, in a deal that spared the CEO Jamie Dimon and his executives from any jail time.

So the next big question I ask myself is: Can money determine the truth?

And the answer is **No**.

MONEY DOES NOT DETERMINE THE TRUTH.

All that has happened through the financial crisis with these circumstances is that the leaders of these banks have been vilified and the public have less confidence and trust in the judicial and financial systems.

Yes, Jamie got off but his bank was forced to pay the biggest penalty of its type in history at that time.

You have got to hand it to Bernie he's breaking records all over the place, and like all great fraudsters, unfortunately, a whole lot of people get tangled up in the melee. Greed on this scale takes hold over everyone exposed to it as the excitement of grand success is intoxicating but equally frightening is the reality that dawns when the illusion is exposed.

I have been lucky to face many challenges in different roles in my working career and have mostly always loved my work and cherished it as real possession in the humdrum of life. I think the words from Desiderata have this concept embodied in it, so I copy a pertinent excerpt from this masterpiece of thought below. It is something I have always loved as a philosophy to live by and it was again another treasure that my dad exposed me too.

"Go placidly amid the noise and haste, and remember what peace there may be in silence.

"As far as possible without surrender be on good terms with all persons.

"Speak your truth quietly and clearly; and listen to others, even the dull and the ignorant; they too have their story."

I hope you get the same sense of serenity from desiderata that I do and I encourage you to Google it and read the full script that is a poem written by lawyer Max Ehrmann around 1920. It is simply wonderful and a really balanced foundation guide to live by in all facets of your life, your personal relationships, your business dealings and your beliefs.

Adopting the mindset of the customer is a powerful business tool and so it is most important that you listen to them and understand what they are saying. When you are deciding whether the quality or design of your product is causing it not to sell, or the inability of sales people, make sure you listen to your customers as they will tell you the truth. Your manufacturing staff and sales team have positions to protect and may well give you sanitised versions of events.

It's always convenient to find excuses and blame people, but you also need to examine whether you went through a thorough process before you launched to test your concept and theories. Also always test your promotional strategy on consumers with focus groups and, in this case, product testing and value testing. By talking to your target audience, you will soon be able to determine whether you are on the money or barking up a tree.

When feedback comes back different to what you think it should be, listen to it. This is the learning development stage of making your dream come true and, ultimately, the truth will be what you believe even though sometimes you have to change, have to get up off the floor, have to find a new partner or even completely restart your vision.

There may be something that the designer fails to do, as they often are blind to criticism of their own ideas. Brutally test the product and face the truth early on to save red faces and red ink later on. Keep believing and never give up.

In a completely different situation, you may be involved in resolving a dispute between a franchisee and you are the franchisor. It's easy to pull the trigger, when you are the only one with the gun, but that will not create harmony or success.

Franchisees can be unbelievably frustrating and at times rude and ignorant, even to the extent they will try to extort and publicly humiliate your company and staff. At all times, you need to deal within the boundaries of the agreement and be fair. You have to listen to them and fully understand their view; however, it doesn't mean you have to agree with them, as the wider truth for the group may well be very different to an independent franchisee's view.

If the circumstance dictates it, you must issue a breach notice and terminate a franchisee, as this part of the discipline that maintains the credibility of the franchise agreement. Always in this process seek out the whole truth of what has happened through a fair and transparent process and then carry out appropriate discipline in accordance with the agreement or rules.

In a franchise-type business, or cooperative, when you are at the group office administering the rules, you have a responsibility to at times use the full force of the agreement for the betterment of the group as a whole. Never weaken and let a strong franchisee that is breaking the rules, and wanting to take the business in a different direction for their own advantage, get their way. This is the road to ruin and not what the system is all about. The constitution and agreements provides the franchisor the ability to determine the truth and decide what is right; this must be the continuous pursuit irrespective of the business type.

The strength of these independent based groups comes from the collective belief that if they all act as one, and follow a proven formula, they will collectively get stronger and succeed. As the group gets bigger, the scale of the organisation generates buying power, margin advantages and efficiencies in structure that can have amazing positive impacts on the bottom line. I know I've seen it. The key always is to have the robust business model first so that expansion is on the basis of profitability from the sale of products and not solely generation of fees. Those franchise systems that drive membership growth to make profits from selling franchises without a robust business model will be sentenced to ongoing disputes and disharmony that will ultimately result in failure, unless the model is transformed.

The process of managing change and improving the franchise system are squarely on the shoulders of the franchisor as the brain of the organisation. Manage this process with care or you will fail and the group will splinter in a variety of directions, diluting the base foundation blocks that built the business in the first place.

Enjoy the challenges because you can be sure if you have the strength to push and drive your chosen competitive advantage, you will succeed if it's real and you have done your homework well. Never stop believing, ever, and success will come and the fruit of all your diligence reveal itself as you drive towards your goal. You will feel great when your company milestones are achieved and so will your staff.

At one organisation, I managed for 14 years I developed a cultural document that used the acronym IFIT meaning that members of the cooperative all fit together to make the whole even though we had many different types of membership. IFIT stood for INTEGRITY, FAIRNESS, INNOVATION and TEAM.

This group had three types of members, and ended up being about 140 stores, so the need for discipline, respect and common direction was paramount to succeed against chain stores that had a single owner, single order book and the ability to quickly make decisions.

The cultural document of the acronym is represented below. I'm sorry I don't have a copy of the original document so I've done my best to replicate it below so that you get the idea behind the culture we were developing.

Integrity – *Always act with honesty in all dealings with all people*

Fair – *Always treat your fellow members, suppliers and Customers fairly and as you would want to be treated. (Basis of Be the Customer ethos)*

Innovative – *DNA is our heart and we will always strive for new ideas to create new successful markets*

Team – *Our strength is in our uniformity*

As you can imagine we had the majority of the network embracing these fundamentals as they were experiencing the success while the organisation grew and plundered market share from opposition that were not as well drilled. However, there are always those who have to have their own way and want more than what is rightly theirs. They are usually the bigger members who will think that their size entitles them to more, even though in some instances they were late joining the group and really should have had more respect for the founding members that toiled to grow the group from its humble beginnings, to what became the market leading group in the industry.

For these members, when they are completely outside the rules and failing to recognise others rights, there was another culture that was applied. One that Genghis Khan would have applauded and we called it FIFO commonly referred to as the FIFO principal.

FIT IN OR FUCK OFF.

I learnt it from the MD of another similar cooperative, in a similar industry, and must confess that we used it in many ways. Once when an errant member, who also was a director, was abusing the rules our lawyer sent him a letter/email advising him of his wrongdoing and reminded him that the society was a voluntary organisation. This was a beautifully worded document which was the subtlest way delivering the FIFO principal I ever saw.

The message got through and the errant member modified his behaviour, for a time anyway. Leopards don't change their spots.

I have also found it resonates well with staff as in nearly all circumstances staff want other employees to be true to the company cause and tend to naturally ostracise those who want to deliberately undermine operations for individual gain.

During this period I wore three hats – general manager and company secretary of the cooperative group, and managing director of a subsidiary that held the intellectual property for a new member type which became our largest individual member. I was constantly under pressure from different member types demanding my time and the only way through that minefield was with absolute transparency and complete integrity at all times.

The group was administered according to the rules no matter how much pressure was applied from an influential supplier or large member, as the basis of the society was that all members had equal rights. No matter what I ensured those principals were applied and made sure that all the group office staff knew that they were always empowered to uphold the constitution and do the right thing, they would have my support and that of the board.

I learnt through this period more than any other time in my life the importance of the telling the truth at all times. I witnessed some appalling behaviour and greed where fellow members acted with total disregard for others. As long as they benefitted financially, they simply didn't care about others or the long-term prospects of the group.

Short-sighted money grabs seldom contribute to the long-term plan and so sometimes, as hard as it may seem, you have to say no to a short-term gain for the long-term good. Remember this advice the next time you face a situation where you know you can make a quick buck now and haven't fully considered the consequences.

Be very aware of those promising quick riches. There is no substitute for hard work.

Some parties in a business I was aware of even built into their business plan an excessive legal fund, so they would simply fight with high-powered legal companies to legitimise their dishonesty, fuelled by greed. When discussing with one company owner over an elaborate take over he was conspiring, I noticed an obvious conflict in his plan and he simply said, "Oh, so there is a gap in the story," and moved on to create an even deeper web of deceit to push on with his objective. Interestingly, the partner he conspired this deception with, later became his bitter enemy.

NO AMOUNT OF MONEY CAN TURN DISHONEST GREED INTO THE TRUTH AND RESTORE INTEGRITY

Are these people happy? I don't know because they fly in the face of most moral values purported by the stoics and most religions as a basis for happiness and contentment. Happiness was always one of the big three things instilled into me by my father as the basis of a decent life. The other two were honesty and health. The big three H's are the code I still live by.

HAPPINESS

So what truly makes a person happy?

I believe that happiness is a self-determined state and that you are the one that ultimately decides your happiness through the decisions you make and the actions you take. This happens every second of every day, it's your choice.

This subject can easily be in the religious section but I have put it here as it seems to flow from the aspect of greed that drives many wealthy people – not all but many.

So what is happiness – Wikipedia describe it as *'a mental or emotional state of wellbeing characterised by positive or pleasant emotions ranging from contentment to intense joy.'*

I think that sums it up as there are so many ways of being happy, depending on what turns you on, in the community or society you associate with.

I know for sure in the work environment that staff work best when they are happy and are most productive. The down time and cost dealing with uncooperative staff and bullies is almost incalculable, so my advice is to get rid of them as soon as you can if they won't conform after proper process. Just watch your productivity and staff morale soar.

In my experience, trying to correct behaviour patterns with this type of people is a slow road to nowhere.

I believe happiness and productivity are indelibly linked. Just watch those that supported the bully, as it was the safest place to be, swap sides and their views when the bully is confronted and ousted. Unfortunately, many weaker people get caught up with these cancerous types and they cannot be blamed for not knowing how to deal with them. The role of the manager is to prevent this happening, and the role of the company is to have a clearly defined code of conduct and an employment contract that allows poor behaviour or work standards to be dealt with justly and appropriately.

It's absolutely vital that you ascertain through a thorough investigation what really happened and present the allegations to the perpetrators, so they have every opportunity to defend themselves. Often the bully will try and attack the manager for upsetting the process as this is how these people operate, they will say and do anything to get what they want. The really sad part is that often they are really good workers but they just can't seem to get their focus right and channel their abundant energy for a common good.

Do not drag the process out as it can often complicate the issue and the bully may use their influence to get corroboration for a lie that will muddy the waters sufficiently to get them off the hook. Back to back interviews with the staff concerned without the opportunity for them to talk to each other is the way to go if you can. Very clearly and concisely present your questions and do so in an objective manner.

When you have found the truth, you can determine the solution. Again it is the truth that is the pivot point that determines everything.

WHEN YOU HAVE FOUND THE TRUTH, YOU CAN DETERMINE THE SOLUTION

Always be firm and fair. Your staff, especially those that have caused the problem will never see your decision as just but that matters not, what matters is that you determine the correct discipline appropriate to the crime that has been ascertained through the investigation.

Use the truth search to eliminate and stamp out destructive behaviour. The perpetrators will fight management but if you follow proper process then you can free your company from this disease which at its very worst can paralyse organisations and at the least wastes time, reduces focus and stunts productivity.

The critical issue in making this all happen is to ensure that your company has the necessary structure, rules and contracts in place so that it can discipline outcomes accordingly. Whether it is a rogue staff member or a supplier that is not meeting expectations of their trading agreement, you must constantly strive to drive out corruption and stand over tactics by constantly pursuing the truth and intent of the agreements.

ALWAYS PURSUE THE TRUTH CONTINUOUSLY, IN EVERY FACET OF YOUR BUSINESS, SO THAT ITS CREDIBILITY IS UNQUESTIONABLE

Philosophers and religions often see happiness as living a good life, not dissimilar to the Stoics, but simpler in its approach and still based on virtuous ethics and not just an emotion.

As I mentioned at the start of this section on happiness, I think it is definitely self-determined and the difference between fear and excitement is the way you react to a situation. The decisions you make when confronted with adversity can become your worst nightmare or your greatest success.

Happiness is the result if you make the right choice and have the courage to see it through.

If you decide wrong, you will be trapped by your fear and wallow in darkness that too many people face every day and don't have the strength to deal with. David Bowie wrote in the *Aladdin Sane* album – ***"Breaking up is hard but keeping dark is hateful."***

To move forward, you need to accept the truth. This applies to both your business and your personal life. Don't let people who think they are stronger than you force you into abandoning your belief. If you do, they will be proven right, be the victor and claim the spoils. If you have the courage, spawned from knowing you are right, when you make a difficult decision whether to sacrifice your integrity over a relationship that has hit rocky waters, you will come out of the failure with your most important asset intact. Mr Bowie is right. Holding on to resentment is horrible and hopeless, far better to move on and end a relationship that has become destructive to both parties.

If you always do the right thing, you have nothing to fear, will sleep soundly at night secure in the knowledge you have acted always with honour.

Mencius was a Confucian some 2300 years ago, 372 to 289 BC, and he argued that if we did not nourish our vital force with righteous deeds, then that force would shrivel up and die. He also argued that this joy can be most heightened when experiencing virtue through music.

This was recently experienced globally in Iran when Pharrell Williams smash hit *"Happy"* was grooved to on YouTube by six Iranians. The happy six were arrested in Tehran by the police and the Tehran Police Chief Hossein Sajedinia was quoted as saying the dance video was a *"vulgar clip which hurt public chastity."* Islamic law enforced in Iran requires women to cover themselves from head to toe.

Pharrell Williams in his song uses the words – *"Clap your hands if you think happiness is the truth"* and so I am sure that this is what the essence of the video was intended to be even though the producer deceived those that participated in the video were told it would not be published. It was probably a protest against the restricted social freedoms that exist in Iran. The International Community caused an uproar about the incident and officials were forced to release the six happy dancers the next day.

The following excerpt is from a YouTube link and shows that the President has the foresight to embrace the changing nature of the world and his comments below reflect this.

"In a speech over the weekend, Mr Rouhani (President) argued that Iran should embrace the internet rather than view it as a threat.

"But conservatives regularly denounce what they see as laxity on the part of the authorities on women covering up or on behaviour deemed offensive to Islam."

Pharrell Williams responded to Iran's decision on his Twitter account, saying, *"It's beyond sad these kids were arrested for trying to spread happiness."*

It is utterly amazing how internet is smashing tradition and boundaries for a six everywhere so you need to be really mindful of this when developing your company's business plan. The music business, like no other, is embraced by the youth of today and music is probably the best way of connecting with them. It was in my day also, but it's just all so much more accessible now at less comparative cost.

You should always have your business goals clearly defined and make them wholesome and based on good values and you will find a greater degree of acceptance and support than goals that are motivated on greed for the owners only. For the righteousness of good endeavour will always succeed over self-serving oppression.

Mahatma Gandhi summed it up this way:

"When I despair, I remember that all through history the way of truth and love have always won. There have been tyrants and murderers, and for a time, they can seem invincible, but in the end, they always fall. Think of it – always."

The think of it always is exactly the point I am trying to make when I say to always pursue the truth continuously in every facet of your business. Not only will your customers realise it, they will thank you for it and continue to support you. It's what creates the invaluable business asset – trust.

Perhaps companies need to measure trust and report on it, many now measure their environmental impact and that is a subset of fully connecting with your customer on all levels.

While Sonja Lyubomirsky concluded in her book, *The How of Happiness*, that 50% is from the genes you inherit, 10% the circumstances that you confront in life and 40% self-control, it is how you react to what happens I believe that it is almost entirely self-determined.

And the prize is significant according to the book *"Happy people live longer"* where the conclusion is a 14% upside or 10 to 14 years extra life. I believe that is most true so you have to be a mug to take the choice to be bummed out about something you can laugh at.

Really, what the hell reason really exists to be down. The essence lies in your ability to determine how you react to external or internal pressures, whatever they may be, or wherever they come from. If your jealous lover is trying to make you feel guilty for something you have not done, choose not to be guilty, choose to be happy in the knowledge that you did nothing wrong, and do not accept bunkum that other people hang on you.

Similarly, if a business colleague is trying to pressure you into a decision that you know is wrong, and is self-motivated, and not for the good of the company, then choose not to do it, choose to do the right thing and be happy in the knowledge that you always do your best.

Cary Grant the famous actor had two great quotes which I copy below:

"My formula for living is quite simple. I get up in the morning and I go to bed at night. In between, I occupy myself as best I can."

"I pretended to be somebody I wanted to be until finally I became that person. Or he became me."

I love this one, it epitomises the essence of this book.

So here I am writing this book and thinking this guy just has to be happy to have a belief system like that because it just embodies so much of what I believe, so I googled "is Cary Grant happy" because when in doubt, consult God always for instant divine wisdom.

This guy was an extraordinary human being who pursued happiness by being the best he could. I was so blown away with the response that I have copied some of this article below for you.

"Do not blame others for your own mistakes." This is one of Cary's most important rules. I remember when I blamed "Mother Nature" for the fact that every bite I take puts weight on me. Cary looked deeply into my eyes – and that I enjoyed and said, "Nonsense. YOU are Mother Nature. You have the power within you to be thin or fat, as you desire." And as I still looked sceptical, he went on, "God is within you, and you can do and have anything you want. You must love yourself more." And then he added, "You can love your fellow man."

"Love – that is a word you hear often when you are around Cary Grant.

"It is the law of life that if you are kind to someone you feel happy. If you are cruel you are unhappy. And if you hurt someone, you will be hurt back."

Cary Grant reached the pinnacle of the cutthroat acting industry with these simple philosophies and his ideology that if you hurt someone you will be hurt back applies in business, but it is the competitive nature of the market that makes this inevitable. To grow and prosper in a static or declining market, you must hurt another company by taking market share from them, or they will do it to your company.

The other option is to change your business model and grow into other market opportunities or create new ones, but always do thorough research before you leap into new ground.

CHANGE

Change in a company, no matter how much it is needed, often cannot be easily seen or wanted by those in their comfort zone. There will be also those who can't see the threat or the opportunity that is driving the need to change.

Often they don't want to recognise the truth about their problems and go into denial, which of course is the worst thing that you can do when a business is beset by financial problems, for whatever reason. This is the time when a strong leader needs to instigate changes and often these leaders need to come from outside the business. This way they can see the existing problems more clearly and can look at the issues confronting the company objectively and through fresh eyes.

Just because something is new doesn't mean it's wrong. The old school will fight the changes as often they feel their power base shifting, and hate to relinquish the influence they wielded, however misguided that may have been. Incredibly, they often refuse to do this even when confronting the real truth of the situation.

DO NOT DENY REALITY, EMBRACE IT. ONLY THEN CAN YOU MOVE FORWARD TO A CREDIBLE FUTURE.

The errors of the past can easily be blamed on others and just like the famous athletes who lied to the public about their drug taking, business people in dire straits act precisely the same way.

It is utterly incredible how they can fabricate a story, that they truly believe, that only faintly resembles what really happened.

When a company needs to change everyone needs to embrace it, and get on and adopt the new direction, cost cutting, new supplier terms, new product lines or whatever it is that has to be done. It's often hard to be completely transparent through the process of restructuring companies, but I encourage that as the best and fairest way but, unfortunately, the time it takes to work through consultation allows protagonists an opportunity to do everything they can to upset the apple cart.

IT IS ALWAYS BEST TO RELAY THE TRUTH OF THE SITUATION THROUGH THE CHANGE PROCESSES AS STAFF WILL TALK TO EACH OTHER AND ANYTHING LESS WILL RESULT IN INCREASED TURMOIL.

THE TRUTH CREATES MORE HARMONY, AND DISHONESTY MORE DISHARMONY – ALWAYS.

Hold the line and execute your well-considered plan and you will succeed.

In one company I managed, the finance department were simply not delivering the results needed so as part of a restructure, that ended up taking over a year, we completely disestablished the finance team in favour of outsourcing a top-line international professional accounting firm and this was absolutely the right move to get the information needed in a timely manner to manage the business.

THE TRUTH IS, IF YOU CAN'T MEASURE IT, YOU CAN'T MANAGE IT.

You have to have a financial team that delivers what you want, when you want it. They also have to know that their role is to count the money and not to spend it. Yes, they can manage the cash flow and the budget, but the CEO and his marketing team need to be the catalyst for spending money in the organisation and they need to take complete ownership of that.

Strangely, how well you spend, dictates how much profit you make, but I'm not going to delve into that now.

Darwin's theory that if you don't evolve you die is increasingly true in business today as product life cycles shorten, Intellectual property is harder to protect and globalisation via the internet and improved transport systems means it's impossible to escape the watching eye of competitors.

So you have to be good at what you do and constantly evolve but don't stray too far away from your core business, especially too fast. History is littered with companies that have had poorly researched leaps of faith into the greener pasture of another industry only to find that they completely miscued.

They didn't do their research nearly well enough and paid the price.

Charles Kettering said, *"If you have always done it that way then it's probably wrong."* Nothing is surer in business. Charles also said, *"The world hates change but it is the only thing that has brought us progress."*

It is not that far from the definition of insanity, doing the same thing again and again and thinking you will get a different result.

So change you must.

Just plan it, budget it, communicate it and do it for the right reasons by being brutally honest about what's good for the business and not what's good for you.

PROGRESS BEGINS WITH THE PRODUCT

In an environment where technology is developing faster than ever, it is increasingly important to stay very close to your competition, so that you are right up to speed with market changes that can destroy brands and companies at alarming speed.

Classic examples are in the mobile phone market where companies like Nokia and Blackberry were slow to adjust to the advent of the touch screen phone and the convenience and brand mystique created around these developments by new market giants like Apple and Samsung.

While you need to have a good hard look at your business model and how you fund technological competitive advantages there is no fixed way of doing this. Some companies like LG pour massive amounts into research and development (R and D) and a leapfrog technology drive that has seen them develop into a true electronic super power from the role of an OEM manufacturer back in the day when they traded under the Goldstar brand.

If you drive hard in R and D and spend heavily you are likely to command a premium price for your goods and LG made the very successful, yet difficult, transition to a single brand company when they launched the LG trademark globally. The big spend in branding and research is offset by brilliant factories that are amazingly automated. I visited a video plant in the 90s which was more or less entirely run by robots and the advantages are many:

a) Everyone turns up on time.
b) No back chat and false sick leave.
c) Quality control is optimised.
d) Cost of production minimises dramatically when the initial capital investment has been recouped.
e) The plant can run 24 hours a day and labour rates do not change.

Interestingly, robotics is now being seen as the new future and how America will be able to seize back the global manufacturing base that resides in China and Asia due to cheap labour.

Watch closely as this new truth emerges as this will be the next big opportunity for manufacturers in the west that have adequate capital to wrestle the manufacturing base away from Asia and China in particular. Since the Industrial Revolution, the countries that have prospered most have been those that have had a strong manufacturing base, and as the global powers wrestle for survival, the countries that develop and use the best new technological innovation, with control of the manufacturing process, will win the market.

To develop markets and then lose the manufacturing base by not moving swiftly enough to read new product trends is to fail like Sony and Sharp have in categories they developed like portable sound and LCD television.

Samsung is another example of a company that has taken enormous strides to the extent that now the two Korean giants, LG and Samsung are heading off the traditional market dominance in consumer electronics previously enjoyed by such Japanese innovators like Sony, Panasonic and Sharp.

Sony made some tragic mistakes and did not enter into LCD television production nor did they produce MP3 players after developing mobile sound, with the Walkman tape player and then the Discman. They followed up this brilliant foresight with … nothing.

It is my view that the best manufacturer always wins, as long as they are clever with their go to market strategies. How could Sony beat Samsung in television when Samsung were producing them for Sony? Samsung developed the technology so enjoyed a market position where they could sell a superior product at a cheaper price and let the market know both brands were made by the same company. No brand could withstand that for long without innovating something new that gave them a competitive point of difference.

To think so would be brand arrogance.

It is also not necessarily the developer of the technology that gets the gain in the market place, it is the company that identifies the opportunity to commercialise a concept that fires the customer's imagination. Always, however, the manufacturer that has the best efficiency and technological capability will get the volume, unless the innovator wraps up the innovation with suitable protection of intellectual property which is very hard to do. If not, this leaves themselves open to attack from rivals that can quickly surpass them in the market place with better quality and design.

CREATIVE INNOVATION THAT STIMULATES HUMANS TO IMAGINE NEW POSSIBILITIES WILL TRULY RESULT IN INCREASED ENTHUSIASM AND SALES.

It is Samsung who supplies Apple with their microchips and processors for their phones and iPads and Apple are finding it hard to replace the technology speed and reliability that Samsung have perfected. Efforts by Apple with Taiwan Semiconductor Manufacturing (TSMC) that started in 2014 was beset with glitches that prevented the chips from meeting the speed and power standards specified according to a TSMC executive.

Apple is one of Samsung's biggest customers and yet they are fierce rivals in the mobile phone category with both companies taking legal action against the other. They were ideal partners when they didn't compete, but when Samsung started rolling out a superior product and eclipsed iPhone sales, the tension escalated to a level that some Apple executives have expressed concern that their dependence on Samsung inhibits their ability to control their future.

Apple's dilemma is that the world's biggest and most sophisticated manufacturer of parts that Apple craves including processors, memory and high-resolution screens is their foe – Samsung. Former Apple executives say that replicating that elsewhere is a daunting challenge and time will tell who will be the dominant force.

The battle will rage on and new players will come and go in a category where the only thing that is sure is that maintaining a market dominant position requires massive resources, forward thinking R and D, exceptional brand strategies resulting in relentless product demand as the consumer appetite for the smartphone lifestyle is seemingly insatiable.

YOU CAN'T BANK MARKET SHARE

Never a truer word uttered!

This was a favourite gem of a mentor of mine, the amazing Bob Toone of Email Ltd.

What this saying means is that when you develop your budgets and product pricing you must not consider volume as your primary driver as it doesn't matter how many products you sell if the Gross Profit does not exceed the total expenses.

In all my years of business, it has never failed to amaze me how many people have no concept of what really drives their business and don't even know what their breakeven costs are. They don't grasp that it is the volume multiplied by the margin that generates the gross profit and it is managing this formula in your forecasting and buying and negotiating that makes this line in the profit and loss way more important than the top-line revenue line when pursuing profitability.

I don't intend to bore into this subject here but wanted to throw it in as a must think about subject, when developing the business plan, that makes up the vision you seek to realise.

THE NUMBERS NEVER LIE. THE DECEPTION IS IN THE PERCEPTION.

Recently, I travelled to Bali for a holiday and had an unbelievably good time and couldn't help but marvel in the amazing friendliness and respect we received from the Balinese people. However, on the way there and on the way back, we encountered the most deplorable service of any company ever, so much so that I want to share the experience.

Unfortunately, a volcano blew its lid in Java and the ash was blowing over Bali airspace, so Jetstar advised us that our flight was to be transferred to Bali via Sydney, and not Melbourne, where we had a day stop over planned. We were advised on time so didn't go to the airport and waste time which was commendable.

It is fair to say that Jetstar positions itself as an airline that is price driven and as a result needs to get market share as the margin formula dictates that if you sell for a lower price, you have to sell more if the expense is assumed to be the same. They sell you value added in-flight service which suits some people, as you only pay for what you want.

They say it is their intention to operate all services to schedule in the apology email they sent me but it seemed that they constantly took the option to fill flights first and do so before they considered how they were doing that impacted their customers. All of the customers we interacted with were getting really agitated at the inconsistency of reasons given for the delays in flights departing.

In all of the four flights to and from Bali, not one left on time and two were delayed something like five times, I just gave up counting in the end.

The excuses varied to people on the same flight as follows;

1. Someone on the flight was sick.
2. The pilot has not had the required amount of sleep.
3. The plane was delayed in arriving and so leaving would be delayed.

So which one was the truth? Let's deal with them in turn.

1. As I understand it from friends working on airlines staff is rostered and their contract has them on short notice call, so if someone is sick, you get someone to replace that person and the sick person in turn replaces that person when they are next on as planned in the roster. Amazingly, Jetstar told us this and said

they would pay for us to all stay at the Mercure Hotel in Legian that night which seemed a good effort. However, when you really consider the hassle of having to get all your bags off the plane and back through customs, and then back to the hotel, you just wish it never happened. You have to wonder how they didn't know they had a sick person before all their customers were put through this drama. But it gets better. We all trudge off to the Mercure and are standing waiting in a really long queue that stops moving so I go up and ask why.

The response was staggering. The hotel had no more rooms and even more alarmingly we were advised by the staff at reception that Jetstar had not advised the hotel they were sending frustrated customers to them!

True!

Would you pay for a planeload of customers in a hotel for the night or would you have a system that made sure you had staff available? Really you have to wonder whether this story had any substance at all as it is entirely implausible or abominably inefficient and time wasting for the customer resulting in serious brand damage.

1. If the pilot had not had the required amount of sleep then he or she should not have been flying, no question. But why did they put us on the plane? Surely, they knew! If they didn't, they are alarmingly incompetent, and if they did, they are alarmingly deceitful as they wasted all our time. They had our email and mobile contact details and were in touch so why didn't they communicate with us all and tell us to only come to the airport when they were ready to fly and had the appropriate resource in place.

2. The next excuse that the plane was late arriving was dispelled by Denpasar Airport staff who confirmed the plane was actually at the airport. I was told by a passenger that Jetstar will often cancel flights if they

don't have full enough flights and in this instance a plane left at 11.15 on the Tuesday when we were scheduled to leave at the revised time of 10 am, as promised the night before. The story being bounced around was the 11.15, flight 44, got our plane and we got a new charter flight 7044 which was scheduled to leave at 2.30 pm that day. Incredibly, it did, only four and a half hours later than plan.

We were hearing stories of people coming to the airport every day for a week and then going back to the hotel in complete frustration. At this stage, you become numb to the process as anger is replaced by a futile resignation that there is nothing you can do.

Clearly in all of this, the truth was not being told as the stories don't align and lack credibility.

When we were leaving Sydney to go to Bali, we were stuck there for an additional two nights due to the volcano initially, but when flights were resumed, it was amazing how badly Jetstar handled the situation. In their effort to put bums on seats first and foremost and obviously ahead of the cost of putting on an extra flight, they tried to shuffle customers into existing available flights with scant regard that for some of these customers this was a dream holiday they had been planning for years. Finally, they organised a charter flight and everyone was happy just to be finally heading on their holiday. Some had saved for ages to make this their dream break and to be treated this way was appalling in deed.

Certainly, I did not come away from the experience thinking it was their intention to fly to schedule. I came away thinking that this was their excuse for their maximising customers on planes time which is why they are cheap, and if this in fact what is happening, then they have an obligation to tell the customer that if the plane is not full you may be delayed. The volcano was a natural disaster beyond control, no doubt about it, but the attempts to make the most of a bad situation revealed serious flaws in the company's ability and intentions.

Jetstar is, in my opinion, the worst company that I have ever had the displeasure of experiencing globally. My rationale is detailed below:

1. They put their staff in the impossible situation of knowing less than the customer. Jetstar's website that updates flight times was proven over this 11-day period to be very accurate and reliably the latest information available on flight times. Staff were on several occasions looking at their screen and telling us different times regarding flight delays than we could see on the Jetstar website, and they thought they were right. Always the website was right. The impact was more wasted time at the airport and confrontations with staff that were protecting a position with good intent that was wrong, as they were working on old or incorrect information.

2. They do not intend to fly to schedule otherwise they would find a way to achieve it. If this is the primary intention, then they should leave on time and not wait for customers who are late jeopardising on time customers who are meeting connecting flights.

3. They don't consider connecting flights as other airlines do and in Bali said they could not advise what the connecting flight in Melbourne would be and we would have to wait until we got there.

4. They are inconsistent about the reasons for delays as evidenced by the contrary stories given above.

5. Their communication skills are epically pathetic. This includes internally to their staff and externally to the customer. I even had a staff member laugh at me when I was expressing to them frustration at their inability to tell us what was happening. They would be better off not committing to a revised time until they knew they could achieve it. I am talking about the period when the airport was open so all headaches in this regard were generated by Jetstar and to top it off what company would send you to some

accommodation late in the evening without checking it was available?

6. The attempt to buy your loyalty for $50 after treating you so poorly is insulting. Would you fly again with an airline because you got a $50 voucher when you know that flying on time is not a priority?

Jetstar's focus on price without being honest with the customer about the method will ultimately not end well as I don't believe the price differential will ultimately be enough for them to succeed unless they improve their service. The number of customers that won't fly Jetstar again has probably risen after this event and I contend that Jetstar's disaster recovery plan is a disaster.

To then compare Jetstar with amazing friendly and honest service we got at EWA Villas in Seminyak, and in every facet of the Indonesian experience was like comparing a Bugatti Veyron with a pushbike with flat tyres. If they didn't have something, they told us. Novel huh! Mostly they simply did exactly what they said they would, on time, in a disarmingly respectful and friendly way.

Bali is the land of gods where free easy honesty and trust prevails. Imagine this population driving on small narrow roads with motorbikes like locusts invading intersections, yet miraculously we didn't see any accidents. The nose in front rule applied at intersections as vehicles could converge from all streets at once and somehow make it to the other side without accident.

Motorbikes have children on the gas tank and bales of goods on the back. No worries. We even saw a child on the handlebars in dense peak hour traffic. The simple beauty of their way of life and how they respect the five main religions is something to behold as it is this that creates the harmony you feel everywhere. They also know that tourism is their lifeblood, so they act like that and treat you with the utmost respect, exactly the opposite of our experience with Jetstar where snide disdain from some staff was a recipe for failure.

Just as the Balinese are open in their simplicity, Elizabeth Holmes was complex in her deception.

Elizabeth became the darling of Silicone Valley with her start-up Venture Company, Theranos, by claiming the company had technology that could run hundreds of blood tests on just a few small drops, thereby giving hope to people that they would have affordable access to their own healthcare. Actually, she was the master of deception and built the company to an estimated value of $9 billion by winning the trust and investment from corporations like Walgreens and world leaders like Henry Kissinger.

The problem was the company never had the technology and Elizabeth now faces a penalty of up to 20 years in prison for federal fraud. Not unlike some of the other fallen stars reviewed Elizabeth seemed to believe her own story. *"One of the more interesting things about Elizabeth was I don't think that … she thought she was doing anything wrong,"* says Jessie Deeter, a producer of the HBO documentary *The Inventor* that investigated Elizabeth and her company.

Dan Ariely, a behavioural expert who was seeing Elizabeth when things started to unravel, commented in the documentary, *"The reality is that data just doesn't sit in our minds as much as stories do."* Actually, the more people tell lies, the more they are likely to believe them especially if they continually get away with it. The deception becomes the creator's own reality and the lie becomes even more convincing as it is perpetuated.

Yet no amount of telling lies makes it the truth and this is what Elizabeth and many others before her have found out, including the infamous Bernie Madoff.

You better believe that understanding that core base of what makes your market tick, and carrying out the service required to fill that demand, is the complete essence of success in your business. In every moment that your company interfaces with another party, whether it be a customer, a colleague or a supplier, there must be an uncompromising ability for all staff to act with integrity and follow the organisation's creed and plans, as that is the key to long-term success.

REAL POWER RESIDES WITH THE TRUTH.

The Truth of Relationships

After the first betrayal – nothing exists.

Nothing but the blinding fog of confusion as it searches for the freedom and understanding that the truth will bring.

There is no question in my mind that the world would be an infinitely better place if the truth was the pervasive reason for action and the old axiom that *"the truth hurts"* was ultimately superseded. The only reason the truth could have hurt is because a lie or treason existed.

When faith is gone, it is gone, and can never truly be repaired to the original state of bliss, as doubt will always be part of the equation in that relationship in the future. Faith is the confidence or trust you have in a deity, partner or even a business venture. When it is broken, suspicion reigns and disharmony prevails.

No relationship will ever be the same when it has reached the pivotal point of no return when a partner has breached the faith obligations that bound the partnership in the beginning or as the relationship evolved.

Relationships, whether they are for love, friendship or business are what bind humans together with a common sense of purpose, whether it is for something as simple to chill with your friend, spend a romantic night with your lover or put a business partnership together that will make millions.

The two fundamentals that need to be present to make a relationship succeed over time are trust and direction. You must trust each other and you must want the same things so that you are heading in the same direction.

If you think trust alone is going to provide the sustenance needed for a long-term sustainable partnership, then think again. Not even a contract will ensure the survival of a relationship if love or market forces erode the essence that made the relationship form in the first place.

What the contract will do is make the split less complicated, so definitely spend time on getting this right and working out what you both want in the times ahead.

The New Zealand Government introduced a three-year relationship property agreement, where after that time of living together everything is divided equally unless you have an agreement establishing asset bases contrary to that law. Prenuptial agreements are a good idea as divorce rates globally are stratospheric in the modern world and this gives you the chance to think through what lies ahead for you both and how you want to manage your differing asset bases when entering the relationship. Property owned prior to the relationship can be maintained as separate property.

Interestingly, a 2011 poll in London revealed a whopping 26.4% of British females said they have cheated on their partner compared with 25.7% of men. And 43% of women think they can have a one-night stand without being truly unfaithful compared to 33% of men. If they aren't being truly unfaithful, then what should we call this? Harmless fun! Or maybe it is just satisfying one's curiosity, which can easily be justified, until you are found out. It's amazing how we can justify our actions to ourselves as being acceptable as long as we feel good about it at the time.

The quicksand of deception doesn't swallow you until your partner discovers you have betrayed them. That is when you will see how quickly you can complicate and destroy something that you may have been better holding onto, and working at, after all there was something there when you started out together wasn't there?

That harmless fun has transformed into what it really was all along, a caustic lie tantamount to the worst form of human behaviour that somebody can inflict on a partner they pledged to respect.

DECEIVING YOUR LIFE-LONG PARTNER FOR
SELFISH LUST COMES WITH A HEAVY EMOTIONAL
AND CREDIBILITY PRICE TAG.

According to the National Archives statistics published in December 2012 estimated that 42% of marriages in England and Wales ended in divorce. That statistic has a remarkable resemblance to the percentage of women who think it's all right to have a one-night stand without being truly unfaithful.

The top five reasons for divorce in the United Kingdom are as follows:

1. Adultery – making up 55% of the reasons for the marriage failure and the clear winner.
2. Lack of Preparation – As outlined above if there is not enough thought into where the marriage is going and what both parties want from it, then the physical attraction that burnt so brightly at the start dims to instability, arguing and general unhappiness.
3. Excessive Arguing – Lack of respect for each other's views or understanding then fuels conflict which ultimately drives dissatisfaction to the level that adultery, or other unreasonable behaviour, terminates the marriage.
4. Unreasonable Behaviour – which is deemed to be excessive drinking, taking drugs, verbal or physical abuse.
5. Lack of Equality – is also a primary reason where males often feel they are providing where the female believes they are trapped at home and have lost their freedom.

Man and women are entirely different from each other in their decision-making process which ultimately defines their existence, and the potential magic of the togetherness that comes with unconditional commitment to each other.

Men predominantly use logic and women often use feelings to determine outcomes. Neither is right or wrong, and the fact that both have different processes for determining courses of action strengthens the relationship as both views add to the decision-making outcome. When they respect each other's view, they live harmoniously and the relationship flourishes.

If man and women were the same, there would be no reason for them to be with each other, will there? The Creator showed infinite wisdom in making all people and all things different, but one at the same time.

The key to reaching harmony is being absolutely truthful with your partner, respecting each other's opinions and cherishing the difference that drew you to each other. Fear not that you disagree but rather nurture the learning's in the difference; it is the greatest treasure when you understand.

IF YOU ABSOLUTELY RESPECT YOUR PARTNER AND CHERISH YOUR INDIVIDUALITY, YOUR LOVE WILL FLOURISH.

When building a company, all the same skill sets would be useless. You need to have different roles and the appropriate complimentary skills to fulfil those roles to make the company prosper.

There are many types of relationships other than that of man and women and the dynamics that flow from that connection. An example of how one of the world's most celebrated artists can be publicly vilified on the global stage that lead to his tragic demise was no more evident than with Michael Jackson.

A GREAT BIG LIE

"A great big lie" was how Michael Jackson referred to the allegations made against him. The unconscionable allegations made against this beautiful human were dragged through the US Legal System for years in search of the substance to them. The truth certainly changes everything, once both sides know what has happened, then the aggrieved person has to grapple with the reasons why, and the one who committed the betrayal has to learn to live with their self.

In Michael's case, his career was ruined by someone's attempt to extort money from a huge star because of his genuine love for children, and the desire to have the childhood that was deprived from him by a father hell-bent on making his very gifted children famous.

I always believed he was innocent.

Unfortunately, Michael was not only battling the deception he also was confronting the media who had a great new story to sell papers with and was largely portrayed as guilty with sensationalist headlines not being supported by fact. The *New York Post* ran the headline *"Peter Pan or Pervert"*, with only minimal information being disclosed by the police.

Hard Copy's Diane Dimond spent nearly 15 years trying to establish Michael as a paedophile. A story ran with this headline: *"And one more shocker, Hard Copy has obtained new documents in the criminal investigation of Michael Jackson, and they are chilling; they contain the name of child movie actor Macaulay Culkin."* Yet the document itself stated that Culkin strongly denied ever being harmed by Jackson.

While the settlement with Chandler could be surmised as an admission of guilt, the settlement agreement specifically stated that Jackson admitted no wrongdoing and no liability. Legally, settlement cannot be used as evidence of guilt in future civil and criminal cases and after the settlement Jordan Chandler was interviewed by detectives to seek evidence of child molestation but no criminal charges arose from that interview.

The police never pressed criminal charges citing a lack of evidence without Jordan's testimony, and the state closed its investigation on September 22, 1994. The grand juries did not find the evidence presented by the Santa Barbara Police and the LAPD to be convincing enough to indict him or subpoena him even though they can indict the accused on hearsay evidence alone.

172

In 2003, further allegations by the Arvizo family were bought against Jackson and ex-disgruntled employees sold allegations to tabloid television shows and the image of Michael Jackson was constantly being tarnished in the news again. Mostly these stories were reported as allegations but the frequency and volume of stories had a devastating impact on public opinion of him.

"A LIE TOLD OFTEN ENOUGH BECOMES THE TRUTH" IS NOT TRUE. TIME WILL REVEAL THE FALLACY.

In December 18, 2003, seven charges of child sex abuse and two counts of administering an intoxicating agent to commit a sexual abuse felony on Gavin Arvizo were bought against Jackson. Michael always denied these allegations even though the judge allowed testimony from previous trials to be admissible.

Jordan Chandler had left the country to avoid testifying. This becomes particularly relevant later in this section around the time of Jordan's father's death.

In a lecture at Harvard after the trial, Thomas Mesereau said, *"The prosecutors tried to get him to show up and he wouldn't. If he had, I had witnesses who were going to come in and say he told them it never happened and that he would never talk to his parents again for what they made him say. It turned out he'd gone into court and got legal emancipation from his parents. June Chandler testified that she hadn't spoken to her son in 11 years. At one point in her testimony, she claimed that she couldn't remember being sued by Jackson (who had counter-sued for extortion) and at another point said that she'd never heard of her own attorney. However, she said she never witnessed any molestation."*

Jackson was found unanimously not guilty of all charges by the jury on June 13, 2005.

The calamity of this sordid sorry saga is that a mild-mannered genius suffered incredible damage from the rapacious selfish intent of a few money hungry despicable opportunists. The general public didn't know what to believe as the media delivered sensationalism that sold papers and destroyed a reputation.

In this instance, the media were reprehensible in their blind quest to persecute an innocent peace-loving megastar to simply get their circulation or ratings up. It doesn't seem to matter to them that they helped destroy someone who touched more people with his kindness, and musical prowess, than ever before in human history.

This from *The Sun* was a fine example of what the squalor reporting had descended to: Britain's biggest newspaper ran an article titled *'He's Bad, He's Dangerous, He's History'*. The piece branded Jackson an 'ex-black ex-superstar,' a 'freak' and a 'twisted individual' and called for his children to be taken into care.

This type of media reporting is both farcical and disgusting, particularly when the role of the media should be to reveal the truth. Michael's fans never stopped believing and you only need to listen to his music to know he was being attacked for selfish gain. His rebuttal in interviews was to me obviously sincere when he talked of his genuine care for children.

Perhaps Donald Trump is on to something with his fake news!

The outcome for the accuser's family was that Chandler's father got a handsome settlement and the mother ended up never talking to the son. There is no amount of anything that is worth the price of being spurned by your children for trying to force them to lie for your own selfish gain, but that was the outcome for the Chandlers. Not dissimilar to the position Armstrong found himself in when the hurtling truth descended on his fantasy.

On June 10, 2015, the following post appeared where Jordy Chandler's guilt finally got the better of him and the truth was finally validated as he admitted he lied about

Jackson molesting him. The father's comments below should be brought to justice as I believe he ultimately destroyed Michael's faith in humanity which led to excessive drug consumption and ultimately his death.

Now maybe for the remorse of his death, Chandler decides to tell us the truth. *"I never meant to lie and destroy Michael Jackson but my father made me to tell only lies. Now I can't tell Michael how much I'm sorry and if he will forgive me."* Evan Chandler (Jordan's father) was tape-recorded saying amongst other things, *"If I go through with this, I win big-time. There's no way I lose. I will get everything I want and they will be destroyed forever…"*

The truth revealed itself and the retched behaviour of Evan Chandler is disgusting. How can a parent be so misguided that they would put greed and wealth ahead of the love and wellbeing of your child?

Spare a thought for Jordy Chandler who has to live with the guilt of his father's conspiracy while also proving the myth to Lenin's theory.

Michael was right, it was all *"a great big lie,"* and the media have blood on their hands for crucifying one of nature's most beautiful instruments and a creative genius the likes of which we will never see again.

It is fitting that in Michael's passing his music has been embraced again by the world, and he will forever be remembered for the love in his voice, the rhythm in his soul and the strength of his heart because, ironically, no one loved children more than Michael.

How can modern society condone and feed on such malicious intent? Even more incredulous is that the perpetrator might succeed. But he didn't succeed as the following Wikipedia article on Evan Chandler confirms.

Evan Chandler committed suicide (via self-inflicted gunshot) on November 5, 2009, in his luxury apartment in Jersey City, New Jersey, four months and eleven days after the death of Michael Jackson. He was 65 years old when he died.

Clearly, the weight of his own guilt and the immense accolades Michael received at his passing turned the blow torch right back on Evan and it was too much for him, and the only way out was to succumb to terminating his own existence.

KARMA IS THE UNIVERSAL BALANCE SYSTEM FOR THE TRUTH. THINK BEFORE YOU LIE.

I hope the media has done everything possible to unwind the damage they inflicted on Michael now that Jordy's statement is there for all to know, especially Diane Dimond and Hard Copy that got it so terribly wrong and seemingly deliberately so. I had to search to learn the truth to get the real conclusion to this story where Evan's guilt was proven by his own cowardly action and the defiance and integrity of his son.

May 6, 2005, Michael Jackson arrives at the
Santa Barbara County Courthouse

The toll on Michael was devastating as seen in the image above. The tortured soul is bare for all to see and yet this, throughout his life, was the source of much of his unbelievable creative energy. A divine instrument of love and harmony like the world has never seen before.

Unfortunately, Michael's torment did not end with his passing as the opportunity to make money from public interest resulted in further allegations against him from Wade Robson and James Safechuck in a controversial HBO documentary. In this documentary, they detail the abuse they say they received from Michael.

Unfortunately, the documentary was one-sided and proved to be factually incorrect as established by Michael Jackson biographer Mike Smallcombe.

In May 2013, Wade Robson, a choreographer who had worked for Jackson, went on television to allege he had been sexually abused by Jackson when he was a child. This was the same Wade Robson who had previously testified under oath in 2005 that Jackson had 'never' touched him. With Jackson no longer around to defend himself, he cited repressed memory for the contradiction.

Statements made by Safechuck in his lawsuit alleged ongoing abuse occurred between 1988 and 1992. In the HBO documentary, he stated that this occurred when he was 14 years old and in the upstairs train station at the Neverland ranch. This was a very poor lapse in memory or worse, a complete fabrication of events as the train station land use permit wasn't processed until September 2 1993.

The documentary did not interview anyone other than the accusers and their families in what has been considered as a one-sided programme that did not once seek a right of reply from the Jackson Estate

The Jackson Estate has proceeded with legal action against HBO in a suit that urges HBO to take part in a public arbitration process that claims could cost HBO up to $100 million.

"HBO could have and should have ensured that Leaving Neverland was properly sourced, fact-checked and a fair and balanced representation," the estate attorney Howard Weitzman told Deadline.

To date, there has not been any evidence proven in court against Michael Jackson and only more inconsistencies in allegations against him.

Does this mean that today's truth for many people is established by the media often-peddling propaganda for sensationalist headlines or political agendas? Has fake news replaced the truth because it isn't as interesting as lies?

HAS FAKE NEWS BEGUILED THE PUBLIC AND REPLACED THE TRUTH IN OUR MODERN WORLD BECAUSE IT IS MORE INTERESTING THAN REALITY? IS PROFITING FROM LIES THE NEW MEDIA NORM?

I have witnessed in media an outpouring of people saying they would not listen to Michael Jackson's music because of his atrocious behaviour, none of which has been established in a court of law. To the contrary, it was actually after extensive investigation determined that he was innocent.

I must be different I guess, I still love his music and will continue to listen to this incredible genius. I won't, however, be watching any more documentaries from HBO.

We love you, Michael.

LOVE

One of the most difficult things to do is determine whether you are truly in love and whether your partner feels like you do. If they don't, is it love?

Let me paint a scene that probably occurs all too often.

A male in his mid to late 40s (let's call him Bob) is happily married with two children and a devoted wife (Kristie), living in relative harmony even though she nags him day or night to the extent he can no longer hear her. He retreats to the safety of his cave and just switches out which merely has the impact on increasing the ferocity and intensity of the nagging.

He is the manager of a large company and is usually quite mentally exhausted when he gets home from a stressful day at the office, dealing with everyone else's problems. He doesn't see that she is busy looking after the kids, part time job, food shopping, keeping the house tidy, and dropping the kids at music and sport.

All he sees is the visa bill and the endless coffees catching up with the infinite number of friends she has, and the shopping competition she has with a friend trying to see who can spend the most.

Yes, it's true, purchases are even made to make the girlfriend jealous and not because of need.

Despite all this, the relationship works, and the children are great and growing up as they should.

Enters the stunning new receptionist at the office, Mandy, who has more than her share of sex appeal and knows it.

She is single and in her mid-thirties and has a well-toned body from hours at the gym and a vivacious free spirit, that can easily be misinterpreted as flirting, which is probably what it really is but she just wouldn't like to call it that. Worse, she's at the age where she doesn't really want children of her own but wants the security of an older man after several bad relationships with guys that have just taken her for a ride. Ahem.

She flirted her way around the office and was the envy of all females and the desire of all normal men. Surely, you can see how difficult it will be for the happily married Bob, with more than a few issues, to resist the temptation that will come his way.

Temptation is the test the devil inside has sent us, to see if we can be true to our core belief system.

When you grow up in a normal family with a mother and father that live mostly happily together that becomes the mental image you adopt of what you will also be like in the future. Conversely, many children that grow up in a family where the parents have split often don't want that to be their future, and will fight to save their marriage, but they are also torn by the fact they have seen parents sometimes happier in themselves after they transitioned to new partners.

Temptation is a dastardly fellow that does not relent and Mandy knows that Bob is attracted to her by the way he looks at her when she walks in and out of his office, sometimes swinging around to catch him looking at her and then laughing playfully as she leaves.

Of course when Mandy is taking notes for him in the office, she makes sure that she turns slightly side on so that he has the best view of her ample cleavage. And Bob cannot resist taking a peak and is finding himself increasingly stimulated by Mandy's obvious flirting.

His dilemma is twofold, he loves his wife and children more than anything and he's not sure that he is reading the signals right and doesn't want to make a fool of himself by making an approach and being declined. Mandy of course is all too aware of this and simply adds to his dilemma by flirting with other men around the office while always being careful to give Bob the most attention if he is close by. She's a real pro and he needs to be really careful.

Mandy has him on a string and starts dropping hints that she is home alone tonight while talking to office staff a little too loudly so Bob can hear, or saying she will stay a little late tonight so she can go straight to hockey practice at 7. The bait is being firmly planted and Bob is increasingly having difficulty with his mental image of himself, as the dutiful husband forever, and he is not even sure of whether Mandy is for real or just teasing him.

However, Mandy is seeing herself with a mature partner and doesn't care about Kristie, Bob's wife, as when she met her, she seemed aloof and ignored her. She believes she can make Bob happier and so has a right to him. That is her truth and she is prepared to live by it.

Bob is playing it outwardly really cool and no one knows what is going on in his head as he continues to act and be the devoted family man that is his true identity up until now.

Suspicion when it's driven by fear can really tangle up your mind.

Right now that's what is happening to Kristie as she is noticing Bob is paying her less attention and has been for quite some time. She doesn't understand why Bob is less interested in her and increasingly nags him to try and force him to feel how she wants him to feel. This is not going to achieve what she really wants, and it is her fear of losing him and her increasingly unacceptable behaviour that is ultimately driving a wedge into the relationship and making Bob notice Mandy more than he normally would.

The reality of his situation is really difficult and he doesn't know how he feels or what to think. Temptation is crying out 'Just try her for one night and see how it feels and it won't do any harm'. Remember 43% of women in the UK think it's okay to have a one-night stand without being truly unfaithful.

Common sense is saying you risk losing everything. *'I'll give it all up for you'* by Simply Red springs to mind. Because that is the dice throw, make no mistake! In the fickle way of the world, some relationships go on being happy ever after as the truth is accepted or not yet discovered, and the others because the cause of heart ache and family upheaval the likes of which you can't imagine, until it's experienced, is driven by the dread of discovery so maintenance of what they are comfortable with is tolerated.

I must admit I admired Ronan Keating who admitted that he deeply regretted his affair, and knew it was a wrong decision. Unfortunately, the marriage was impossible to repair once the trust was broken, even though both Ronan and his incredible wife Yvonne decided to give it another go.

Francine, who was the dancer that had an affair with Ronan for seven months before it came to a sudden end, when his wife Yvonne found out about it, thought Ronan was telling the truth when he said they would be married in 20 years' time. This just absolutely endorses my view that:

THE TRUTH IS WHAT YOU BELIEVE AT THE TIME, AND MAY CHANGE

He may have genuinely believed that he intended to marry Francine, or he may have been having his cake and eating it too.

Only Ronan will know as it was he who knew the sincerity of his commitment at the time he said what he did. Whichever way you cut the story, his credibility is badly impaired as he lied to his wife and so one has to consider whether it is likely he was telling the truth to Francine, or just using his influence as a star to have his way. This is common with successful famous people and is something we look at in both the Truth of Business and the Truth of Sport.

In the end, he fesses up, and that is the only thing to do if you really want to move on to where ever it is you will land, after committing betrayal on your partner. One thing is for sure, it will not be in the relatively harmonious place you were before you did it.

No matter what Ronan Keating, Lance Armstrong and others delude themselves to believe, to justify their actions, the real truth will emerge and they will have to face it. Some choose to deny it and live on in their fantasy, but this is simply not a sustainable position as the truth ultimately determines your Karma.

YOUR INTEGRITY SHOULD NOT BE FOR SALE OR EVER RISKED, IT IS THE GREATEST TREASURE YOU OWN.

Ronan realises that what he did was wrong and how he was caught in that state of confusion, where he was not happy with what he had and didn't know how to resolve it, so he committed an act of betrayal and that, unfortunately, never ends well. Not only for him, but his wife family and children all get caught up in resolving the deceit, and, ultimately, the search for the truth, which is the only way back to harmony.

Ronan had the following to say on *Piers Morgan's Life Stories* admitting he was sick of conforming to the need to be the perfect husband.

"I had spent so long trying to be the perfect husband. I woke up and decided I didn't want it," he said. *"I was wrong. I made a choice and, because of that choice, there were devastating effects in people's lives."*

He said, *"I was honest. They're your kids, you have to be and with something like this, they were going to find out anyway. As a parent you're never wrong in your children's eyes. So you feel like a failure."*

He explained, *"She took me back. That was a huge step. But I don't think it can ever work after something like that. 'The trust was gone.'"*

No matter how you try to forgive, the absolute faithfulness that is an essential ingredient of real lasting love, when gone can never be fully resurrected. You can try and carry on, and many people do because they lack the courage or financial wherewithal to do what they know they should. So a brave face and a story are concocted to make it all right but it isn't, that is the bleak reality.

There can be deep learning from other people's actions but many people can't help but take advantage of a situation even though they know it's wrong. Whoever you are and whatever you do, there is a credible way to resolve conflict, and if you ultimately want peace in your life, you will choose it. Be sure you know what you really value before you risk the relationship with your loved ones.

IF YOU CHOOSE TO ADOPT A NEW BELIEF THAT IS CONTRARY TO YOUR CURRENTLY KNOWN PERSONA, YOU WILL HAVE TO LIVE WITH THE CONSEQUENCE OF THAT DECISION FOR THE REST OF YOUR LIFE. GOOD OR BAD.

The tipping point was when Ronan woke up and didn't want to be the perfect husband anymore. Once he had made that decision, he then allowed himself to make a whole series of decisions that ultimately lead to his family being magazine news.

The final reality for Ronan was when his loyal wife moved on, and found love with another partner and he fully realised that his marriage was over and there was no going back. This is when the 'truth really hurts' because the dawning of what he has lost, and can never get back, has hit home in more ways than one. His relationship with his children will never be the same and that is something that becomes really difficult for the whole family as they transition to a new existence, where both parents need to realise there is nothing more precious in this world than the love and respect of your children.

Let's now look at where Bob is at, having churned through a real-life celebrity family disaster.

We should commiserate with poor Bob who is only human after all; he's not a rock star with heaps of fame and fortune to fall back on! In the end, I don't believe Ronan having fame and fortune makes the failure of his family any worse than what Bob confronts as an ordinary everyday man, they both face the same decisions and suffer the same consequences. If anything, having to play that out in public probably more than offsets financial independence as your public reputation is besmirched and it is difficult to face trial by the media.

Bob's head is messed up, and his left-brain analytical thought processes are doing flip-flops with the abstract thoughts flowing through him by his utterly free and emotionally sensitive right brain.

The confusion that results can be what some misconstrue as love.

It's when you are attracted to someone and your left-brain logic tries to understand what is happening in the emotive right brain. You want to proceed with the relationship because it's exciting and risqué and you wonder whether this will be true love.

LOVE BRIDGES INTUITION (right brain) AND INTELLECT (left-brain).

Aristotle said that, *"Love is composed of a single soul inhabiting two bodies."* Personally, I don't believe that's possible and I think we each have an individual soul but I fully agree with the concept that having that same value base is what can really bind couples tightly for a long time. Plato's original theory in his work *Symposium* said that we were originally formed with four legs and four arms and were half female and half male. After planning to climb Mount Olympus, Zeus ordered the humans to be cut in half which resulted in us searching for our other half to find true love and contentment.

When you are really in love, the harmony of your feelings and thought processes creates a euphoria that is so simple and natural that you feel nothing else matters other than your partners happiness and wellbeing. Your partner in turn feels the same with you and the physical intimacy that comes along with this euphoria is exquisite, fulfilling and timeless.

A *soul mate* is a person with whom one has a feeling of a deep and natural bond, and a physical, mental and spiritual compatibility.

Perfect relationships are often when you meet your soul mate when you are both single and free of any other emotive and physical relations with a partner. This can occur at any age in your life. Complications will hinder perfect harmony when jealousies and possessiveness overshadow your commitment to each other which often occurs in young people as they are still discovering themselves, the world they live in and how to love each other.

TRUE LOVE CAN ONLY EXIST BETWEEN TWO PEOPLE.

Bob is having feelings for Mandy that he can't explain to himself and she is increasingly leading him on and gently teasing him which he finds dangerously exciting. Having someone pay him compliments is a world away from the incessant belittling he confronts daily with his wife, who is frustrated because Bob's self-esteem is strong enough to survive the attacks. He knows the abuse is baseless but cannot find common ground where his wife Kristie will deal with the reasons behind her anger.

But resist Mandy he does, such is his loyalty to his wife and family. He knows that his children would never forgive him for leaving their mother for another woman having seen this first-hand, many times. Bob could never look into his children's eyes and know that the admiration and trust for their dad had gone. James and Ella are the meaning of life for Bob as he was lucky enough to come from a stable home with two amazing parents. Bob's parents were always there for him, no matter what, and he knows the support he got as a child is essential to a balanced emotional upbringing.

Life always has its curve balls, and there are people that can't live by the ethos that the core of any family is the integrity and family creed that binds them. Bob is determined that he will not succumb to the modern-day standards that have allowed promiscuity to become acceptable. It simply isn't, in fact, it is only a short step to debauchery and is one of the ultimate forms of dishonesty that can cause harm on so many different levels.

The office staff is starting to notice that the two always sit next to each other on staff outings and admiring looks at each other are just a little too long and often. They are still unsure of each other's feelings but are aware of a connection between them and of the dynamics and risks. Mandy can quickly become the family wrecker and Bob could easily be in exactly the same position as Ronan.

The risk profile is high for Bob as he has it all to lose and Mandy only has upside as she can easily convince her own friends that she did it all for love, and Bob was unhappy anyway so he was looking for someone like her. In fact, he wasn't, but opportunity was unfolding as the great man said.

The only drama will be to convince Bob's friends that she is not the blame for the split, and Bob will have to be the one who does the most of that, once she has him around her little finger. As soon as he makes a move, she will own him and she knows it. Mandy can tell Bob is interested but she wants to be really careful before she makes the big move that she doesn't want to backfire. He is the only man she has met that can match her father for looks, humour and all-round presence and while she doesn't realise it that is what attracts her to him.

Her attire on some days is a little more saucy than usual and Bob likes it but tries not to notice. Today it's a see-through white blouse with a coloured bra that shows off her assets and leaves little to Bob's imagination. The top doesn't quite reach her jeans so her taut midriff is revealed so he sneaks a peek when he thinks she is not looking.

Her jeans are the low-rider style so that her panties show when she is moving around the office or bending down for files in front of Bob. Always she whirls around quickly to see if Bob is watching and sometimes he's just too slow looking away, so she knows he is on the line. Her long auburn hair hangs loose and she is constantly adjusting it to attract attention and poor old Bob isn't the only one who thinks Mandy is hot.

Bob's finance manager, Geoff, also can't help but admire her and Mandy knows it so she gently gives him some attention just to see whether it affects Bob. A little bit of a jealousy test to see whether Bob really is attracted to her but Bob can spot this game. He's a proud man and sees this for what it is and does not feel threatened or jealous of Geoff. In fact, this is a mistake from Mandy, her first so far, as Bob sees her flirting for what it is and tells himself that he must be stark raving mad to ever think that he could have a relationship with Mandy as it wouldn't be long and she would be off flirting with someone else.

And then where would he be.

But the desire is strong.

Bob hasn't crossed the line as he doesn't see himself as Mandy's partner but the thought has crossed his mind what it would be like to be with her. Yet even though he can fathom this whole situation quite rationally in his left brain, his right brain isn't listening.

In fact, the more he realises that she isn't for him, the more he wants her. His right and left brain are symmetrically balancing each other in exact opposite solutions based on different fundamentals. His creative intuitive pull is telling how amazing it would be and his logical reasoning is saying it will be your biggest ever mistake.

Who inflicted this perversion on mankind that we should want what we can't have?

Was it the Creator?

Or did it come from the evolution of apes when they decided ice cream was more desirable than a banana?

What is the moral of this tale and what is Bob's truth. Will Bob decide to run off with Mandy and live an exciting new life because that is what he believes will make him happy? Will he get what he can't have because he no longer decrees that it is out of bounds? Is he able to really see the fall out if he makes the move to betray his partner?

Will Bob set his moral compass for the heart of the sun in the quest of what might be true love, or will he realise that he is being a fool and stay with loyal wife Kristie. Bob has a check and balance in place every time temptation comes to play and that is the unconditional love of his two beautiful children.

Then fates cruel hand twists a dagger deep in Bob's core as while Bob has decided to put his family first and wrestling with his identity and flirtations from his secretary, his lovely wife has started having an affair with his next-door neighbour who just happens to be his son's best friend's father.

So while Bob is wrestling with doing the right thing, his wife was being seduced by Winton, the neighbour, with an eye for the main chance and known philanderer.

Bob noticed that they were flirting a bit too much when they were at neighbourhood functions but didn't initially think too much of it. Then she started to visit his house more often and, for strange reasons so, at a quiet moment he stole a look at Kristie's mobile and low and behold the texts between each other were more than normal when arranging events for the kids at school with xxx's to each other. Bob confronted Kristie and she denied it all and said she did that with everyone.

A couple of weeks later, just before Kristie was off on a girlie week away to Bali, paid for by Bob, she denied his question whether she was having an affair on her children's grave, and did so looking him square in the eye. Bob believed her but a nagging suspicion remained. You cannot run away from the truth as it will always catch you when you least expect it, and in a way that you never imagined.

SUSPICION REQUIRES REASON, IS SELDOM BASELESS AND OFTEN THE EMBRYO OF A TRUTH DISCOVERY.

The meetings carried on and Bob checked the phone from time to time and noticed the texting had stopped, so being the trusting loyal husband, he convinced himself to believe his wife, as any husband should. So at this stage the truth was what he believed but soon he was to be confronted with a horrible reality that shattered his world and that of his family and his treasured children.

Kristie had grown up in split marriage and had always told Bob that she would never do to her children what her parents had done to her. They had a marriage that had lost its sexual attraction in recent years and Bob thought this dated back to the month and year when their daughter Ella was born and around the same period as her father died.

Ella's birth was a complicated emergency caesarean and both Ella and Kristie's lives were at risk. Perversely, it bought the family even closer for a while as Kristie went into post-natal depression and suffered a double dose as the loss of her father cut her deeply and opened wounds of yesteryear in her childhood. Her dad was the one part of her family that she could rely on as he was always there for her. The mother had a different agenda and was mostly interested in her own existence and that of her new partner Jim.

Life between Bob and Kristie was not perfect but it was good enough and Bob always valued the deep love he had based on the trust he shared within the family unit. Trips overseas together, family lunches with parents and the joy of watching the children grow in a stable family environment and with the love of their parents was enough for Bob. He knew that Utopia did not exist and was happy to make the most of what he had and was content within himself and what he was achieving in life. First and foremost always was the wellbeing and support of his family. Like his father before him, it was his primary focus and reason for existing and what provided him with his most enjoyment.

Then out of the blue Bob's life was turned on its ear. He arrived home from work to find his son James visibly distressed and learnt that he had been strangled by his neighbour's son, and best friend Matt, that morning on the way to school. Thankfully, he was saved by his other best friend, Jimmy, who pulled the confused and raging angry adolescent off James stomach, forcing him to release his grip choking Bob's son's neck.

Bob was horrified and when James told him that a similar thing happened on the weekend. He wanted to know why and believed that it would be something to do with a dysfunctional family environment. Bob said he thought the father, Winton, was a weirdo as he could see it in his eyes, and this was a view shared by neighbours. In the distant reaches of his mind, a thought was growing like a coiled spring about to be released. He did not want to shatter James' vision of Winton, which was being carefully cultivated by both Winton and Kristie with school adventures, pickups, drop offs and any excuse to be together as it was becoming increasingly obvious they were attracted to each other. Kristie felt she needed the attention because she didn't feel Bob's love and Bob was tired of the relentless test of his affection. He was numb to her attempts to put him down, as this happened daily, however, he remained stoic in his commitment to her and the children.

Kristie wanted to feel like a woman but would never accept Bob's offer of weekends away, or even a dinner, so he was confused as to what she really wanted and whether she really loved him.

So Bob dived onto the internet and contacted the new-age god, Google (see Religious Truth) for the answer and sure enough there it was.

"Anger in people with depression often stems from narcissistic vulnerability, a sensitivity to perceived or actual loss or rejection. These angry reactions cause intra-psychic conflicts through the onset of guilt and the fear that angry feelings will disrupt relationships. These conflicts lead to anger being directed inwards, further lowering self-esteem, creating a vicious cycle. Defence mechanisms that are triggered, including passive aggression, reaction formation, denial and identification with the aggressor, are ineffective at managing these conflicts and further prevent the appropriate expression of anger."

Bob thought that probably Winton had done something that had triggered the anger in his son, Matt, and that it was probably not really directed at James. Bob was devastated to see his son shaken like this.

The idea in the back of his mind was forming into full-blown suspicion like a hurricane at sea and his mind started exploding with fear and anger at what might be the cause of this appalling action. They were just trading harmless boys' put-downs, and Matt then lost it and raged at James taking him to the ground and choking him.

James had a strong belief that Winton was a great guy but Bob could sense the cocksureness in his eyes as he wanted to gloat to Bob as he flirted with Kristie, knowing that Bob could not fight back because he believed in his wife. She had told him nothing was going on and he believed her as that was the basis of the family they built together – trust and support for one and another. Blood runs fast and wounds cut deep when deceit arrives in the family unit.

Bob and Kristie had a pact from the beginning that any betrayal would result in the end of their relationship, so Bob thought that Kristie wouldn't go that far and was just seeking attention, as she had so many times before. She would always push him away to test his love.

Winton, for some reasons, was probably jealous of Bob's stylish new home and seemingly perfect life and decided to destroy it by having an affair with his wife. After all, he has had affairs before and gotten away with it and he didn't like it that his son Matt seemed to like Bob either. He knows his lovely wife won't do anything and believes his family is immune to his ways by now. He holds the purse strings of power over his wife who will not leave the children and lacks the courage to risk leaving him. She is trapped in a loveless marriage where sex is dutiful, and love rots in the dust of what was their dream cottage by the beach.

The children are loyal to him and don't want to see him as the sad, pathetic nothingness he really is. Who wants to admit to themselves that their dad has no moral fortitude and is selfish to his own end?

That is why Matt attacked James. He was venting his hatred for his father's abuse of his best friend's family, who had only been generous to him because he couldn't direct it at his father. The pain of that reality is more than he could bear as the basis of his entire belief and reason for love and life had become a lie.

MANY CHOOSE TO LIVE A LIE AND AVOID THE PAIN OF THE TRUTH. THIS LEADS TO NOWHERE AS THERE IS NO REAL MORAL BASE FOR LOVE WHICH IS A FOUNDATION BLOCK OF MEANINGFUL RELATIONSHIPS AND ESSENTIAL FOR SPIRITUAL NOURISHMENT.

No son or daughter would ever want the image of their parents to be fractured by the unconscionable treason of everything they owed them by making the commitment to conceive them.

What is it that makes the parent think that it's okay to do this to their child, more than once; convince themselves it's all right and have a complete and callous disregard for the impact on others. Only someone who is so self-absorbed that they have lost the ability to distinguish, or care about, what is right and what is wrong could act in this way. The need for emotional sustenance has divorced the brain from balanced emotions and the sanctity of life is abandoned. Loyalty is discarded for self-gratification.

James then had a dawning after Bob explained to him what harm split parents can cause their children. The new light hit him hard and he was no longer angry at his best friend and ran downstairs to get his phone and show his dad a text that had been sent to him in error. The text is below:

"I can't stop thinking about you and was really worried about you last night when you were alone in the crazy storm that hit the Coast. Wish I could have been with you to take care of you. Today I will be busy with business and travel commitments so apologise for not being in touch again today, so sorry, Shona."

Fates cruel hand was starting to unravel the master deception. No doubt Winton's erection in life comes from the power he gains from preying on the weak. The text was really intended for Kristie, James' desperate for affection mother, and dyslexic Winton had sent it to James in error. As Bob and James read it, their world started to spin into a web of confusion that stayed with them for months. There is no escaping the dilemma that a reality shift of this magnitude in your life causes, and your brain just won't let go of the questions that bombard you day and night, questions that you don't know the answer to.

And so the birth of a new life begins with the discovery of betrayal.

The good news is for everyone going through this is that it passes. Just knowing that makes it easier. Bob was distraught and he, initially, didn't want to believe it was true even though he knew it was because reality was staring him in the face. He quickly pieced together that Shona would have been another identity set up by Winton and Kristie, so that Bob would not recognise them on her phone, so intent were they on having their deceitful dalliance undiscovered.

Kristie's denials were now nothing more than dirty lies.

LIES BREED LIES AND DESTROY ANY HOPE OF REDEMPTION.

Everything is now about to unravel while the truth is discovered. Redemption comes at a price and both Winton and Kristie were about to realise that, in spades, as the hand they played was being trumped by the truth. The road to redemption is long and hard as the families involved were about to find out. Winton turns out to be a serial low-life and the owner of several phones. How perverted is this when the use must be known by the family, a dysfunctional unit that is limping along in the confusion of compromised identities.

Bob phones Kristie in Bali to let her know what has happened to James and explain why he thinks so. Amazingly, Kristie is most concerned about defending the affair first and foremost saying it was just a few harmless texts. She shows little concern about what happened to her son and goes into denial, which is exactly what Bob doesn't want to happen. He wants and needs to know the truth, as only through that understanding can he reconcile his feelings. James feels the same and the incredible bond that father and son have becomes a strength that helps them deal with the litany of lies that Kristie tells over the next few weeks, as she goes into damage control and tries to come to terms with what she has done. Deep down she knew the risk, but cold hard reality is different to the warm retreat of a lover's arms.

The fallout is now coming home to roost. Kristie can only accept it little pieces at a time, so she can only reveal the truth a little bit at the time as her moods swing from defiance to helplessness. Bob insists on knowing as he believes that the truth will come out anyway and doesn't want to talk to anyone other than Kristie's brother Chad until he knows the whole story. This takes several weeks after Kristie gets home as she wrestles with what she has done and is struggling to deal with the consequences she now wants to avoid.

Karma will do its thing and Winton and Kristie will not know where and how that will come, until it arrives in its many shapes and forms.

Karma is the Sanskrit word for deed or action and applies whether it is a physical or mental action. The ways of Karma are not simple in that an action now will be bound to some future experience or reaction. There is no direct link of punishment or reward for any particular action, but if you sow good seeds, you will reap goodness, and if you sow evil, you will attract evil and is more about your total existence than any particular deed or action. To conquer Karma, one needs to consider one's actions carefully and also eliminate emotion from responses.

In this regard, there is a remarkable similarity to the belief of the Stoics covered later.

In life we all reap what we sow and Bob knows that the time has come for him to truly face up to his relationship with Kristie, and her demons. He has lived with her incessant manipulation and constant desire for control and power because of her own feelings of inferiority for too long. She deeply resents his success, and that of their children, who have inherited his drive and intelligence. Bob has understood this but has always strived to help Kristie deal with her issues and thought that she will conquer them. His hope was obliterated when he learnt he could not trust her, and that she was prepared to blame him for the reason she soaked up Winton's attention. It was what she needed she said, someone to show her attention while she grappled with the black dog.

Bob's support and commitment to a future was not enough, and the regression process Kristie was having with her psychiatrist meant she was reliving her childhood, whether she realised it or not.

Life experiences and challenges that we all confront from time to time are what determine you on your life journey. We define our own happiness and misery by the choices we make.

"Whatsoever fortune or misfortune experienced is all due to some previous action," the Buddha said.

"So, then, according to this view, owing to previous action men will become murderers, thieves, unchaste, liars, slanderers, covetous, malicious and perverts. Thus, for those who fall back on the former deeds as the essential reason,

there is neither the desire to do, nor effort to do, nor necessity to do this deed, or abstain from this deed.

"Karma does not necessarily mean past actions. It embraces both past and present deeds. Hence in one sense, we are the result of what we were; we will be the result of what we are. In another sense, it should be added, we are not totally the result of what we were; we will not absolutely be the result of what we are. The present is no doubt the offspring of the past and is the present of the future, but the present is not always a true index of either the past or the future; so complex is the working of Karma.

"It is this doctrine of Karma that the mother teaches her child when she says, 'Be good and you will be happy and we will love you; but if you are bad, you will be unhappy and we will not love you.' In short, Karma is the law of cause and effect in the ethical realm."

The article above is fascinating and totally in accord with my thoughts, however, I believe there is another dimension to Karma than the past and present and that is the machination that occurs in our minds that has intentions for the future. It may be that I am misunderstanding the great Buddha's meaning, but the interesting part in all this to me is the creation of the future based on our existing beliefs and what we are projecting the future will be like in our mind. Humans have a phenomenal ability to visualise and this is an extremely powerful force that shapes outcomes of lives.

Is this what has happened in this circumstance with Bob and Kristie?

Let's examine what Kristie's motivations are and whether she realises what it is that really is driving her life. The more I dwell on this I think the Karma explanation above is very on the money as it is the past that shapes our current thinking, whether we realise it or not, and our current thinking is shaping our destiny. Remember Buddha said, *"I am the sum total of everything I thought."* That's it right there and so it then must also apply to our future visions as what we believe will shape our destiny. The mysterious machinations of

Karma's distribution of ethical retribution plan encompass all time zones, the past, present and the future.

Another incredible Chinese philosopher Lao Tzu who lived from 571 BC to 531 BC, in a similar time to Buddha, had a not dissimilar view but expressed it this way;

"Watch your thoughts; they become words. Watch your words; they become actions. Watch your actions; they become habit. Watch your habits; they become character. Watch your character; it becomes your destiny."

The torment continues to engulf Bob, however, his number one concern is for that of his children so he contacts Shan, Winton's wife, and asks her to seek treatment for Matt so that he does not attack James or anyone else again, while in the distressed state he is in. Matt and James are best mates and innocent victims in this stupidity.

Amazingly, the next morning, a contrite Winton rings Bob and leaves a message for Bob that he thinks he knows why his son Matt attacked James, and that it was all due to the text he sent in error. His son was reacting badly to it when it was really only a relationship of harmless flirty texts. Winton then tries to convince Bob that there was nothing to it in what can only be described as a series of unwanted texts to Bob that there was nothing to it, no kisses, nothing just flirty fun.

Bob's instincts have told him differently, and Kristie is now also in full denial as she literally tries to cover her ass! Phone calls to her in Bali end badly and she doesn't want to talk anymore, until she gets back. Then she wants to come back early but Bob needs the time and space to think, so he tells her to just come back as planned while he tries to assemble his feelings and thoughts in one cohesive manner.

Shan and Bob work through the confusion and piece together the puzzle that their spouses had created through their craving and need for attention that overrode rational thought. Kristie was lapping up the attention and feeling great so why should she care about what would happen, her juvenile emotions were not being policed by reason and she felt young again and desired. She can justify anything to herself because she feels good and has a right to. Responsibilities and commitment to her family mean little when these feelings nourish her craving to be desired.

When Bob caught up with Kristie's psychologist, he wanted to know what he had advised his wife and whether he knew that Kristie was having an affair? Robert (the psychologist) confirmed to Bob that he had told Kristie what she was doing would end in tears, and that she had been depressed since her childhood traumas. Kristie cannot accept that truth and it makes the basis of living with her near impossible for Bob as her insecurities, and inability to tell and confront the truth, make having a conversation with her difficult to conclude. Robert also advised Bob that when Kristie's parents split up in her adolescent years, her emotions never developed properly after that and, in those days, there were no psychologists to help, or hinder depending on how they treat the patient. Robert said that Kristie was reliving her childhood as Bob was keen to learn the motive as to why she chose to betray him.

Was Kristie out to hurt him, and their children, so that they would share and understand the misery that she had as a child? Bob asked Robert this and he replied that Kristie did not know what she was doing and that it was in her subconscious driving her behaviour. Bob told him that Kristie had on occasion said to the family that she was leaving the family because no one loved her, and she would be best living on her own. This is what she believed in her mind and no amount of discussion or devotion would change it. Ironically, the belief became true but not for the reason she had invented in her mind.

THE TRUTH IS WHAT YOU BELIEVE, SO BE CLEAR WITH YOUR VISIONS.

This just wasn't something Bob was prepared for. He has gone from fending off the attentions of Mandy at the office to being insulted and lied to by his wife and he just couldn't understand why. The anger and abuse he got from his wife as she battled and refused to admit her depression had long since burnt out his flame of desire for her and so she felt unloved and that was a circle they constantly rotated in. Bob was hurt, so if that was Kristie's intention, she had achieved her goal, but he was not the type to stay down. Kristie had once said to him that he was hard to hurt which staggered Bob, why would his wife try to hurt him? Bob also was having visions of what it would be like to be separate from Kristie, so it was probably inevitable that they parted as neither was truly happy and it was the children that bound them.

Bob was aware that his hurt was mostly for the breakdown of the family unit, as he cherished that, but he knew in his heart there was a new dawn and he had to seek the sunlight.

Robert also advised Bob that his wife thought she was still her father's little princess and that she wanted Bob to be the person her father was. This identity confusion further compounded the erosion of the relationship as Bob increasingly had been unable to fathom Kristie's actions. Kristie had bigger issues emotionally and mentally than he had realised and this whole situation was just blowing up in his face. On one hand, he knew it was an option that he should forgive her and try to rebuild the relationship as that was the best for the kids. But was it?

If Bob was not going to be happy, how could the children grow up in a normal family environment and what did Kristie really feel. Did she still want to be with Winton? She said no, but Bob doesn't believe anything she says anymore. Bob has always said that if Kristie is so unhappy that she wants to leave, he would not hold her back but it had never gone this far. Partly because of their beautiful children, and partly because like in so many relationships the fact she is not currently employed and would find life very difficult without everything provided for her. Financially, they are in good shape, but to have to buy another home would dent their savings, and increase expenses, but this is part of the process they both need to go through to get freedom and ultimately a love that nourishes each other. Both idolise their children who are the real victims.

The fallout over the next few months is ugly and Bob wants Kristie to tell their daughter, Ella, what she has done but she is aware of James' reaction and doesn't want to risk her daughter feeling the same. Kristie is trying to deny the truth and bury the pain. She can't, and is just living day to day and hoping that she won't have to face Ella with what she has done, but that day will come.

Bob believes that not telling Ella is just making the lie worse, and he hates being caught up in it. His skin crawls at the thought of it. He doesn't know how Ella will react either, and her heart is the most precious thing in the world to him right now, and he wants to protect her above all else so he confides in James who knows the situation and provides a valuable perspective.

WHEN YOU KNOW THE TRUTH – FACE UP TO IT. DENIAL ONLY PROLONGS THE INEVITABLE JUSTICE THAT KARMA WILL DETERMINE.

SO WHAT IS TRUE LOVE?

It is the pure, faithful trust that two partners have when they share and commit to each other. True love has no place for abuse, does not include emotional or sexual affairs, does not have a dominant selfish partner and does not exist within dishonesty.

True feelings change, as we are human after all with all our silly frailties, jealousies and insecurities that blow out of proportion when we get tired or overexcited and stimulated by an attractive partner of the opposite sex paying attention to us. The fact that you are doing something wrong when having an affair probably increases the excitement, as the danger element heightens your senses and makes you forget that consequences exist around the corner for all of those who don't live an honest life. This is one of life's traps for the weak who allows the instant gratification of temptation to blind them from real principals of lasting value.

The trouble is innocent people get their lives dragged through the gutter of deception that is the fun of a harmless fling in someone's selfish existence. Always put your children first in everything you do in life, or don't have them. It is a tragic sin to have children and not love them fully and, unfortunately, modern society has normalised family failures due to unfaithfulness, so much so that it is the start of the breakdown of humanity as we knew it, especially in the Western world. I admire some friends who have decided not to have children as they are not prepared to make that sacrifice. I also feel deeply sorry for those that want them and can't because of biological problems.

Be careful who you love as that decision can have a very big impact on how you can maintain the commitment to your children.

Temptation is leading Bob to explore his feelings. Only through the right decisions and commitment over time will he discover the truth about those feelings, and to a large extent, his conscious thoughts will dictate those feelings.

Statistically, up to 50% of marriages end in divorce, so there is a strong chance Bob will go and pursue Mandy or another new partner.

The fallout from adulterous relationships is not something that can be managed easily and there is no perfect way to handle the children and keep a harmonious relationship with your ex. The quandary for many is whether they are better off with the status quo, and often hedge their bets and have an affair to see whether there is some substance to the attraction.

It is never worth approaching it in this way! Your children are always affected and if you really love them you will go through this whole gambit of love breakdown with honesty to your partner, and your children, as it is the cheating that causes the lingering scars and subsequent relationship void.

If you put yourself before your children, which you must do when you cheat on your partner, you create the biggest lie of them all. It is a grand deception you will always have to live with, that will create a hollowness that no amount of kidding yourself you did the right thing will replace. You might be getting some awesome whoopee but rest assured the universe will balance the ledger, and the truth will be the balancing determiner that Karma uses.

Your children will know that you chose your new partner ahead of them, and that will never go way, and it will be harder to explain than you imagine as your lust hunger will dissolve into the fog of reality.

LIES ARE FOREVER, SO THINK TWICE BEFORE YOU ABANDON THE TRUTH.

The truth is that true love takes a lot of commitment and that is the key to surviving the challenges of children, attention from the opposite sex and just plain old familiarity that sets in too many couples' relationships. Never under estimate the power of physical intimacy as it is the pivot to completeness.

THE TRUTH IS YOUR CHOICE. OTHERS MAY NOT AGREE, AND THAT MATTERS NOT AS OFTEN THEY DO NOT UNDERSTAND THE COMPLEXITY OF HOW YOU HAVE REACHED YOUR DETERMINATION. YOU CAN ONLY EXPLAIN IT TO THEM AND THEY CAN THEN RESPECT YOUR DECISION, OR OTHERWISE, WITH THE RESULTING CONSEQUENCES.

When you have an affair, it is done by choice, and if the decision is made because of romantic feelings that may at the time seem overwhelming, then this is when you will find that a lot of people will not agree with your choice. When you choose to forsake your wife/husband and your children because of your feelings (however substantial they may be) and you use this as the basis of your decision, others will not understand. Many won't believe that you could give up everything for sexual gratification or what may even be love, and most especially this will be your children and your partner.

You actually chose to leave them and give up the very basis of their existence and reliance on you as their ultimate source of support, and teacher of the truth, being the basis of their life code. If you have a friend who is encouraging you in an affair, then have a good look at your friend.

THE ROLE OF PARENTS IS TO TEACH TRUE VALUES TO THEIR OFFSPRING AND NEVER DEVIATE FROM THAT LOVE CONVICTION. THE PARENT SETS THE MORAL COMPASS THAT BECOMES THE CHILD'S LIFE CODE.

The dereliction from that duty is destroying lives and is a cancer in our world that we must fight with every breath we take to uphold love, honour, faith, respect and freedom being the five pillars of the truth.

I have seen first-hand in friends and family what happens when a family breaks up due to an unfaithful parent – the damage is always deep, irreversible and lasting. Yes, that's right, it stays forever and shapes the future – the sum total of everything you thought, remember!

So you will be confronted with this new truth, a new life and everything will change at a speed and on a basis that you never could have envisaged. Time will ease some of the hurt but it doesn't go away as the most basic element of their love has been destroyed – TRUST.

So let's examine what I call the five pillars of the truth. Without them it doesn't exist.

1. LOVE – Love is a subset of the truth and that is because as already explained love is the pure, faithful trust that two partners have when they share and commit to each other. In the greater sense of the truth, as the instigator and glue of global harmony, we must all love each other if we want peace.

2. FAITH – Faith is the confidence or trust in a person, thing or deity or in the doctrine or teachings of a religion. It can also be belief that is not based on proof. This is a really important consideration as to what the truth really is as it is misunderstood by many, it can be what you believe without fact to support it, which is most evident in religion and love.

3. RESPECT – Respect is a positive feeling of esteem for another person, entity, country or religion. This is pivotal for truth to really exist in the sense that the truth is not always based on fact or proof. If we can reach the state where we all can respect other's views, we will achieve a far more peaceful existence than currently exists, where we have a global war on terrorism which at its core is based on fanatical belief differences. For the truth to truly be what we believe we need to let people reside within their own philosophies in the absolute freedom of not having to react to the judgement or rules of others.

4. FREEDOM – The meaning of freedom will vary depending on who you ask. Sartre claimed that we are free to do whatever we want 100% of the time. This is probably true as in a non-physical sense we are free to choose whatever course of action we like, even if it leads to jail because it is against the law, like choosing to murder. However, you might get away with it and then be only constrained by the bounds of your conscience. For the truth to always exist I believe that we must be free to believe what we want to, but must always respect others. The truth cannot exist when someone has determined for you what it is. You have to determine that yourself, and that is only done when you act out and experience in your life what it is that makes you the special individual you are.

5. HONOUR – Honour is the integrity of acting out one's beliefs, or in other words, to accept and acknowledge personal responsibility for one's actions. A very wise friend once told me that your integrity is not for sale at any price to anyone, after too many ports late one night in Adelaide. This is so right and that is why it must be a foundation pillar of the truth. Not only must we respect others but we must act with honour to our own ideologies. Always, no matter how difficult that can be at times.

Whatever transpires, and however you choose to live your life, and whatever decisions you make along the way will become the fabric that you are determined by, from the people you love and associate with. This is undeniable. There is no retracing time, and you don't get another go so be sure of what you really value and try to balance your mind's rational thought with the madness and fun you may be experiencing, driven by temptations cruel wand.

Society is having its standards eroded constantly, as what was a moral embarrassment of epic proportion in the middle of last century has been reduced to an everyday event. It is almost as if it's okay to cheat on your partner, to be a promiscuous teenage girl getting obliterated on booze, to be a thug and bully to disadvantaged people or to be a corporate criminal who steals from people under the guise, it's okay because he wears a ritzy suit.

The Presidential candidate of the United States, Hillary Clinton, did not even know what the truth is. In an interview with Scott Pelley from the CBS in February 2016, he stated that, *"You know in 76, Jimmy Carter famously said (to the American public) I will not lie to you."* Hillary replied *"Well, I have to tell you, I have tried, in every way, I know how literally, from my years as a young lawyer, all the way through my time as secretary of state to level with the American people."*

She was then asked if she's always told the truth to which she responded, *"I've always tried to."*

After anchor Scott Pelley stated, *"Some people are gonna call that wiggle room that you just gave yourself."* Hillary said, *"You're asking me to say, 'Have I ever?' I don't believe I ever have. I don't believe I ever have. I don't believe I ever will. I'm gonna do the best I can to level with the American people."*

You don't try to tell the truth, the truth is a definitive state that you believe based on all the five pillars I outlined above. Hillary's truth blows in the wind and is by definition not the truth as she should know if she has not told the truth. This is something you have complete control over, given what you know at the time. The difference between Carter's statement and Hillary's is gargantuan and one of the real reasons she ended up losing the election. Too many of the American public didn't believe or trust her.

Democracy at its core requires the truth to be told and of the two candidates this must have been Trump. People may not like the truth he tells but he sincerely believes it and there lay the difference at the time. Whether anything comes of the conspiracy investigation that Trump's team were collaborating with the Russians will come out in time. Real evidence to date, July 17, is flimsy but there is a growing discord. We will see.

There is a link on YouTube dedicated to 13 minutes of consecutive lies by Hillary Clinton. If you feel so compelled, the link is below:

https://www.youtube.com/watch?v=-dY77j6uBHI

There is a phenomenal relationship transition occurring globally and what happened in the US 2016 Presidential Election is a breakdown in the connection between the historical way the country has been run and the brash unbridled bluntness that comes with the truth Donald Trump lays bare in many of his policies. He is no saint and both he and Clinton were the most disliked presidential nominees in history for different reasons.

Hillary can't be trusted and Donald is breaking all the rules of the old guard so they were even prepared to go so far as to rewrite the rules to maintain their grip on power. Trump ended up prevailing in a most comprehensive victory in the end as he connected with people better and their votes for him represented a substantial backlash against the establishment. The public no longer believe the stories they are told from Capitol Hill, as it is them who pick up the tab. They want to believe America can be great again and like with most great movements it begins with a belief and not a plan.

THE GREAT MOVEMENTS IN HUMANITY HAVE STARTED WITH A BELIEF AND NOT A PLAN. THE PLAN IS DEVELOPED AND THE NEW TRUTH EMERGES.

The relationships in Europe are all experiencing similar stress as the refugee crisis and terrorist attacks have driven a rethink away from liberal policies and a strong surge back to nationalism is occurring.

When refugees that you have welcomed with open arms turn on you with bombings, like in Paris and assaults on women in Koln, then this movement triggers a momentum all of its own. The people now have a different belief and the majority belief will prevail as it has throughout history. That majority belief, as Gandhi articulates below, will be based on love and truth despite the many-headed beasts that try to bring humanities most basic core to demise.

"When I despair, I remember that all through history the way of truth and love have always won.There have been tyrants and murderers, and for a time, they can seem invincible, but in the end, they always fall. Think of it – always."

Immigration has turned out to be one of the core issues that have determined the Brexit outcome on 24 June 2016, a day when the world shook with the voice of real England. The people decided to leave the European Union despite threats and stories of the disaster that will follow. At the end of the day, the people believed in themselves and their values and voted to *"take back control"* from Brussels and the power the combined Union had over their daily existence.

Trump was in town for the happening as he launched a new golf course in Scotland at Turnberry and he lauded the British people for voting for independence and claimed that he believed the US will do the same in the following statement:

"Come November, the American people will have the chance to re-declare their independence. Americans will have a chance to vote for trade, immigration and foreign policies that put our citizens first," he said. *"They will have the chance to reject today's rule by the global elite, and to*

embrace real change that delivers a government of, by and for the people."

British voters did indeed deliver a crushing rejection of political, business and media elites and Trump's prophecy rang true. Power and strength comes from an indomitable will and like it or not Trump has that. In this regard, he is very different to Obama who tended to adopt a conciliatory path. Trump's direct tweet of news approach and fake news story has rattled the media so much that reporting is seldom unbiased anymore as it seems to me. Social media has provided him with a new voice to the public without the filter of the press. It's an interesting new landscape and clearly one many established media giants are not relishing.

Trump has proven to be the leader that America needed as he has the fortitude and courage to confront China where they are not playing by globally accepted fair principals. He has also been found to have not criminally conspired with Russia by the extensive Mueller investigation he labelled as a *"witch hunt"*. The investigation engaged 19 lawyers who were assisted by approximately 40 FBI agents and supporting staff over two years, with nearly 500 witnesses interviewed, and yet it still failed to produce sufficient evidence that the Attorney General William Barr determined would meet the requirement of an obstruction charge.

The swamp is being drained as Trump promised meaning the removal of federal bureaucracy.

William Barr also appears to not be afraid of the relentless attacks and smears on his position and is now conducting an investigation into the origins of the Mueller report which links back to Hillary Clinton, the FBI and the Democrats. His strength and conviction is driven by a desire to find the truth, which for so long has been hidden from Congress, in their attempts to uncover what really happened. No doubt Barr will lead the law as it should be, focused on the truth determined by evidence and not fuelled by deceit and political ideologies.

Different times call for different leaders. One wonders how long Pelosi will remain the Speaker of the House when she says with apparent glee that Trump is impeached forever. It's as if her sole endeavour is to besmirch him irrespective of any real evidence to help the Democrats in the coming election.

On Wednesday, February 5, 2020, Trump was acquitted by the Senate of the charges of abuse of power and obstruction. He was acquitted forever, in what was very clearly a partisan impeachment from the outset and not what the framers of the Union had originally envisaged.

David Cameron, who staked his career and reputation on the UK staying in the European Union, was supported by Obama and Hillary Clinton as they wanted the status quo, but clearly there is a growing discord globally with this hollow rhetoric. Cameron resigned following the vote to support the exit which reflects his disconnect with the people of Britain and a failure to provide them with a vision that would take them into the future and address their economic and immigration issues.

That is the truth of the matter, it is no different to any relationship, both parties must trust each other and want the same thing. In this situation, the British didn't want the same old spin that is a proven failure and the public and the government were just talking past each other with neither party connecting to the other. The government must take responsibility for the communication failure as it is their role to represent and govern for the people and clearly, they weren't.

Only the strong have the courage and ability to adopt a view that breaks down the accepted norm to create a new truth and a new future. Weak people tend to accept, and are happy to exist in a world of lies, as it is often easier and cheaper to delude yourself than confront reality head on. The British have reached the tipping point and no one could ever accuse them of being weak, history reveals their fortitude. They have shown backbone in their decision and will no doubt have challenges ahead but what is new in that. Nothing worthwhile was ever easy.

ONLY THE STRONG WILL FIGHT FOR WHAT
THEY BELIEVE.

Relationships, whether they are for love, friendship or
business, are what bind humans together with a common
sense of purpose and the European Union and Britain now
need to go through a defining transition where they find new
ways to coexist. It will be silly indeed for Europe to force the
British to direct trade elsewhere as this will only further
weaken a fragile community that is grappling with weak
member states, terrorism and a refugee crisis that is
threatening to topple the initial ideology.

A most unlikely supporter against the rampant refugee
problem and resulting move to nationalism throughout
Europe, the US and the wider Western world is none other
than the Dali Lama who reportedly has said there are *"too
many"* refugees in Europe.

*"Europe, Germany in particular, cannot become an
Arab country, Germany is Germany,"* he said. The logical
extension of this statement I believe to be right, we are at risk
of changing centuries of natural evolution by letting this crisis
evolve to the extent that our natural identities and racial
characteristics are homogenised into oblivion.

The European Union philosophy that for free trade you
must allow free immigration is the core policy that will
ultimately unravel the Union. The logical conclusion of free
immigration and no borders is not peace; it is simply the
destruction of the various races and societies that have
developed since the beginning of man. We will all end up as
some blend of white, black, brown and yellow and the
differences and rivalry that exist to develop innovation and
creativity for the betterment of us all will be lost in a diluted
sameness that stunts our senses. Whether the leaders of the
Union learn this in time to prevent the economic meltdown
that is looming and maintain humanities natural order remains
to be seen.

HOMOGENISATION OF RACES WILL STUNT
INNOVATION AND CREATIVITY, THROUGH LACK
OF FUNDAMENTAL DIFFERENCES TO STIMULATE
NEW THOUGHT AND COMPETITION.

Brexit marks the beginning of a new world order where globalisation, and other phenomenon like political correctness, terrorism and even feminism are going to take a back seat to nationalism and pride in one's heritage and country.

In my opinion, the British have made the right decision and the mood that the British have expressed has been bubbling in much of the European Union for years. Fortune favours the bold and those that choose to hide behind false protectionism that is not market competitive will fail. Theresa May, the new British Prime Minister, in her speech on Brexit January 17, 2017 spoke of a new Global Britain that would achieve its goals while maintaining its nationality, in the courts and with immigration. This I believe is the right course for the world. Ironically, the protectionism and trading collective of Europe is destined to fail because its foundation stones don't suit the purpose of the Union as a whole.

Breaking down borders will not create the harmony we seek, the solution is in determining the truth of the opposing views and working through them to reach a state where love, faith, respect, freedom and honour can exist and flourish on both sides of the fence and where all nationalities are respected with equal opportunity. Individual currencies and independent cooperative economies also need to be part of the new solution.

PEOPLE ARE INCREASINGLY ADOPTING THE
TRUTH BECAUSE IT PROVIDES THEM WITH THE
STRENGTH AND SECURITY OF KNOWING THEY ARE
DOING WHAT IS RIGHT FOR THEM.

A situation like Brexit can completely divide the people as nearly equal levels of the population believe different things. If it is right to assume that all European members should have to sacrifice their sovereignty in order to trade with each other, then ultimately the Union will succeed in its current form and Britain will find new markets, and both parties will go through a difficult transition.

I believe that the European Union is really just a great big cooperative that is being very badly managed and out of tune with its membership. Any cooperative requires a strong set of rules, strong leadership that will enforce the rules at all times but the management and governing committee must recognise failings and have the ability to change the constitution. Darwin's theories reside even in relationships like this, change or die.

If a member wants to leave, it is because the system is flawed. The answer is to work and find a solution with that member, not try and force other disaffected members of the Union to follow what increasingly is becoming a failed system and an ideology that is no longer shared by them all.

The mind-boggling part to me is that it all seems so simple. Remove the foundation basis that free trade can only exist with free immigration, and return rights of member state economies to have their own currencies and economic development rights.

What piffle! How did freedom of migration ever become a foundation for free trade?

Actually, the exercise to change that broken formula is an opportunity to bring all members of the Union closer together in the quest of an efficient, growth seeking common trading group that relishes competition. Yes, it will be scary to the existing leaders and the members but it will be exciting and invigorating also.

Britain continues to address its leadership issue, with the appointment of Theresa May and subsequent election process which, when writing, was between Boris Johnson and Jeremy Hunt. The EU now needs to follow suit. The new leaders need to talk and find the common ground that unites them, and remove the foundation stones that are not necessary, or Britain will not be the last to leave. This is a basic truth Europe needs to confront.

Boris Johnson ultimately succeeded with his election as Prime Minister and astounding support for his Conservative Party removing any doubt that Nationalism is on the rise in the 2019 election.

It is like time is turning on itself as much of this movement can be seen in the belief in Stoicism that started way before Christ was known.

The theory of Stoicism was developed around 300 BC in Athens by Zeno of Citium. The Stoics taught that destructive emotions resulted from errors in judgement and that a sage, or person of "moral and intellectual perfection," would not suffer such emotions and therefore hold the key to happiness.

Stoics concerned themselves with the relationship between cosmic determinism and human freedom and the belief that it is right to maintain a will that is in accord with nature. The Stoic philosophy became a way of life and they thought that it was best to determine a person's philosophy, not by what they said, but by what they did. To me, this philosophy is something that the world today needs to behold and the common aphorism "actions speak louder than words" is the modern-day mirror of this part of the theory. You know it's true because people will lie to you as easily as falling off a log if it suits them, but they won't often do something that is contrary to what they really believe as the consequence of an action is far greater than simply correcting a misstatement if you get caught out, in the unlikely event someone bothers to confront the truth.

Hillary Clinton in the YouTube video is a classic example of the case in point.

An action is an easy and obvious statement reflecting something that has been done and is easy to analyse. A lie is much more complex to determine and is by far the preferred method of fraudsters, as it is harder to prove and is often concealed in a web of deceit that takes time and perseverance to unravel. Fraudsters rely on this and often bully their way to an outcome they want relying often on the theory that they

213

will succeed if they are more persistent than their foe irrespective of the truth.

How dare you question their integrity! This is just an all too accepted practice in today's world where embellishing stories to suit one's end for financial or emotional gain is widely accepted practice. But the tide is turning and nowhere is this more evident than in global sport and the crackdown on drugs.

Stoicism has at its core belief determinism so that everything is or was meant to occur and that we have little or no influence over events. Commonly, this is now referred to as fate or destiny. It is important to know, however, that Stoics believed that underneath horrible tragedies that occur in life there was a living and divine being in charge of it all. This was known as the 'Logos' and was ruled by reason.

The 'Logos' is a rational plan where each person gets benefit from a tragic circumstance. The death of your father is an undeniable tragedy leaving most people feeling a sense of loss and loneliness but Stoics claim this is a good event as it teaches you to learn to be more independent and stand up for yourself.

They also believed that one should control and even eliminate emotions and attachments, not dissimilar to the Buddhist theory. We, and everything we know has its own end, so when we over-evaluate things or people or become too attached to them, their loss will cause a great sense of unhappiness. They believe that we cannot change our environment, the outside world, but do have influence over our own internal world.

One of the key advantages of a Stoic belief system is that it makes you strong in times of stress and confrontation and this is why the Romans believed in it.

Christians, on the other hand, were more interested in the belief that one should devote their life to a higher purpose and were able to endure terrible torture, persecution and horrible death with a sense of calm and seeming lack of fear through the devotion to their cause. Life was just a temporary state on the path to the never-ending afterlife in heaven.

Stoicism should not be used as an excuse to be lazy and check out of life's responsibilities but, in my view, provides a confidence and empowerment to push on with your calling in life, whatever you determine that to be.

It is you who responds to adversity and the way you respond dictates your destiny and Stoicism can provide you with the courage to go ahead and realise your dream instead of being strangled by a fear that prohibits you from realising what you might become. Learn from your experience and always move forward with integrity. This is how ultimately a Stoic life bias will help you in your world of exciting adventures.

Embrace and cherish every experience knowing that there is a reason for it.

This is what the British have done and they would probably be the most Stoic race on earth. They have charged into an uncertain future based on the belief that they will be better off and will be able to deal with whatever comes. And they will, just watch them. In fact, they will be stronger by maintaining their core identity which is at the heart of how the decision was made.

"Stoicism does not mean an escape from reality; it means facing the truth while not letting it wrestle us to the ground." The British, say no more.

It's easy to dodge the truth, if it's going to cause trouble or pain, but the fact remains in all false states we are creating disharmony whether it is an inner turmoil that we deal with alone leading to confusion, and depression, or deceit that leads to offense being taken by others.

Confusion is the lack of distinction in your mind between right and wrong and the lack of clarity that impedes progress.

So it follows that if you can't distinguish a direction of thought by crystallising your feelings on a matter, how on earth can you progress yourself. You have stunted yourself at step one by choosing to not accept the reality at hand by facing the facts. That in turn stunts us all as we are all connected, and only by us all moving to acceptance of one and another's beliefs can the real truth emerge and harmony prevail.

This is where Bob now finds himself, in his own mini universe, caught in a web of lies that broaden by the day as Kristie starts to tell her friends about the affair so she can justify her actions and feel good about herself again. Their divided base core values are being increasingly exposed through this deception, so Bob tells Kristie that he will tell Ella the truth if she continues to avoid this responsibility.

Weeks later, he eventually does this and feels an immediate liberation of his feelings. He is no longer trapped in someone else's emotions and can move forward with doing what is best for the children and equally importantly find happiness again for himself.

THE TRUTH MAY HURT YOU, IT MAY BE UGLY, IT MAY MAKE YOU FEEL THINGS THAT YOU NEVER WANTED TO FEEL BUT UNTIL YOU FACE IT, YOU WILL BE TRAPPED IN YOUR MISERY FOREVER.

Bob thought Kristie was so scared that he would leave her that she kept pushing him away to test his love. A psychiatrist explained it that her inability to commit was because of her fear of loss, which she deals with all the time. These deep feelings of loss, developed in childhood trauma, have trapped her in her fear and that is why she resents Bob's family and success as he didn't experience this in his stable family.

She says she didn't love Winton, and Bob believed this to be true but it didn't dilute the betrayal, so he decided he was going to leave her now that Ella was aware of the situation and seemed to be handling it well, outwardly anyway.

Kristie displayed satisfaction when she said Bob had failed at his marriage and to Bob seemed especially pleased, because she had caused it. Bob countered that he believed he had done nothing wrong, certainly nothing intentionally. In fact, he now thought he had been a complete fool because he always retained hope that Kristie would progress and they could have a normal loving relationship like they did in the early years.

FEAR IS A GREAT PROMOTER OF LIES.

Much like the relationship between Cameron's party and the British public, there is a wall between Bob and Kristie that neither party will admit is of their making, but both of them are not being really honest with their feelings.

The very same relationship misunderstandings occurred when the Great Chief Seattle from what is now known as Washington State responded by letter to an offer by US President Pearce to buy his tribe's land.

The great Indian Chief Seattle summed up the differences he saw with the following remarkable insight. I have copied only the first three paragraphs but fully recommend you taking time to read fully his wisdom on the link below. It is stunning in its depth of sincerity and understanding.

http://www.context.org/iclib/ic03/seattle/

The following excerpt is from a letter Chief Seattle of the Washington based Duwamish Tribe sent to President Franklin Pearce, the 14th President of the United States in 1855.

"THE GREAT CHIEF in Washington sends word that he wishes to buy our land. The Great Chief also sends us words of friendship and good will. This is kind of him, since we know he has little need of our friendship in return. But we will consider your offer, for we know if we do not so the white man may come with guns and take our land. What Chief Seattle says you can count on as truly as our white brothers can count on the return of the seasons. My words are like the stars – they do not set.

"How can you buy or sell the sky – the warmth of the land? The idea is strange to us. Yet we do not own the freshness of the air or the sparkle of the water. How can you buy them from us? We will decide in our time. Every part of this earth is sacred to my people. Every shining pine needle, every sandy shore, every mist in the dark woods, every

217

clearing, and every humming insect is holy in the memory and experience of my people.

"We know that the white man does not understand our ways. One portion of land is the same to him as the next, for he is a stranger who comes in the night and takes from the land whatever he needs. The earth is not his brother, but his enemy, and when he has conquered it, he moves on. He leaves his father's graves and his children's birth right is forgotten. The sight of your cities pains the eyes of the Redman. But perhaps it is because the Redman is a savage and does not understand."

In my mind, it was the white man who did not understand. The Redman was at complete harmony with nature and this is a state of perfection that people in our modern world now cherish, as it is all too fleeting with our sprawling urbanisation and industrialisation destroying the trees, the sparkling water and morning mist that Chief Seattle and his people loved so much.

Bob's position is not dissimilar to that of the Great Chief Seattle; he realises that he cannot satisfy Kristie in the same way as the Great Chief realises he will not be able to satisfy President Pierce. Kristie can't accept Bob for who he is and nor can the president accept the chief's way of living.

When different belief systems collide from alternate histories or cultures, a new belief will emerge. It will take time for everyone impacted to find the way forward, but if the collision is handled with honour, respect and genuine love, then the faith that builds will lead to freedom and the fertile ground that the new way can germinate in. Understanding each other will strengthen both parties.

Bob and Kristie and the EU and UK can find a new order that will work. It is not worth believing in anything else, so the endless stream of negativity I heard on the radio talkback about the decision to leave the EU is far better directed to a positive solution for all, which is attainable, with both parties looking for a solution that works for each other. Brussels needs to understand Britain can leave and that they need to work to retain as much of their support as they can, not dictate it. Those days are over.

Similarly, Kristie will need to learn that Bob is no longer at her beck and call as Bob does exactly that and starts to build a new life, first and foremost looking after his children and then engrossing himself in his work. It wasn't long before he met someone that turned out to be someone very special. He continued his drive for doing the right thing and only concerned himself with the genuine people he enjoyed from his time with Kristie, and they have remained good friends to this day.

Those that did not take time to understand both sides of the story and made judgement on Kristie's dark imaginings meant nothing to him. He didn't need to tell them the truth, as he knew it and what they believed was of little consequence to him.

BY CONDONING A LIE, YOU EMBRACE IT.

Bob had no great need for a wide friendship base and preferred to develop the deep relationship with his new partner that is based on complete openness and trust. He was not interested in adopting or participating in deception for the sake of friendship, as it was not what he believed in.

His world is a simple existence really, where his Stoic beliefs allow him to experience life in a most sincere way without fear. Temptation was beneath him and something he could resist by rationalising the fall out that would occur.

However, the temptation of sex can be more than the need to uphold one's integrity for some people, as they do not really have that absolutely clear understanding of themselves that it takes to know when an action you make will unravel your credibility.

Rita Mae, the American writer and ex-lover of tennis great Martina Navratilova has a really interesting perspective on all this. She wrote…

"Sex makes monkeys of us all. If you don't give into it, you grow up to be a cold, unfeeling bastard. If you do, you spend the rest of your life picking up the pieces."

This is a fairly narrow perspective, however, as many can enjoy sex as long-term lovers. You just need to meet the right person, have the courage to love them and believe that sex is an expression of your love, not just a pursuit in physical gratification.

Affairs are becoming more accepted, so much so that Public Office no longer upholds the standards that they should as elected representatives of the people. On October 15, 2013, the Mayor of Auckland, Len Brown, admitted he had an affair and became embroiled in a fight to keep his newly re-elected position. His grubby behaviour with the much younger Asian women, Bevan Chuang, involved him masturbating while talking to her on the phone, sex in the City Chambers, lying to his wife and family and then the contriteness to think he is still fit for Office. It is more possible that if you are a liar and a cheat in your personal life that the same standard of ethics will apply in your business life. Len had already proved this when he was caught manipulating expenses in his favour and also made an election promise to cap City rates at 2.5% and promptly failed to honour that commitment.

The really absurd aspect of this is that once someone is elected to Public Office in Auckland City there is no way to get rid of him as he was elected by the Public. This scandal is quite deeply contrived and may well have been part of his competitor's plan to destroy him, BUT, Len, you did it and so you have to pay the price, whatever that turns out to be.

Len politically relied on the brown vote of South Auckland to support him and hypocrisy is involved here as they typically are Polynesian people with strong Christian values that frown on this type of behaviour. But Len has been their left-wing supporter so they are rallying behind him because the alternative right-wing contender is likely to bring a move to the right which may upset current policies working in their economic advantage.

THE TRUTH CAN BE ESTABLISHED BASED ON NEED. IF THE NEED IS GREATER THAN THE MORAL FIBRE OF THE PERSON OR PEOPLE, THEN THE TRUTH WILL BECOME BASED ON NEED NOT MORALITY.

In my holistic view, this is the wrong outcome from this situation as I contend that is not really the truth. The real truth is that Len Brown does not meet these people's standards but some are changing their own belief for financial gain. Having said that if they believe that it is best for Len to stay mayor and they are the majority of the voice then that is what will occur as the truth is what you believe and it is driven by many motivations – see the Truth of Business and the Stock Market. The majority rules in democracy, the ultimate political system for the fair existence of truth reflecting the people's will.

THE TRUTH IS THE CURRENT STATE OF EXISTENCE BASED ON THE PEOPLE'S CURRENT PERCEPTION AND NEED.

Like so many theories in this book, this concept leads back to Ancient Greece. The excerpt below from Wikipedia looks at exactly what I am interpreting in this situation and I have bolded the part where the sense of the fundamental truth is identified as the key recognisable characteristic of holism. As always, the determining element of the outcome is what the majority of people believe to be the truth. With the truth this will change as new information emerges, and it seems as I write that even some of Len's die-hard media supporters are waning with their support of him as he is now failing to front the media. So what is he hiding? Not even someone as thick-skinned and ignorant of public sentiment as Len can contain the truth.

In November 2015, Len Brown confirmed he was not seeking re-election to the position of Mayor of Auckland.

"Holism (from ὅλος holos, a Greek word meaning all, whole, entire, total) is the idea that natural systems (physical, biological, chemical, social, economic, mental, linguistic, etc.) and their properties should be viewed as wholes, not as collections of parts. This often includes the view that systems function as wholes and that their functioning cannot be fully understood solely in terms of their component parts.

"In philosophy, any doctrine that emphasises the priority of a whole over its parts is holism. Some suggest that such a definition owes its origins to a non-holistic view of language and places it in the reductivist camp. Alternately, a 'holistic' definition of holism denies the necessity of a division between the function of separate parts and the workings of the 'whole'. It suggests that the key recognisable characteristic of a concept of holism is a sense of the fundamental truth of any particular experience."

Relationship truth is the most important truth of them all as it is every second and every moment that you have interacting with someone that shapes the destiny of you and your connections. If you live your life trapped by wrongs in the past that you can't face, you will forever be unhappy and searching for something external, that can only be solved within – where true happiness and contentment resides.

To never lie is to never compromise the truth and it requires real strength because so many people hide from themselves so they can't be hurt. This is hollow comfort as only when you fully understand what it is that drives you can you reach contentment, even if that is nothing.

The legendary Chinese military General Sun Tzu that lived from 555 to 496 BC, or thereabouts, used this type of concept as part of his strategy for war – be formless so you can't be attacked. If the enemy doesn't know where you are, what you look like or how strong you are, how can they plan to beat you in battle? They can't but conversely how can anyone love you?

Sun Tzu's strategy created a huge psychological advantage that allowed him to win wars without fighting which is the ultimate victory. No loss of life!

And so it is with you every day and every moment. You make decisions based on what you are afraid of, or believe in, and build facades so you can protect yourself if a relationship fails. But the reason it fails is because you built walls of fear which ultimately become the truth or belief system of your life; the defining essence which is you.

We all do it and Sun Tzu knew it. So he played on it masterly by being the most terrifying foe anyone could imagine, except for maybe Genghis Khan, who also fully grasped the power in this idcology.

Love as mentioned earlier is the pure, faithful trust that two partners have when they share and commit to each other. This state relies on pure honesty all the time, and every time a little white lie is deployed, the chasm of a future failed relationship starts to open. The lies get bigger and, more often and before you know it, you are in the arms of your lover without even the slightest concern that you have done anything wrong.

Relationships don't usually just implode; they slowly unravel, inch by inch with deception and lack of faith. It is a difficult road to travel when your partner keeps changing course, and ultimately, when the fork in the road finally appears and you both go your separate ways, trying to reflect on what happens invariably causes anger and animosity.

The domineering habitual liar bully-type struggle with being confronted with the truth more than most as they are simply used to being able to assert their opinion aggressively and continuously, until the other weaker party just gives way. That is why the weak lose, they don't have the stamina to fight what they know is right.

These bullies take correction to their stand over tactics very personally and being bought back to the reality of the situation is a real dent to their self-image and ego. They tend to hold grudges and will spiral the confrontation on to different people so that they can end up with the final say so they satisfy themselves as a victor. Their need to do this will transcend their ability to reason.

I am not referring to Genghis Khan and Sun Tzu in this example as they fully understood the reason for their posturing and had honourable endeavour.

Keeping the peace with bullies in a group dynamic is not easy but as Edward Deming advised you need to **drive out fear** to create success in his theories on total quality management. The same applies to relationships; you need to remove fear to have an honest relationship and a successful one. Having the cojones to confront troublesome bullies in your environment, whether it is social or business is a key trait that must be very evident in the leader so that the honour of the truth is preserved and harmony prevails. The weak are then not abused, their voice is heard and the best possible balance is achieved for the greater good.

This is what the great Khan and Tzu fully appreciated and is one of the reasons they were among the greatest leaders in history.

Edward Deming was also a phenomenal leader and transformed post-WW2 Japan from a manufacturer of cheap low-quality merchandise with his focus on statistical quality control. He also had this view on change and how to affect it.

"It is not necessary to change. Survival is not mandatory.

"If you can't describe what you are doing as a process, you don't know what you're doing.

"It is not enough to do your best; you must know what to do, and then do your best."

The same theories apply to relationships. If you do not keep adjusting and developing your relationship to suit the changing environment and the changing needs of your partner, your relationship will die. Further, to progress the relationship, you must understand what it is that makes it work, and makes it fail, and do your best to maintain it if in fact you still believe that keeping it alive is in your best interests.

So what happens when you come face to face with a critical make or break moment of truth?

Do you run and hide or do you face it and deal with it?

You can go on believing your own deception but you will not be happy. Facing the truth at first won't be easy and you will have to believe that it is for the best and have the courage to work through the dilemma. Establishing what the truth is can in itself be a journey, and one you can face alone, but it is best with support from someone who will take the time and understand.

It can be very difficult if your partner can't be honest for fear of being hurt from the consequences of a lie. The bigger the lie, the bigger the consequences, and there is no way to avoid it.

THE BIGGER THE LIE, THE BIGGER THE CONSEQUENCES, AND THERE IS NO WAY TO AVOID AN ACTION OR STATEMENT ONCE MADE.

If one partner in love can't be honest with the other, then love and respect does not exist, and so then the only thing keeping them together is fear of the future for either themselves or their children or staff whatever the case may be.

After the split, Bob and Kristie continued to have differences and Bob just preferred to have no contact other than as necessary for the children as he no longer felt compelled to accede to her wishes just to make her happy to his own detriment. The betrayal has been realised and it is over and he feels nothing for her, not even contempt. Just nothing, whatever there was is gone.

His love and admiration for James and Ella grows as he focuses on them developing and achieving their potential in life and making good life decisions by teaching them the right way to act and think, as they progress through the millions of decisions that shapes their destiny. Those consecutive momentary decisions shape your existence and build your friends and family and are the moments of truth that determine your happiness.

There was an absolute killer line in the second Wall Street movie with Michael Douglas delivering the punch: *"If you don't stop telling lies about me, I'll start telling the truth about you."* Great line, Michael, and delivered with exactly the right level of cynicism that the creep deserved. The inference also from this line that is underwritten is that the truth is more powerful than lies as it was going to bring an end to the lies. Those who don't believe that have rude awakenings in their life.

In some instances what people say can be really funny; it's funny because it's true. You know when someone says exactly what everyone is thinking, but everyone is scared to say it. Spike Milligan was a master of making nonsense of the truth and it is unbelievably funny when you get it.

The fear of the unknown can have the entirely opposite impact and can create a sad existence. Face the reality, square on and you will see that you really had nothing to fear except your own dark imaginings.

WHEN THE TRUTH IS KNOWN, A BRIGHT FUTURE CAN BE REALISED.

This is at the heart of what Deming is saying; you must understand your current position or process to be able to improve.

The truth fears no questions and this knowledge when understood is what makes a relationship strong. Getting defensive, falling into denial and distorting facts for selfish gain is no way forward. This is what the European Union needs to grapple with, what Kristie should have done, what Len Brown refused to face and what Michael Jackson's accusers blindly ignored.

THE TRUTH FEARS NO QUESTIONS. WHY SHOULD IT? IT IS THE ULTIMATE DETERMINER OF RIGHT AND WRONG.

If you don't know the truth, keep searching and you will find it.

The truth is everywhere. It is in your mind, in your heart and soul, in the vision you have for the future, in the idea that came from nowhere, and in the relationship that binds you to your loved ones.

Loyalty comes from the love and respect of those who believe in you, and the pivotal link in all relationships is the truth. When one relationship breaks down, another one will form, because the truth always prevails over dishonesty, as good always prevails over evil.

In essence, they are the same thing.

The truth is the God Particle of relationships binding everything that is good in human nature.

The erosion of standards caused by not recognising the importance of the truth is denigrating societies, religions, families, sports and businesses globally. Anywhere we humans interact must be governed by the foundation of honesty and the endeavour to do the right thing.

My hope is that by shining light on the truth, people of all life's equations will stop and take a look at themselves, and readjust their respect and integrity levels for themselves and their fellow men. The truth is forever, and a lie is just a dirty stain in a moment of time that introduces the negative impact of Karma in your future existence.

Living a true life is a value that is beyond any measurement form we know. It is God's way of testing how we will react, the scorecard we meet our maker with, and truly worth believing in.

References

The Big Religion Chart – Religion Facts,
Published: January 10, 2016
Website name: Religionfacts.com
Publisher: The publisher of the document
URL: http://www.religionfacts.com/big_religion_chart.htm

Religious war
Page last modified: March 12, 2017
Website name: En.wikipedia.org
Publisher: The publisher of the document
URL: http://en.wikipedia.org/wiki/Religious_war

World Religions War and Peace
Website Name: War and Religions
Publisher: Peace Pledge Union
URL: http://www.ppu.org.uk/learn/infodocs/
    st_religions.html

Barua, Pradeep P.
Year published: 2017
The State at War in South Asia
Website name: Google Books
Publisher: The publisher of the document
URL: https://books.google.co.nz/
    books?id=FIIQhuAOGaIC&pg=PA316&lpg=PA316
    &dq=Al-Utbi,+Tarikh+Yamini&source=bl&ots=-
    2GODP3YsO&sig=2xiwIzgu6M9wyRu-
    4c5xUyL8pR8&hl=en&sa=X&ved=0ahUKEwiwyca
    Ww9XSAhXBw7wKHWCtCvQQ6AEILzAE#v=one
    page&q=Al-Utbi%2C%20Tarikh%20Yamini&f=false

Fairless, T. (2014)
U.S. Expresses Concern Over EU Antitrust Debate on
Google
Website name: WSJ
Publisher: The publisher of the document
URL: http://online.wsj.com/articles/u-s-expresses-concern-
over-google-antitrust-debate-in-europe-1416943414

Olson, P. October 17, 2011
Googles Fundamental Flaw is Search
Website name: Forbes.com
Publisher: The publisher of the document
URL: https://www.forbes.com/sites/
parmyolson/2011/10/17/googles-fundamental-flaw-is-
search/#7c87d7cd76d5

Mulder, P. September 19, 2014.
5 Whys analysis
Website name: ToolsHero
Publisher: The publisher of the document
URL: https://www.toolshero.com/problem-solving/5-whys-
analysis/

Elizabeth 1 of England
Website name: En.wikipedia.org
Publisher: The publisher of the document
URL: https://en.wikipedia.org/wiki/Elizabeth_I_of_England

Ellis, I.
Page title: J. Robert Oppenheimer Quotes - 28 Science
Quotes - Dictionary of Science Quotations and Scientist
Quotes
Website name: Todayinsci.com
Publisher: The publisher of the document
URL: https://todayinsci.com/O/
Oppenheimer_Robert/OppenheimerRobert-
Quotations.htm

Islamic State of Iraq and the Levant
Website name: En.wikipedia.org
Publisher: The publisher of the document
URL: http://en.wikipedia.org/
    wiki/Islamic_State_of_Iraq_and_the_Levant

Sunni Islam
Website name: En.wikipedia.org
Publisher: The publisher of the document
URL: http://en.wikipedia.org/wiki/Sunni_Islam

Kumar, M. (2014)
Difference Between Islam and Muslim
Website name: Difference Between
Publisher: The publisher of the document
URL: http://www.differencebetween.net/
    miscellaneous/difference-between-islam-and-muslim/

Sunni Islam
Website name: En.wikipedia.org
Publisher: The publisher of the document
URL: http://en.wikipedia.org/wiki/Sunni_Islam

Temporarily Unavailable | Military.com
Website name: Military.com
Publisher: The publisher of the document
URL: http://www.military.com/video/operations-and-
    strategy/terrorism/a-second-message-to-
    america/3763859346001/

Phillips, A. (2013)
America Produced More Oil Than It Imported For The First
Time Since 1995
Website name: Think Progress
Publisher: The publisher of the document
URL: http://thinkprogress.org/
    climate/2013/11/14/2942361/produces-oil-imports/

Albert Einstein quotes on truth - Google Search
Website name: Google.co.nz
Publisher: The publisher of the document
URL: https://www.google.co.nz/
search?q=albert+einstein+quotes+on+truth&espv=2&
biw=1366&bih=667&tbm=isch&tbo=u&source=univ
&sa=X&ei=WCswVfaAL4bq8AXqp4GICQ&ved=0C
BsQsAQ#imgrc=NK1LAi4-
c1MjwM%253A%3BgOA3an12TO6HEM%3Bhttp%
253A%252F%252Fizquotes.com%252Fquotes-
pictures%252Fquote-be-a-loner-that-gives-you-time-
to-wonder-to-search-for-the-truth-have-holy-curiosity-
make-your-albert-einstein-
226628.jpg%3Bhttp%253A%252F%252Fizquotes.co
m%252Fquote%252F226628%3B850%3B400

Deity
Website name: En.wikipedia.org
Publisher: The publisher of the document
URL: http://en.wikipedia.org/wiki/Deity

Social media and suicide
Website name: En.wikipedia.org
Publisher: The publisher of the document
URL: http://en.wikipedia.org/
wiki/Social_media_and_suicide

Terrorist groups recruiting through social media
Website title: CBC News
Publisher: The publisher of the document
URL: http://www.cbc.ca/news/technology/terrorist-groups-
recruiting-through-social-media-1.1131053

Terrorism and social media
Website name: En.wikipedia.org
Publisher: The publisher of the document
URL: https://en.wikipedia.org/
wiki/Terrorism_and_social_media

Atheists face death in 13 countries, global discrimination: study
Website name: Reuters
Publisher: The publisher of the document
URL: http://www.reuters.com/article/2013/12/10/us-
    religion-atheists-idUSBRE9B900G20131210

Sport
Website name: TheFreeDictionary.com
Publisher: The publisher of the document
URL: http://www.thefreedictionary.com/sport

Lance Armstrong 'stripped' of Tour de France titles and banned
Website name: BBC Sport
Publisher: The publisher of the document
URL: http://www.bbc.com/sport/cycling/19369375

Epstein, D. January 18, 2103.
Mike Anderson, former bike mechanic of Lance Armstrong, speaks out
Website name: SI.com
Publisher: The publisher of the document
URL: https://www.si.com/more-sports/2013/01/17/mike-
    anderson-lance-armstrong#

Website name: Nydailynews.com
Publisher: The publisher of the document
URL: http://www.nydailynews.com/sports/i-team/vicious-
    cycle-doping-admission-legal-rish-lance-article-
    1.1233875

O'Keefe, M. (2017)
Vicious cycle? Doping admission could be legal risk for
Lance
Website name: NY Daily News
Publisher: The publisher of the document
URL: http://www.nydailynews.com/sports/i-team/vicious-
cycle-doping-admission-legal-rish-lance-article-
1.1233875#ixzz2HHFTLt18 legal trial

Ben Johnson 1988 100m - YouTube
Website name: YouTube
Publisher: The publisher of the document
URL: http://www.youtube.com/watch?v=cCh5QswxQ6k

The Ben Johnson story
Website name: YouTube
Publisher: The publisher of the document
URL: http://www.youtube.com/watch?v=l-
    il82AfPGY&feature=related

Ben Johnson: The story that shook the world
Website name: ESPN.co.uk
Publisher: The publisher of the document
URL: http://www.espn.co.uk/
    athletics/sport/story/241555.html#
    z0DoTSjdaLVtoPsI.99

Linford Christie
Website name: En.wikipedia.org
Publisher: The publisher of the document
URL: http://en.wikipedia.org/wiki/Linford_Christie

Mackay, D. April 24, 2003
Lewis: 'Who cares I failed drug test?'
Website name: The Guardian
Publisher: The publisher of the document
URL: https://www.theguardian.com/
sport/2003/apr/24/athletics.duncanmackay
https://www.youtube.com/watch?v=dGiEKeJnmpg&f
eature=related
Unable to cite this page as this has been withdrawn since
initial access due to multiple notifications of copyright
infringement

Ryan, N. September 12, 2103.
Johnson urges Lewis: Come clean
Website name: Fox Sports
Publisher: The publisher of the document
URL: http://www.foxsports.com.au/more-sports/ben-
johnson-urges-carl-lewis-to-come-clean-and-admit-
using-performance-enhancing-drugs/news-
story/9ef649bc00f5c020aa83deb7aea1a39e#.UjTbC8
ZONvo

Fotheringham, W. January 26, 2015
Lance Armstrong: I would probably cheat again in similar
circumstances
Website name: The Guardian
Publisher: The publisher of the document
URL: https://www.theguardian.com/sport/2015/jan/26/lance-
armstrong-cheat-again-doping-cycling

Lewis a Drug Cheat? Documents suggest cover up.
April 19, 2003 London
Website name: The Age.com.au
Publisher: The publisher of the document
URL: http://www.theage.com.au/
articles/2003/04/17/1050172707806.html

Lao tzu quotes - Google Search
Website name: Google.co.nz
Publisher: The publisher of the document
URL: https://www.google.co.nz/
search?q=lao+tzu+quotes&oq=lao+tzu&aqs=chrome.
1.69i57j0l5.6649j0j1&sourceid=chrome&ie=UTF-8

Hodgkinson, M. October 30, 2009.
Boris Becker: I'm struggling to understand why Andre
Agassi wanted to confess
Website name: Telegraph.co.uk
Publisher: The publisher of the document
URL: http://www.telegraph.co.uk/
sport/tennis/atptour/6461555/Boris-Becker-Im-
struggling-to-understand-why-Andre-Agassi-wanted-
to-confess.html

Website name: FOX Sports
Publisher: The publisher of the document
URL: http://www.foxsports.com/tennis/story/pete-sampras-
upset-about-remarks-in-andre-agassi-book-011410

Telegraph staff and agencies, January 14, 2010

Pete Sampras eager to hold 'man-to-man' meeting with
Andre Agassi about book
Website name: Telegraph.co.uk
Publisher: The publisher of the document
URL: http://www.telegraph.co.uk/
sport/tennis/6991088/Pete-Sampras-eager-to-hold-
man-to-man-meeting-with-Andre-Agassi-about-
book.html

Mcevoy, J. May 1, 2013.
Biggest cover-up in sports history? Murray blasts court order
to destroy blood bags after doping doctor Fuentes verdict
Website name: Mail Online
Publisher: The publisher of the document
URL: http://www.dailymail.co.uk/sport/tennis/article-
2317353/Andy-Murray-enters-Eufemiano-Fuentes-
row-calling-court-order-cover-up.html

AFP updated May 3, 2013
Drug cheats should be named: Nadal
Website name: DAWN.COM
Publisher: The publisher of the document
URL: http://dawn.com/2013/05/03/drug-cheats-should-be-
named-nadal/

Govan, F. January 29,2013.
Cycling's 'Doping Doctor' Eufemiano Fuentes says he
worked with 'football, boxing, tennis and athletics'
Website name: Telegraph.co.uk
Publisher: The publisher of the document
URL: http://www.telegraph.co.uk/sport/
othersports/cycling/9835576/Cyclings-Doping-
Doctor-Eufemiano-Fuentes-says-he-worked-with-
football-boxing-tennis-and-athletics.html

Gordon, I. May 3, 2103.
Murray blasts judge's decision to destroy 200 blood samples
Website name: The Sun
Publisher: The publisher of the document
URL: http://www.thesun.co.uk/sol/
homepage/sport/tennis/4909830/Andy-Murray-blasts-
Spanish-judges-decision-to-destroy-over-200-blood-
samples-from-Operation-Puerto.html

Ben Johnson (sprinter)
Website name: En.wikipedia.org
Publisher: The publisher of the document
URL: http://en.wikipedia.org/wiki/Ben_Johnson_(sprinter)

Has Nadal Run Afoul of the Doping Laws? · Tennis-
Prose.com
Website name: Tennis-prose.com
Publisher: The publisher of the document
URL: http://www.tennis-prose.com/bios/has-nadal-run-
    afoul-of-the-doping-laws/

Eufemiano Fuentes
Website name: En.wikipedia.org
Publisher: The publisher of the document
URL: http://en.wikipedia.org/wiki/Eufemiano_Fuentes

Tennis has a Steroid Problem
http://tennishasasteroidproblem.blogspot.co.nz/2011/02/curi
ous-case-of-rafael-nadal.html

Macur, J. April 30, 2013.
Judge Orders Blood Bags Destroyed in Puerto Doping Case
Website name: Nytimes.com
Publisher: The publisher of the document
URL: http://www.nytimes.com/
    2013/05/01/sports/cycling/spanish-doctor-sentenced-
    in-operation-puerto-doping-case-in-cycling.html?_r=0

Fuentes found guilty in Operacion Puerto case - Goal.com
30 April, 2013
Website name: Goal.com
Publisher: The publisher of the document
URL: http://www.goal.com/en-
    gb/news/2885/europe/2013/04/30/3943269/fuentes-
    found-guilty-in-operacion-puerto-case

Vinton, N. August 9, 2012.
Tainted cyclist Hamilton wants out of Olympic record book
Website name: NY Daily News
Publisher: The publisher of the document
URL: http://www.nydailynews.com/sports/i-team/tyler-
       hamilton-won-gold-u-s-athens-2004-requests-erased-
       olympic-record-book-article-1.1133076

Vinton, N. October 9, 2013.
New book claims Crow sang to feds about Armstrong
Website name: NY Daily News
Publisher: The publisher of the document
URL: http://www.nydailynews.com/sports/i-team/new-book-
       claims-crow-sang-feds-armstrong-article-1.1481152

Vinton, N. November 19, 2013.
Armstrong accuses ex-cycling chief of covering up his
positive drug tests
Website name: NY Daily News
Publisher: The publisher of the document
URL: http://www.nydailynews.com/sports/i-
       team/armstrong-accuses-cycling-chief-covering-
       positive-drug-tests-article-
       1.1521191#ixzz2mqv5kJGZ

Controversy in Australian Open 2014 Men's Final between
Stan Wawrinka and Rafa Nadal
Website name: YouTube
Publisher: The publisher of the document
URL: https://www.youtube.com/watch?v=mtfyaG8SRJA

stan wawrinka - Google Search
Website name: Google.co.nz
Publisher: The publisher of the document
URL: https://www.google.co.nz/
    search?q=stan+wawrinka&espv=2&biw=1366&bih=6
    62&source=lnms&tbm=isch&sa=X&sqi=2&ved=0ah
    UKEwiTwfTO55fRAhXFlZQKHe0eCogQ_AUIBigB
    #tbm=isch&q=stan+wawrinka+us+open+2016&imgrc
    =UpOc5D_8H1jv0M%3A

The 2015 ATP Tour Official Rule Book
URL: http://www.atpworldtour.com/
    ~/media/files/rulebook/2015/2015-atp-
    rulebook_sept15.pdf

Mahler, J. September 9, 2013.
Let's Hope Drugs Prolong Rafael Nadal's Great Career
Website name: Bloomberg.com
URL: http://www.bloomberg.com/news/2013-09-09/let-s-
    hope-drugs-prolong-rafael-nadal-s-great-career-.html

Mahler, J. September 9, 2013.
Let's Hope Drugs Prolong Rafael Nadal's Great Career
Publisher: The publisher of the document
Website name: Deadspin.com
URL: http://deadspin.com/lets-hope-drugs-prolong-rafael-
    nadals-great-career-1279047223

Emmett, M. March 22, 2013.
"Is There a Connection between Rafa and Lance?" |
oncourt.ca
Website name: Oncourt.ca
Publisher: The publisher of the document
URL: http://oncourt.ca/news/2013/03/22/michael-emmett-is-
    there-a-connection-between-rafa-and-lance/

Associated Press in Johannesburg, Monday 23 March 2015

Website name: The Guardian
Publisher: The publisher of the document
URL: http://www.theguardian.com/
world/2015/mar/23/tennis-player-bob-hewitt-
convicted-of-rape

Valerie Adams: Olympic champion calls for life bans for
drug cheats, November 20,2014
Website name: BBC Sport
Publisher: The publisher of the document
URL: http://www.bbc.com/sport/0/athletics/30135259

Cockroft S, Burrows T. November 10, 2015.
Russia's doped athletes 'sabotaged' 2012 Olympics, say
drugs chiefs
Website name: Mail Online
Publisher: The publisher of the document
URL: http://www.dailymail.co.uk/news/article-
3310332/Athletics-faces-darkest-day-drugs-
investigators-publish-bombshell-report-accusing-
sport-s-chiefs-extortion-doping-cover-ups.html

Jenkins, S. November 12, 2015.
It's not just Russia: Britain helped create this corruption in
sport | Simon Jenkins
Website name: The Guardian
Publisher: The publisher of the document
URL: http://www.theguardian.com/
commentisfree/2015/nov/12/not-just-russia-britain-
corruption-allegations-athletics-sport

FIFA bans Sepp Blatter and Michel Platini from football-related activities for eight years
Website name: Stuff
Publisher: The publisher of the document
URL: http://www.stuff.co.nz/sport/football/world-game/75350818/sepp-blatter-and-michel-platini-banned-from-footballrelated-activities-for-eight-years.html

Vladimir Putin says FIFA's Sepp Blatter 'a respected person', deserves Nobel prize
Website name: Stuff
Publisher: The publisher of the document
URL: http://www.stuff.co.nz/sport/football/world-game/75248231/Vladimir-Putin-says-Fifas-Sepp-Blatter-a-respected-person-deserves-Nobel-prize

Miller, M. Barbash, F. May 27,2015.
U.S. indicts world soccer officials in alleged $150 million FIFA bribery scandal
Website name: Washington Post
Publisher: The publisher of the document
URL: https://www.washingtonpost.com/news/morning-mix/wp/2015/05/27/top-fifa-officials-arrested-in-international-soccer-corruption-investigation-according-to-reports/

Schlein, L. December 21, 2015.
FIFA Chief to Fight 'Unjust' Eight-Year Suspension
Website name: VOA
Publisher: The publisher of the document
URL: http://www.voanews.com/content/blatter-platini-banned-from-soccer-for-8-years/3111645.html

Bagchi, R. December 21, 2015
Sepp Blatter demands termination of his FIFA ban
Website name: Telegraph.co.uk
Publisher: The publisher of the document
URL: http://www.telegraph.co.uk/sport/football/sepp-
blatter/12057261/Sepp-Blatter-demands-termination-
of-his-Fifa-ban.html

Holt, O. December 27, 2015.
Year of the downfall: Great and the good saw reality bite in
2015
Website name: Mail Online
Publisher: The publisher of the document
URL: http://www.dailymail.co.uk/sport/football/article-
3374882/Year-downfall-Sepp-Blatter-Michel-Platini-
Stuart-Lancaster-Jose-Mourinho-12-months-saw-
reality-bite.html

Sepp Blatter: Former FIFA president loses appeal against
six-year ban after Court of Arbitration for Sport case
Website name: talkSPORT
Publisher: The publisher of the document
URL: http://talksport.com/football/sepp-blatter-former-fifa-
president-loses-appeal-against-six-year-ban-after-
court

Tremlett, G. May 10, 2013.
Spanish doping doctor ready to reveal role in major sports
Website name: The Guardian
Publisher: The publisher of the document
URL: http://www.theguardian.com/
sport/2013/may/10/spanish-doping-doctor-reveal-
sports

Tucker, B. December 13, 2015.
UFC 194 post-fight press conference video
Website name: MMA Fighting
Publisher: The publisher of the document
URL: http://www.mmafighting.com/
2015/12/13/10021252/ufc-194-post-fight-press-
conference-video

'Juiced to the gills': Brock Lesnar accused of doping by
Mark Hunt ahead of UFC 200
Website name: RT International
Publisher: The publisher of the document
URL: https://www.rt.com/sport/346161-ufc-lesnar-hunt-
doping/

Edwards, J. December 29.2016.
Why Ronda Rousey is doing no media ahead of UFC 207
Website name: The Independent
Publisher: The publisher of the document
URL: http://www.independent.co.uk/sport/general/mma/ufc-
207-news-latest-preview-dana-white-ronda-rousey-
no-media-amanda-nunes-a7499906.html

Domin, M. November 13, 2016.
UFC 205 breaks pay-per-view record as Connor McGregor
KOs Eddie Alvarez
Website name: mirror
Publisher: The publisher of the document
URL: http://www.mirror.co.uk/sport/other-sports/mma/ufc-
205-breaks-pay-per-9250937

Daniel Cormier on Jon Jones' failed drug test for steroids: 'I
don't know what to think anymore'
Website name: MMAjunkie
Publisher: The publisher of the document
URL: http://mmajunkie.com/2017/08/daniel-cormier-
reaction-jon-jones-positive-steroids-test-ufc-214

Al-Shatti, Shaun. December 27, 2018.
Jeff Novitzky reveals that USADA first found adverse
findings in Jon Jones' drug tests back in August
Website name: MMA Fighting
Publisher: The publisher of the document
URL: https://www.mmafighting.com/
2018/12/27/18158305/jeff-novitzky-reveals-that-
usada-first-found-adverse-findings-in-jon-jones-drug-
tests-back-in-august

Evan and Babcock. June 24, 2019.
Jon Jones Talks DC, McGregor vs Khabib 2, and Tests
Elbow on Staffer | TMZ SPORTS
Website name: Youtube
Publisher: The publisher of the document
URL: https://www.youtube.com/watch?v=YxDD77OZc9A

Rothernberg, B. Glanz, J. January 24, 2016.
Match-Fixing Suspicions Raised at Australian Open After
Site Stops Bets on Match
Website name: Nytimes.com
Publisher: The publisher of the document
URL: http://www.nytimes.com/
2016/01/25/sports/tennis/match-fixing-australian-
open-mixed-doubles-betting.html?_r=0

Friedell, D. April 28, 2016.
Maria Sharapova May Get a Second Chance
Website name: VOA
Publisher: The publisher of the document
URL: http://learningenglish.voanews.com/a/maria-
sharapova-meldonium/3306562.html

Rogovitskiy, D. April 13, 2016.
WADA makes meldonium U-turn, could affect Sharapova ban
Website name: Reuters
Publisher: The publisher of the document
URL: http://www.reuters.com/article/us-doping-wada-meldonium-wada-idUSKCN0XA14G

Capriati unleashes Twitter tirade on Sharapova after failed drug test
Website name: ABC News
Publisher: The publisher of the document
URL: http://www.abc.net.au/news/2016-03-08/maria-sharapova-jennifer-capriati-twitter-drug-test/7229972

Rumsby, B. June 8, 2016
Maria Sharapova's career left in ruins after two-year ban for taking meldonium
Website name: The Telegraph
Publisher: The publisher of the document
URL: http://www.telegraph.co.uk/tennis/2016/06/08/maria-sharapova-given-two-year-ban-for-doping/

The International Tennis Federation v. Maria Sharapova Decision
Website: ITFTennis.com
Publisher: The publisher of the document
URL: http://www.itftennis.com/media/231178/231178.pdf

Brown, A. May 12, 2016
Website: sportsintegrityinitiative.com
Publisher: The publisher of the document
URL: http://www.sportsintegrityinitiative.com/over-3600-athletes-test-positive-for-meldonium-in-year-before-ban/

Brown, A. April 14, 2016.
Athletes face uncertainty after WADA meldonium clarification
Website name: Sports Integrity Initiative
Publisher: The publisher of the document
URL: http://www.sportsintegrityinitiative.com/athletes-face-uncertainty-after-wada-meldonium-clarification/

Sharapova may escape drug ban
Website name: Theaustralian.com.au
Publisher: The publisher of the document
URL: http://www.theaustralian.com.au/sport/tennis/maria-sharapova-lifeline-as-wada-makes-meldonium-uturn/news-story/e0b19501b5fd9779adc527846cdff128

Sports Integrity Initiative - Meldonium
Website name: Sports Integrity Initiative
Publisher: The publisher of the document
URL: http://www.sportsintegrityinitiative.com/?s=meldonium

Melbourne, 15 October, 2015.
Speech by WADA Director General, David Howman, Challenges to the Integrity of Sport, Melbourne (October 15, 2015)
Website name: World Anti-Doping Agency
Publisher: The publisher of the document
URL: https://www.wada-ama.org/en/media/news/2015-10/speech-by-wada-director-general-david-howman-challenges-to-the-integrity-of-sport

Mitchell, K. April 25, 2016.
Rafael Nadal to sue former French cabinet minister over
doping allegations
Website name: The Guardian
Publisher: The publisher of the document
URL: https://www.theguardian.com/
sport/2016/apr/25/rafael-nadal-sue-french-cabinet-
minister-doping-allegations

Press Association, November 16, 2017
Rafael Nadal awarded damages over French former
minister's doping claim
Website name: The Guardian
Publisher: The publisher of the document
URL: https://www.theguardian.com/
sport/2017/nov/16/rafael-nadal-damages-over-french-
minister-doping-claim

Dopage: Roselyne Bachelot met en cause Rafael Nadal
Website name: Rtl.fr
Publisher: The publisher of the document
URL: http://www.rtl.fr/sport/autres-sports/dopage-roselyne-
bachelot-met-en-cause-rafael-nadal-7782184716

Rabanal, V. September 19, 2016
FANCY BEARS Nadal defends himself: "I have permission,
so it is not illegal"
Website name: Tenis
Publisher: The Publisher of the Document
URL: http://www.puntodebreak.com/2016/09/19/rafa-nadal-
tomo-sustancias-prohibidas-permiso-ama-2009-2012

Tandon, K. September 19, 2016
Rafael Nadal the latest tennis star to have confidential
medical data leaked: Spaniard responds
Website name: Tennis.com
Publisher: The Publisher of the Document
URL: http://www.tennis.com/pro-game/2016/09/rafael-
    nadal-wada-russian-hackers-rio-tues-tennis-
    performance-enhancing-drugs/61215/

Fuentes recognizes 'some top sports names' could be owners
of Puerto blood bags
Website name: Cyclingnews.com
Publisher: The publisher of the document
URL: http://www.cyclingnews.com/news/fuentes-
    recognizes-some-top-sports-names-could-be-owners-
    of-puerto-blood-bags/

Price, R. January 10, 2014.
Rusedski: If I'm Guilty of Drug Taking Then So Are Half of
All the World's Top Tennis Players: Website name:
Highbeam.com
Publisher: The publisher of the document
URL: https://www.highbeam.com/doc/1G1-112056768.html

Website name: YouTube
Publisher: The publisher of the document
URL: https://www.youtube.com/watch?v=tU5vs-_rreQ

September 27, 2013.
Koellerer Accuses Nadal of Doping
Website name: Theultimatetennisblog.com
Publisher: The publisher of the document
URL: http://theultimatetennisblog.com/koellerer-accuses-
nadal-of-doping/

Gilbert, P. April 27, 2016.
Rafael Nadal sues Roselyne Bachelot over doping allegation
Website name: Sky Sports
Publisher: The publisher of the document
URL: http://www.skysports.com/
     tennis/news/12110/10258692/world-no-5-rafael-
     nadal-sues-over-doping-allegation

French ex minister Bachelot to stand trial in 2017 over
Nadal doping scandal
Website name: www.efe.com
Publisher: The publisher of the document
URL: http://www.efe.com/efe/english/destacada/french-cx-
     minister-bachelot-to-stand-trial-in-2017-over-nadal-
     doping-scandal/50000261-2970530

Defamation case against politician who accused Nadal of
doping is postponed
Website: www.marca.com
Publisher: The Publisher of the Document
http://www.marca.com/en/more-
sports/2017/07/06/595eaab2e2704e6f0e8b45cf.html

de Punto de Break 19/09/2016 16:14
Rafa Nadal took prohibited substances with permission from
the AMA in 2009 and 2012
Website: Puntodebreak.com
Publisher: The Publisher of the Document
URL: http://www.puntodebreak.com/2016/09/19/rafa-nadal-
     tomo-sustancias-prohibidas-permiso-ama-2009-2012

Tandon K. September 19, 2016
Rafael Nadal the latest tennis star to have confidential
medical data leaked: Spaniard responds
Website: tennis.com
Publisher: The Publisher of the Document
URL: http://www.tennis.com/pro-game/2016/09/rafael-
    nadal-wada-russian-hackers-rio-tues-tennis-
    performance-enhancing-drugs/61215/

July 24, 2016.
Website name: International Olympic Committee
Publisher: The publisher of the document
URL: https://www.olympic.org/news/decision-of-the-ioc-
    executive-board-concerning-the-participation-of-
    russian-athletes-in-the-olympic-games-rio-2016

Uddin, L. Walker, A. July 26, 2016.
How world sport governing bodies have reacted to the IOC's
Russia decision
Website name: The Guardian
Publisher: The publisher of the document
URL: https://www.theguardian.com/
    sport/2016/jul/25/russia-doping-scandal-ioc

Wilson S, April 26.2016.
Rafael Nadal wants his drug-test results made public
Website name: AP News
Publisher: The publisher of the document
URL: https://apnews.com/7d6ca6f2df8f4c0aa666
    f93f11630665/rafael-nadal-wants-his-drug-test-
    results-made-public

Harris N, Draper R. July 16, 2017
London 2012 was an Olympics sabotaged by Russian drugs
cheats.
Website name: Mail Online
Publisher: The publisher of the document

URL: http://www.dailymail.co.uk/sport/doping/article-
    4699804/London-2012-sabotaged-cheats-invite.html
https://fancybear.net/

Briggs, S, August 15, 2016
Simone Biles human after all as five-gold medal Rio
Olympic dream is dashed on the balance beam
Website name: The Telegraph
Publisher: The publisher of the document
URL: http://www.telegraph.co.uk/
    olympics/2016/08/15/simone-biles-human-after-all-
    as-five-gold-medal-rio-olympic-drea/

Tingle, R. September 14, 2016.
Website name: Mail Online
Publisher: The publisher of the document
URL: http://www.dailymail.co.uk/news/article-
    3787665/Anti-doping-bosses-ALLOWED-Williams-
    sisters-gymnast-Simone-Biles-banned-
    substances.html

Website name: Google.co.nz
Publisher: The publisher of the document
URL: https://www.google.co.nz/webhp?sourceid=chrome-
    instant&ion=1&espv=2&ie=UTF-
    8#q=oxycodone%20uses

Prendisone
Website name: Letsrun.com
Publisher: The publisher of the document
URL: http://www.letsrun.com/
    forum/flat_read.php?thread=1085708

USADA Media contact. September 19, 2014.
Website name: U.S. Anti-Doping Agency (USADA)
Publisher: The publisher of the document
URL: http://www.usada.org/us-track-field-athlete-spearmon-
accepts-sanction-rule-violation/

This site on 27/5/17when I tried to access it again showed the following message:

This site can't be reached

www.usada.orgus-track-field-athlete-spearmon-accepts-sanction-rule-violation's server DNS address could not be found.

Try running Windows Network Diagnostics. Attempts with this did not succeed either.

DNS_PROBE_FINISHED_NXDOMAIN

Antidoping - ITF
Website name: ITF Tennis.com
Publisher: The publisher of the document
URL: http://www.itftennis.com/
         antidoping/education/overview.aspx

Is Serena Williams on Steroids
Website name: Quora
Publisher: The publisher of the document
URL: https://www.quora.com/Is-Serena-Williams-on-
         steroids

Serena Williams joins clamour against drug-testing
Website name: Telegraph.co.uk
Publisher: The publisher of the document
URL: http://www.telegraph.co.uk/
         sport/tennis/williamssisters/4606356/Serena-
         Williams-joins-clamour-against-drug-testing.html

McEnroe admits steroid use; Agassi stunned
Website name: ESPN.com
Publisher: The publisher of the document
URL: http://www.espn.com/sports/tennis/
         news/story?id=1708055

Gibson, O. September 20, 2016
Mo Farah and Rafael Nadal named in latest leak from Fancy
Bears hacking group
Website name: The Guardian
Publisher: The publisher of the document
URL: https://www.theguardian.com/sport/2016/sep/19/mo-
farah-named-fancy-bears-leak

Hacker group 'Fancy Bears' releases new WADA batch
Website name: RT International
Publisher: The publisher of the document
URL: https://www.rt.com/sport/361466-fancy-bears-new-
wada-batch/?utm_source=rss&utm_
medium=rss&utm_campaign=RSS
Access date: 21/8/17

How athletes can use medical exemptions to beat drug
testers
Publisher: The publisher of the document
URL: http://www.economist.com/blogs/
gametheory/2016/09/doper-s-dupe

Schilken, C. March 11,2017.
Rafael Nadal defends self from doping allegations, says
Maria Sharapova 'must pay' for testing positive
Website name: latimes.com
Publisher: The publisher of the document
URL: http://www.latimes.com/sports/sportsnow/la-sp-sn-
rafael-nadal-doping-maria-sharapova-20160311-
story.html

Gibson, O. September 18, 2016.
Bradley Wiggins faces a fight for his reputation in wake of
Wada hack
Website name: The Guardian
Publisher: The publisher of the document
URL: https://www.theguardian.com/
sport/2016/sep/18/bradley-wiggins-world-anti-doping-
agency-hackers-russian-leak

MacInnes, P. August 22, 2107.
Tevez, Verón and Kuyt named as using TUEs at 2010 World
Cup
Website: The Guardian
Publisher: The publisher of the document
URL: https://www.theguardian.com/
football/2017/aug/22/fancy-bears-accuse-25-players-
of-being-given-tues-during-2010-world-cup

Cycling News, June 17,2017
Spanish court stops identification of Operacion Puerto
athletes
Website: Cycling News.com
Publisher: The publisher of the document
http://www.cyclingnews.com/news/spanish-court-stops-
identification-of-operacion-puerto-athletes/

Cycling News, February 16,2017
WADA struggling over legality of naming Operacion Puerto
athletes
Website: Cycling News.com
Publisher: The publisher of the document
http://www.cyclingnews.com/news/wada-struggling-over-
legality-of-naming-operacion-puerto-athletes/

Mayeda A. October 6, 2016
The IMF Is Worried About the World's $152 Trillion Debt Pile
Website name: Bloomberg.com
Publisher: The publisher of the document
URL: https://www.bloomberg.com/news/articles/2016-10-05/a-record-152-trillion-in-global-debt-unnerves-imf-officials

October 4, 2016.
Gold medal Kiwis Mahe Drysdale, Peter Burling first Kiwis namcd in Fancy Bears data leak
Website name: The New Zealand Herald
Publisher: The publisher of the document
URL: http://www.nzherald.co.nz/
        sport/news/article.cfm?c_id=4&objectid=11721984

Dobbs, R. Lund, S. Woetzel, J. Mutafchieva, M. February, 2015.
Debt and (not much) deleveraging.
Website name: Mckinsey and Company
Publisher: The publisher of the document
URL: http://www.mckinsey.com/global-
        themes/employment-and-growth/debt-and-not-much-
        deleveraging

There is way more debt in the world than there is money to repay it.
Website name: AboveTopSecret.com
Publisher: The publisher of the document
URL: http://www.abovetopsecret.com/
        forum/thread934808/pg1

McFadden, J. September 12, 2008.
Website name: The Huffington Post
Publisher: The publisher of the document
URL: http://www.huffingtonpost.com/joyce-mcfadden/the-
    psychology-of-hope-an_b_141856.html

Viser, M. October 20, 2015.
For presidential hopefuls, simpler language resonates
Website title: BostonGlobe.com
Publisher: The Publisher of the document
URL: https://www.bostonglobe.com/
    news/politics/2015/10/20/donald-trump-and-ben-
    carson-speak-grade-school-level-that-today-voters-
    can-quickly-grasp/LUCBY6uwQAxi
    LvvXbVTSUN/story.html

Leadership
Website name:En.wikipedia.org
Publisher: The publisher of the document
URL: https://en.wikipedia.org/wiki/Leadership

Dessert, L.
Norman Schwartzkopf's 14 Rules on Leadership
Website name: Elephants at Work
Publisher: The publisher of the document
URL: http://www.elephantsatwork.com/norman-
    schwartzkopfs-14-rules-on-leadership/

Article title: iPhone4 vs HTC Evo
Website title: YouTube
URL: https://www.youtube.com/watch?v=FL7yD-0pqZg

Iggulden, C
Lords of the Bow
Publisher; Harper Collins 6th edition

Hoilday, R. May 7, 2012.
Lessons on Power and Leadership from Genghis Khan
Website name: Forbes.com
Publisher: The publisher of the document
URL: https://www.forbes.com/sites/
    ryanholiday/2012/05/07/9-lessons-on-leadership-
    from-genghis-khan-yes-genghis-khan/#57544456996f

Cohn, S. January 23, 2015.
In new emails, Madoff defends his dead sons
Website name: CNBC
Publisher: The publisher of the document
URL: http://www.cnbc.com/id/102364320

Cohn, S. December 11, 2013.
Five years later, Madoff still trying to control the story.
Website name: NBC News
Publisher: The publisher of the document
URL: http://www.nbcnews.com/business/five-years-later-
    madoff-still-trying-control-story-2d11724273

Happiness
Website name: En.wikipedia.org
Publisher: The publisher of the document
URL: https://en.wikipedia.org/wiki/Happiness

©1927 Max Ehrmann (renewed) Bell & Son publishing,
LLC
Website name: Desiderata.com
Publisher: The publisher of the document
URL: http://www.desiderata.com/desiderata-poem.html

Mencius
Website name: Iep.utm.edu
Publisher: The publisher of the document
URL: http://www.iep.utm.edu/mencius/

Ensor, J. May 21, 2014.
Young Iranians arrested for 'vulgar' Pharrell Williams'
Happy dance
Website name: Telegraph.co.uk
Publisher: The publisher of the document
URL: http://www.telegraph.co.uk/
news/worldnews/middleeast/iran/10845573/Young-
Iranians-arrested-for-vulgar-Pharrell-Williams-
Happy-dance.html

Mahatma Ghandi Quotes
Website name: Goodreads
Publisher: The publisher of the document
URL: http://www.goodreads.com/quotes/739-when-i-
despair-i-remember-that-all-through-history-the

The How of Happiness: Chapter by Chapter
Website name: Adventures in Reading
Publisher: The publisher of the document
URL: https://baltimorebookworm.wordpress.com/
2008/05/01/howofhappiness-2/

Graham, S. June 1964.
Website name: Carygrant.net
Publisher: The publisher of the document
URL: http://www.carygrant.net/articles/thinks%20about.htm

Website name: BrainyQuote
Publisher: The publisher of the document
URL: http://www.brainyquote.com/quotes/
authors/c/cary_grant.html#V8BbdxwpxSGUoxUX.99

Lessin, J. Luk, L. Osawa, J. July 1, 2013.
Apple Finds It Difficult to Divorce Samsung
Website name: WSJ
Publisher: The publisher of the document
URL: http://online.wsj.com/news/articles/
SB10001424127887324682204578513882349940500

Ginsberg, Leah. Huddleston Jr, Tom. March 21, 2019.
The psychology of deception: How Elizabeth Holmes fooled
everyone about Theranos for so long
Website name: CNBC
URL: https://www.cnbc.com/2019/03/20/hbos-the-inventor-
how-elizabeth-holmes-fooled-people-about-
theranos.html

What percentages of Marriages end in Divorce?
Website name: Webarchive.nationalarchives.gov.uk
Publisher: The publisher of the document
URL; http://webarchive.nationalarchives.gov.uk/
20160106011951/http://www.ons.gov.uk/ons/rel/vsob
1/divorces-in-england-and-wales/2011/sty-what-
percentage-of-marriages-end-in-divorce.html

Top 5 causes of divorce and separation in the UK.
Website name: Singleparents.org.uk
Publisher: The publisher of the document
URL: http://www.singleparents.org.uk/
information/legal/top-5-causes-of-divorce-and-
separation-in-the-uk

Website name: Wikipedia
Publisher: The publisher of the document
URL: https://simple.wikipedia.org/wiki/
1993_child_sexual_abuse_accusations_against_Micha
el_Jackson

Thompson, C. May 25,2011.
One of the Most Shameful Episodes In Journalistic History
Website name: HuffPost
Publisher: The publisher of the document
URL: http://www.huffingtonpost.com/charles-thomson/one-
of-the-most-shameful_b_610258.html

Evan Chandler
Website name: En.wikipedia.org
Publisher: The publisher of the document
URL: https://en.wikipedia.org/wiki/Evan_Chandler

Admin, June 10, 2015.
Jordy Chandler; "I lied for my father, I'm sorry Michael"
Website name: Jews News
Publisher: The publisher of the document
URL: http://www.jewsnews.co.il/2015/06/10/jordy-
        chandler-i-lied-for-my-father-im-sorry-michael/

Guardian staff. February 21, 2019.
Michael Jackson estate suing HBO for $100m over tell-all
documentary
Website name: The Guardian
Publisher: The publisher of the document
URL: https://www.theguardian.com/
        music/2019/feb/21/michael-jackson-leaving-
        neverland-documentary-lawsuit-hbo

Tale Of A Train Station – James Safechuck's Abuse Story,
in Leaving Neverland, Doesn't Add Up
Website name: mjjjusticeproject
Publisher: The publisher of the document
URL: https://mjjjusticeproject.wordpress.com/
        2019/04/01/tale-of-a-train-station-james-safechucks-
        abuse-story-in-leaving-neverland-doesnt-add-up/

Smallcombe, Mike. January 18, 2019.
Website name: Cornwalllive.com
Jackson Leaving Neverland HBO documentary and why we
shouldn't be free to destroy the reputations of the dead
Website name:
Publisher: The publisher of the document
URL: https://www.cornwalllive.com/news/cornwall-
        news/michael-jackson-leaving-neverland-
        documentary-2438824

Sheridan, E. October 6, 2012.
Website name: Mail Online
Publisher: The publisher of the document
URL: http://www.dailymail.co.uk/tvshowbiz/article-
2213769/Ronan-Keating-opens-reason-cheated-wife-
Yvonne.html

Love is composed of a single soul inhabiting two bodies.
Website name: philosiblog
Publisher: The publisher of the document
URL: http://philosiblog.com/2012/10/29/love-is-composed-
of-a-single-soul-inhabiting-two-bodies/

Busch, F. June, 2009.
Anger and Depression
Website name: BJPsych Advances
Publisher: The publisher of the document
URL: http://apt.rcpsych.org/content/15/4/271.full

Explore love betrayal Quotes
Website name: Pinterest
Publisher: The publisher of the document
URL: https://nz.pinterest.com/pin/510384570250702503/

Karma
Website name: En.wikipedia.org
Publisher: The publisher of the document
URL: http://en.wikipedia.org/wiki/Karma

Ven. M Sayadaw.
The theory of Karma
Website name: Buddhanet.net
Publisher: The publisher of the document
URL: http://www.buddhanet.net/e-learning/karma.htm

Karma: God's Law of Action, Fruit and Rebirth
(Reincarnation)
Website name: Buddhanet.net
Publisher: The publisher of the document
URL: http://www.thekundaliniyoga.org/karma/karma_gods_
      law_action_fruit_rebirth_reincarnation_hindu_perspec
      tive.aspx

A quote from Lao Tzu
Website name: Goodreads
Publisher: The publisher of the document
URL: http://www.goodreads.com/quotes/7459328-watch-
      your-thoughts-they-become-words-watch-your-words-
      they

Hillary: I've always tried to tell the truth and don't believe
I've ever lied or ever will-Brietbart.
Website name: Breitbart
Publisher: The publisher of the document
URL: http://www.breitbart.com/video/2016/02/18/hillary-
      ive-always-tried-to-tell-the-truth-dont-believe-ive-
      ever-lied-or-ever-will/

Casalino, A.
BREAKING: Donald Trump Issues A Call To ALL
AMERICANS...HERE Is What He Is Asking...
Website name: Patriot Journal
Publisher: The publisher of the document
URL: http://patriotjournal.com/breaking-trump-issues-call-
      to-americans/

Ward, Alex. April 19, 2109.
The Mueller report, explained in only 500 words
Website name: Vox
Publisher: The publisher of the document
https://www.vox.com/world/2019/4/19/18507580/mueller-
report-trump-russia-obstruction-summary

By the New York Times, March 24, 2019.
Read Attorney General William Barr's Summary of the
Mueller Report
Website name: NYtimes.com
Publisher: The publisher of the document
https://www.nytimes.com/interactive/2019/03/24/us/politics/
barr-letter-mueller-report.html

Anderson, T. April 6, 2107
Dalai Lama Warns 'Europe Has Taken Too Many Migrants'
Website name: Knights Templar International
Publisher: The publisher of the document
URL: http://knightstemplarinternational.com/2017/02/dalai-
lama-warns-europe-has-taken-too-many-migrants/

Explore Dominant Philosophy, Philosophy God and More
Website name: Pinterest
Publisher: The publisher of the document
URL: https://nz.pinterest.com/pin/570127634048649433/

Farzaneh, A. September 21, 2008
How Stoicism can change your Life
Website name: Arashworld.blogspot.co.nz
Publisher: The publisher of the document
URL: http://arashworld.blogspot.co.nz/2008/09/how-
stoicism-can-change-your-life.html

Chief Seattle: 1855
Website name: Context Institute
Publisher: The publisher of the document
URL: http://www.context.org/iclib/ic03/seattle/

Thomas, P. October 25, 2013.
One monkey business won't stop the Show.
Publisher: Weekend Herald

Slater, C. October 15, 2013.
EXCLUSIVE: Len Brown's Town Hall to Downfall –
Whale Oil Beef Hooked | Whaleoil Media
Website name: Whale Oil Beef Hooked | Whaleoil Media
Publisher: The publisher of the document
URL: https://www.whaleoil.co.nz/2013/10/exclusive-len-
    brown-sordid-affair-run-town-hall/

Holism
Website name: En.wikipedia.org
Publisher: The publisher of the document
URL: http://en.wikipedia.org/wiki/Holism

Website name: Google.co.nz
Publisher: The publisher of the document
URL: https://www.google.co.nz/webhp?sourceid=chrome-
    instant&ion=1&espv=2&ie=UTF-
    8#q=edward%20deming%20quotes

CPSIA information can be obtained
at www.ICGtesting.com
Printed in the USA
LVHW052207270121
677519LV00008B/235